Advance Praise for *Fath*

"This book invites us to enjoy an illuminatin
of a classic Tibetan text on the nature and pra

"Like an experienced trekking guide who k   ....y well, Alan
Wallace points out features of the landscape with easeful erudition and the
deft use of analogy. Along the way, he comes up with all sorts of useful tools
and materials just when the reader needs them—these being the words of
Western scientists and philosophers, and Eastern sages and adepts, which he
draws on with equal familiarity and adroitness.

"Although it can be a rocky and dusty path, and despite any unfamiliarity
and difficulty with the ground that is covered, by the time the end is reached
I suspect the reader will have less dust in their eyes than when they started
out."

—**Ajahn Amaro**, abbot of Amaravati Buddhist Monastery, UK

"*Fathoming the Mind* lucidly focuses Buddhism's present-day encounter
with modernity on one of the most potent possibilities: that cognitive science
is poised on the threshold of major revolution and the Buddhist worldview
offers a profound opportunity to expand into radically new and necessary
territory. This book contains a map of what Buddhist teachings about mind
and reality can offer contemporary science. And Alan Wallace, with his deep
understanding of both physical science and Buddhist philosophy and practice, is an exceptional guide."

—**David E. Presti**, University of California–Berkeley,
author of *Foundational Concepts in Neuroscience* and *Mind Beyond Brain*

"This is a fascinating book. Continuing his impressive unpacking of the leg-
acy of Düdjom Lingpa, Alan Wallace has produced a fine contribution to
the long history of oral commentary on source texts. His grasp of the subject
matter is impressive, as is the way he weaves in references to Western thought
and scientific enquiry that places Düdjom Lingpa's text in a more relevant
context. I highly recommend this book to all who are serious about having a
mind and working with it."

—**Richard Barron** (Chökyi Nyima), translator of Longchenpa's *The
Precious Treasury of the Way of Abiding* and *The Precious Treasury of the
Basic Space of Phenomena* with its autocommentary

FATHOMING
THE MIND

INQUIRY AND INSIGHT IN DÜDJOM LINGPA'S
Vajra Essence

TRANSLATION AND COMMENTARY BY
B. Alan Wallace

EDITED BY
Dion Blundell and Eva Natanya

Wisdom

Wisdom Publications
199 Elm Street
Somerville, MA 02144 USA
wisdompubs.org

Library of Congress Cataloging-in-Publication Data is available.
Names: Bdud-'joms-gliń-pa, Gter-ston, 1835–1904, author. | Wallace, B. Alan, translator. | Natanya, Eva, editor. | Blundell, Dion, editor.
Title: Fathoming the mind: inquiry and insight in Düdjom Lingpa's Vajra essence / translation and commentary by B. Alan Wallace; edited by Dion Blundell and Eva Natanya.
Description: Somerville, MA: Wisdom Publications, 2018. | Includes bibliographical references and index. |
Identifiers: LCCN 2017057635 (print) | LCCN 2018024302 (ebook) | ISBN 9781614293408 (e-book) | ISBN 9781614293293 (pbk.: alk. paper)
Subjects: LCSH: Rdzogs-chen.
Classification: LCC BQ7662.4 (ebook) | LCC BQ7662.4 .B3422174 2018 (print) | DDC 294.3/420423—dc23
LC record available at https://lccn.loc.gov/2017057635

ISBN 978-1-61429-329-3   ebook ISBN 978-1-61429-340-8

22 21 20 19 18
5 4 3 2 1

Cover design by Phil Pascuzzo. Interior design by Tony Lulek. Set in DGP 10.5/14.25.

Please visit fscus.org.

Publisher's Acknowledgment

The publisher gratefully acknowledges the generous help of the Hershey Family Foundation in sponsoring the production of this book.

Contents

Foreword by Dzongsar Khyentse Rinpoché ix

Foreword by Tsoknyi Rinpoché xiii

Preface xv

Introduction 1

   A Serviceable Mind 2

   The Current Dark Age of Materialism 11

1. The Nature of the Mind 29

   The Phenomenological Nature of Consciousness 30

   The Essential Nature of the Mind 38

   The Ultimate Nature of the Mind 44

   The Transcendent Nature of Consciousness 48

2. Revealing Your Own Face as the Sharp Vajra of Vipaśyanā 55

3. Revealing the Ground Dharmakāya 71

   Determining the Identitylessness of Persons as Subjects 71

   Determining the Identitylessness of Phenomena as Objects 85

   Coarse and Subtle Considerations for Determining Emptiness 116

   How All Phenomena Arise and Appear 124

   The Point of Realizing the Emptiness of Phenomena 180

Epilogue 191

Afterword:

   New Frontiers in the Collaboration of Buddhism and Science 197

Glossary   209
Notes   231
Bibliography   245
Index   257
About the Translator   269

Foreword

by Dzongsar Khyentse Rinpoché

It is said that to bump into or hear the term Mahāsandhi or Dzokchen even accidentally will supposedly make our precious human bodies worthy and meaningful. So in that context, I rejoice that Alan Wallace's translation of the Vipaśyanā chapter of *Vajra Essence* is now making some of these extraordinarily precious teachings available to a wider audience. I can only pray that at least a handful of those with the good fortune to seize this opportunity will not only hear but fully understand, practice, and realize the wisdom these teachings convey.

In this text, Düdjom Lingpa—one of the greatest masters and treasure revealers of the nineteenth century—explains the quintessential view of Buddhism with utmost clarity. But he does so in a unique way that requires no blind leap of faith on the part of the reader and practitioner.

On the contrary, in Düdjom Lingpa's pure vision, the teacher, Samanta-bhadra, manifesting as Padmasambhava, engages with interlocuters who give eloquent voice to the coarse and subtle doubts and objections to the Buddhist view that arise in our very own mind and practice as projections of our reasoning intellect. In the ensuing dialogue, we recognize all our own qualms, worries, questions, and uncertainties to which Samantabhadra responds with precision, skill, and patience. Through the method of that remarkable interchange, this treasure teaching is perfectly suited to our present age of doubt and questioning.

But there is another dialogue that pervades virtually every chapter of this book. It's a dialogue with science and its various branches and methods—

from physics, behaviorism, and neuroscience to empiricism and quantum mechanics.

It's a dialogue that I confess I have avoided like the plague, mainly because I despair that Buddhists, let alone Mahāsandhi practitioners, and scientists can even speak the same language in order to communicate genuinely. And so I am intrigued to see Alan Wallace engage in that discourse with such personal passion. I also find myself both cheering on his trenchant critique of scientific materialism and being a bit skeptical of his hopes for genuine collaborative research between Buddhists and scientists.

In my observation, what scientists generally miss is so basic as to make real interchange extraordinarily challenging. For example:

- ❖ Scientists generally reject the possibility of transcendence—that there is anything beyond what is observable.

- ❖ The method of yogic direct cognition that is fundamental to Buddhist logic and practice, which I think goes further than what Wallace calls "introspection," is generally unknown to scientists.

- ❖ In general, scientists do not seem to grasp the view of nonduality. As a result, they also don't understand the meaning of selflessness and wisdom, and they are therefore uninterested in what we Buddhists call "liberation."

- ❖ The distinction between ultimate and relative truth—so fundamental to Buddhism—seems alien to most scientists. Yet without that understanding, it seems impossible to engage scientists in discussion on rebirth and on past and future lives, which they say cannot be proved through analysis. In fact, the Buddhist distinction between teachings that require interpretation and those that do not is strange to most scientists.

- ❖ And therefore, though they claim to share the Buddhist approach of exploring the relation between causes and conditions and their effects, I have yet to meet scientists who really understand cause and effect at the most subtle level. And therefore they also cannot understand practices like offering, praise, torma, mandala, and more, which they disparage as "religious" or "superstitious."

Of course, none of this is reason to reject dialogue with scientists. In my view, we should engage in such discourse for very pragmatic, even saṃsāric, reasons. For example, I think Buddhist teachers can take advantage of the fact that Western intellectuals are attracted to Buddhism's reliance on reason and logic rather than belief.

At the same time, I think the gaps in understanding between Buddhism and science are so wide that we should never portray Buddhism as science, as many people these days seem prone to do. It might sound chauvinist, but I am convinced that Buddhism has something unique to offer that science simply doesn't have in its arsenal.

For all these reasons I am delighted to applaud Alan Wallace's courage in exposing and dissecting the smug assumptions, dogmatic beliefs, and narrow measurement tools of scientific materialism that masquerade as empiricism and that he rightly says "are fundamentally incompatible with all schools of Buddhism throughout history."

Commenting on his thirty years of experience participating in Buddhism–science conferences, Wallace remarks:

> Time and again, experts from diverse fields, including psychology, neuroscience, and philosophy, have presented their cutting-edge research to Buddhists and then invited their response to these advances in modern science. In virtually all such meetings, it is the Western scientists who dominate, speaking for over 90 percent of the time.... Overall, I have found much greater openness on the part of Buddhists to learn about scientific discoveries in the mind sciences than I have found open-mindedness on the part of scientists eager to learn about Buddhist discoveries.

And yet Alan Wallace remains remarkably hopeful about the potential for genuine collaborative endeavors between scientists and Buddhist scholars, and he sees a particular openness toward Buddhist views in the field of quantum mechanics. And so, a good part of this book is geared to furthering, expanding, and deepening that Buddhism–science dialogue based on genuine empiricism.

Call me conservative and old-fashioned, but I have to confess I remain much more enthralled with Samantabhadra's dialogue with his bodhisattva disciples, which to me makes Düdjom Lingpa's *Vajra Essence* one of the most powerful, relevant, and practical treasure teachings we could ever wish to have.

I cannot and will not dismiss the other dialogue that Alan Wallace is so determined to further. Indeed, if I were to do so, I would be as dogmatic and close-minded as the scientists he so roundly condemns. On the contrary, I truly aspire that Wallace's plea for scientists to respect Buddhist insight be taken seriously.

On that front, it is past time to puncture the subtle implication in Buddhism–science dialogues to date that we Buddhists somehow have to prove our validity in scientific terms if anyone is to take us seriously. I am glad to see Wallace show that to be impossible so long as the instruments of measurement and verification are decided by scientists.

But if Wallace can persuade scientists to open their minds to the possibility of transcending the observable, to the method of yogic direct cognition, to the view of nonduality, to the notion of liberation, and more, then I'll be delighted to see them explore our world and engage in whatever dialogue is needed.

In the meantime, I am happy to bask in the glory of Düdjom Lingpa's extraordinary *Vajra Essence* and am deeply grateful to Alan Wallace for bringing that brilliant and remarkable dialogue to a wider English-speaking audience. May all who touch and read this treasure benefit, and may its truth and power liberate all beings.

Dzongsar Jamyang Khyentse

Foreword

by Tsoknyi Rinpoché

When seeing this book's title I didn't know, as a non-native speaker, what the word *fathom* meant. A student of mine said that it could mean, in the context of Dharma, a kind of knowing that goes deeper and deeper while simultaneously opening and expanding, leading to an awareness that is vast and profound. And certainly this is what we need to fathom—the profound visions and teachings of the great tertön and meditation master Düdjom Lingpa. It is said he received his visions from many enlightened beings, including Avalokiteśvara and Longchenpa. The collected teachings of Düdjom Lingpa span over forty volumes.

This book comes at a critical time in our shared history, to a world that is in crisis and, as Alan so clearly and concisely puts it, "is in desperate need of rescue from the clutches of reductionism, with its triadic juggernaut of materialism, hedonism, and consumerism, which is rapidly despoiling human civilization and the ecosphere." In this translation and in Alan's commentary, the power and breadth of Düdjom Lingpa's wisdom provide an urgently needed antidote to the dangerous extremes of materialism and nihilism. He gives us profound practices that transform the mind, allowing us over time to see that mind is primary and the root of our individual and collective experience.

I have known Alan for many years through Mind and Life Institute conferences with His Holiness the Dalai Lama, who has been Alan's root teacher for close to fifty years, and I have bumped into him here and there at various teachings around the world. Alan is a respected scholar who has written on the philosophy of science and has a deep understanding of the philosophy of mind. He is a former monk of fourteen years and was a professor at the University of California; he is a long-term serious practitioner, seasoned translator, and experienced Dharma teacher with students around the world. He is also a student of the Nyingma Dzokchen master Gyatrul Rinpoché, from whom he has received teachings on the Great Perfection for almost thirty years.

I have also learned so much from Alan's excellent introduction to this volume, where he presents the philosophical, scientific, and historical trends of our times and presents the setting in which *Fathoming the Mind* was born. This book is a commentary to the Vipaśyanā chapter of Düdjom Lingpa's *Vajra Essence* and is the companion volume to Alan's earlier book, *Stilling the Mind*, which provides an extensive commentary to the earlier śamatha section of the *Vajra Essence*.

Ngawang Tsoknyi Gyatso

Preface

The contemplative discoveries achieved by the Buddha on the night of his enlightenment, the many teachings he gave based on his direct knowledge, and the extraordinary abilities he revealed over the course of his life were revolutionary in the early history of Indian civilization. And he knew how deeply challenging, unsettling, and difficult to fathom his discoveries would be for his contemporaries. In particular, he recognized that his unprecedented insights into dependent origination, which he himself had acquired with great difficulty, were "profound, difficult to perceive, difficult to comprehend, tranquil, exalted, not within the sphere of logic, and subtle," and that they could be perceived only by the wise, those who had "little dust on their eyes." But his discoveries, which he declared went "against the stream" of all the philosophical and religious beliefs of his time, would remain incomprehensible and threatening to those whose minds were dominated by attachment and hatred, and who unquestioningly clung to their own beliefs, hedonistic values, and materialistic way of life.[1]

The impact of the Buddha's discoveries constituted a kind of "contemplative revolution," first in India, and over the next two millennia, throughout much of Asia. In the West, we have had similar revolutions triggered by the discoveries of Galileo, Darwin, and Einstein. In each case, these revolutions brought about an irreversible change in the outlook on reality of those who have fathomed their authenticity and implications. But every revolution meets with fierce resistance when it is first presented. People don't like to have their beliefs, values, and way of life challenged from the core, and those who are attached to the status quo, including the power structures that are already in place—with all the wealth, prestige, and influence that they entail—resist such revolutions tooth and claw. In India, some who clung to their traditional Vedic beliefs simply rejected the Buddha's claims about his own unparalleled enlightenment and his many teachings that challenged their beliefs and practices, while others sought to assimilate him into the Vedic pantheon by claiming that he was an avatar of Viṣṇu.

In the twentieth century, the Buddha's life and teachings have made their way to the West, and if they are taken seriously, they are even more profoundly revolutionary to modern religious, philosophical, and scientific beliefs than they were to his contemporaries. Specifically, his firsthand reports regarding his "direct knowledge" of his own and others' countless past lives, the natural laws of causality pertaining to actions committed in past lives and their results in future lives, the role of the mind in nature, and the path to freedom from suffering and its causes all challenge modern worldviews to their very core. Some who are resistant to questioning their beliefs, values, and accustomed way of life understandably reject his discoveries and extraordinary abilities, and chalk them off as myths, superstitions, and mere conjecture. Others who are drawn to some aspects of the Buddha's teachings but refuse to take his deeper claims about his enlightenment seriously, seek to assimilate his teachings into the contemporary framework of materialist beliefs, hedonic values, and a consumer-driven way of life, viewing him as a kind of avatar of atheism and agnosticism. The Buddha counseled his contemporaries not to accept beliefs simply because they are widely held and often repeated or rumored, because they accord with one's cultural heritage, or because they are found in some scripture. Likewise, one should not adopt beliefs based solely on conjecture or spurious reasoning unsupported by compelling evidence.[2] Nevertheless, contemporary assimilationists, often calling themselves "secular Buddhists," are prone to claiming that the Buddha's teachings on rebirth and karma, for example, were ones he appeared to adopt simply because they were commonly held beliefs at the time. So his own reports of his enlightenment are often dismissed as later fabrications, and he is depicted as a hypocrite who failed to follow his own counsel of open-minded skepticism toward the prevailing beliefs of one's time. In this way, self-styled secular Buddhists carve out from his life and teachings a "filet of Buddhism" by carefully removing all the bones of his revolutionary discoveries that stick in their throats. In many cases, his teachings have thus been tamed and downgraded into one more form of psychotherapy, and psychologists and neuroscientists are given the authority to determine the benefits and limitations of the meditative practices he taught, while rejecting anything that doesn't conform to their own research methods and beliefs. Yet is this not simply an ideological and methodological extension of the colonialism that has long characterized the West's exploitation and domination of the East? Buddhist meditation is thus reduced to a few psychological techniques that have been simplified, relabeled, commodified, and marketed to the world as new and improved, freed for the first time of all the mumbo-jumbo and claptrap of any claims that go against the stream of modernity.

Many contemporary Buddhists, both East and West, reject such ethnocentric reductionism and misrepresentation of the life and teachings of the Buddha, which rationally and experientially challenge modern beliefs even more than those of ancient India. This book is written in such a spirit of open-minded, but critical, evaluation of Buddhist theories and meditative practices, specifically with reference to the Indo-Tibetan tradition of Dzokchen, the "Great Perfection," as revealed by the great nineteenth-century contemplative Düdjom Lingpa. My earlier work, *Stilling the Mind: Shamatha Teachings from Düdjom Lingpa's Vajra Essence*, is based on an oral commentary I gave to the opening section of the *Vajra Essence*, which focuses on the development of attention and introspective skills in preparation for applying such refined mindfulness to the experiential exploration of the mind and its role in nature. This companion volume also stems from an oral commentary I gave to the next section of the *Vajra Essence*, in which Düdjom Lingpa shares the teachings revealed to him in a pure vision of Padmasambhava, elucidating the cultivation of contemplative insight, or vipaśyanā, into the nature of existence as a whole.

I am indebted to Dion Blundell for editing my original oral commentary presented in December 2012 at the Caminho do Meio Institute in Brazil. This present volume would not have been launched without his dedication to bringing Düdjom Lingpa's teachings to the English-speaking world, which he so ably facilitated in his meticulous editing of my translations of the three volumes of *Düdjom Lingpa's Visions of the Great Perfection*. But this turned out to be only the first step in the evolution of this volume. As I continued to reflect on Düdjom Lingpa's writings and their relevance to the modern world, I was inspired to elaborate extensively on my original commentary and to add the introductory essays and afterword. These provide a historical and philosophical context to the root text and commentary, which the earlier volume *Stilling the Mind* does not. It was during this second phase of writing this work that Eva Natanya once again provided her extraordinary skills as a translator, thinker, and scholar to editing all these further additions to this volume. During our work together, we made a number of revisions to my earlier translation of the *Vajra Essence*, some of them simply stylistic in nature, while a few are more substantive. I'm deeply indebted to her for her inimitable contribution to this book. I wish to extend my thanks to Michel Bitbol and David Presti for their critical comments on my essay "The Current Dark Age of Materialism." I am happily indebted, as well, to the general editor David Kittelstrom, the editor Mary Petrusewicz, and the entire staff of Wisdom Publications for their unflagging, enthusiastic support refining and publishing my writings. Above all, I am inexpressibly grateful to my root lama, His Holiness the Dalai Lama, for the personal guidance and inspiration he has given me since I first met him in 1971, and to the Venerable Gyatrul Rinpoché, who has been my principal guide in understanding and practicing the Great Perfection since 1990. This work is my offering to them, to all my other lamas and teachers, and to all those who seek liberation and enlightenment by following in the footsteps of the Buddha and his awakened disciples. For all those with little dust on their eyes, may our efforts be of benefit.

Introduction

The *Vajra Essence* belongs to the class of teachings called *pure visions*. Unlike scholarly treatises and commentaries, such teachings come from the visionary experiences of a treasure revealer, or *tertön*,[3] in this case, one of nineteenth-century Tibet's foremost masters of the Great Perfection, Düdjom Lingpa. His writings transmit profound teachings by the "Lake-Born Vajra," who was the speech emanation of the Indian master Padmasambhava, who in turn is known in Tibet as Guru Rinpoché. The revelation appears in the form of a fascinating dialogue occurring within Düdjom Lingpa's mind. Various aspects of his mind pose questions to his own primordial consciousness, and the pithy and provocative replies elucidate what could today be called depth psychology that taps into the very ground of being!

Düdjom Lingpa's inspiring autobiography has been translated into English as *A Clear Mirror*.[4] From a very young age, his visions of Padmasambhava, Mandarava, Yeshé Tsogyal, and other enlightened beings guided his spiritual progress. Nonhuman deities, ḍākinīs, and accomplished adepts became his primary teachers. He remembered his past lives, including being one of the youngest of Padmasambhava's twenty-five principal disciples, Khyeuchung Lotsawa, or the "boy translator."

The *Vajra Essence* was revealed in a state of vividly clear meditation when Düdjom Lingpa was twenty-seven. In his pure vision, the primordial buddha, Samantabhadra, manifests as the Lake-Born Vajra—an eight-year-old youthful form of Padmasambhava—surrounded by a circle of bodhisattva disciples. One by one, the bodhisattvas rise from their seats, pay homage, and pose questions to the Teacher, who responds with brief and extensive explanations, including pointed questions of his own. The ensuing dialogue explores every stage of the path to buddhahood in this lifetime, from the very beginning to the unexcelled result of the rainbow body, signifying enlightenment. Everything you need to know to attain buddhahood is complete in this text.

To give a panoramic overview of the *Vajra Essence*: A brief introduction leads immediately into the practice of śamatha, or the cultivation of meditative quiescence, which was the subject of my earlier commentary,[5] and then the text moves directly into vipaśyanā, or the cultivation of contemplative insight, the subject of this current volume. Next come the stages of generation and completion, followed by the two main Great Perfection practices—cutting through[6] to pristine awareness and direct crossing over[7] to spontaneous actualization. Finally, through following these practices, one would be able to realize the rainbow body.

On the basis of śamatha and vipaśyanā, the Teacher explains that there are two possible ways to identify the nature of the ground, Samantabhadra: "directly identifying it in your own being, and identifying it in dependence upon the expedient path of the stage of generation."[8] The latter, more gradual path, revealed in its entirety in the *Vajra Essence*, includes elaborate descriptions of various practices within the stages of generation and completion. However, in pure visions that Düdjom Lingpa revealed subsequent to this one, the *Sharp Vajra of Conscious Awareness Tantra* and the *Enlightened View of Samantabhadra*, Padmasambhava indicates that for practitioners who are drawn to simple, direct practices, only four are indispensable: śamatha, vipaśyanā, cutting through, and direct crossing over.[9]

Here we will be discussing the *Vajra Essence* section concerning vipaśyanā, for which I received the oral transmission, teachings, and empowerment from the Venerable Gyatrul Rinpoché. He authorized me to teach this section of the text to serious students, even though they may not have received the Great Perfection empowerments or completed the traditional preliminary practices.

A Serviceable Mind

In this text, the practice of vipaśyanā is referred to as "taking ultimate reality (Skt. *dharmatā*) as the path." One nice metaphor for this is cutting down the tree of ignorance with the axe of wisdom. To chop down this huge tree, you must first be able to plant your feet in a firm stance—this means having a solid foundation in ethics (Skt. *śila*). Then you must be able to swing your axe and repeatedly strike the right spot—this means meditative concentration (Skt. *samādhi*). Finally, you must have a very sharp axe that can cut through ignorance—this means wisdom (Skt. *prajñā*).

In order to derive the full benefits of vipaśyanā, the essential preparation is the practice of śamatha, with the goal of rendering the body and mind serviceable: relaxed, stable, and clear. On this basis, one is well prepared to venture into the profound discoveries and insights of vipaśyanā, which, unlike śamatha, invariably entails an element of inquiry. Such inquiry may be primarily experiential, as in the four close applications of mindfulness,[10] or it may be deeply analytical, as in the Madhyamaka, or Middle Way, approaches to vipaśyanā.[11] Śamatha is exemplified by three practices that have been thoroughly described elsewhere.[12] These are *mindfulness of breathing, taking the impure mind as the path*, and *awareness of awareness*. The Buddha taught that it is our close identification with, or grasping to, the five aggregates, and implicitly the body, speech, and mind, that fundamentally makes us vulnerable to suffering. In his pith instructions on śamatha presented in *The Foolish Dharma of an Idiot Clothed in Mud and Feathers*, Düdjom Lingpa writes that in following the śamatha practice of taking the impure mind as the path, meditators "observe their thoughts 'over there' like an old herdsman on a wide-open plain watching his calves and sheep from afar."[13] The theme of observing the tactile sensations of the body, the "inner speech of the mind" expressing itself in discursive thoughts, and of observing all mental processes and mental consciousness itself as if "from afar" occurs throughout each of these three śamatha practices.

The first of these, mindfulness of breathing, is itself taught in three phases, focusing on the sensations of the respiration throughout the entire body, on the sensations of the rise and fall of the abdomen with each in-breath and out-breath, and on the sensations of the breath at the nostrils. By closely applying mindfulness to the sensations of the respiration, one observes these bodily sensations in a detached manner, thereby counteracting the deeply ingrained tendency to identify with these sensations. In this way, one achieves some degree of separation from the body, which can open the way for the radical shift in perspective that takes place in a much more advanced Vajrayāna practice known as "isolation from the body."[14]

The second śamatha practice, known as taking the impure mind as the path, or *settling the mind in its natural state*, is the principal method taught in the preceding section of Düdjom Lingpa's *Vajra Essence*. This entails *observing* the movements of thoughts rather than *identifying with* them, and in its much higher evolution could be seen as analogous to the Vajrayāna practice of "isolation from the speech."[15]

The third practice is awareness of awareness, for which Padmasambhava provides a detailed explanation in *Natural Liberation: Padmasambhava's Teachings on the Six Bardos*, where he calls it śamatha without signs.[16] In this practice one releases grasping to all the subjective impulses of the mind and observes the flow of mental consciousness itself, thereby counteracting the habit of identifying with any aspect of the ordinary mind. Though certainly not identical with the Vajrayāna practice of "isolation from the mind,"[17] the practice of awareness of awareness can, in its ultimate evolution, lead to the direct realization of pristine awareness. Once breaking through to this level of primordial consciousness, awareness of awareness could become analogous to the Vajrayāna completion-stage realization of the indwelling mind of clear light.

There is a smooth progression among these three śamatha practices. Engaging in mindfulness of breathing, we withdraw our attention from the environment and turn it inward, to the space of the body. While the primary object of mindfulness consists of the sensations correlated with the respiration throughout the body, we also use introspection to monitor the flow of the mind to see if it has fallen into laxity or excitation. Progressing to settling the mind in its natural state, we further withdraw our attention from all five sensory domains, including tactile sensations, and limit it to the mental domain alone. The primary object of mindfulness is the space of the mind and whatever thoughts, images, and other mental events arise within this space. In awareness of awareness, we withdraw our awareness even further; instead of the objects in the mental domain, we invert awareness exclusively upon itself.

You might imagine this to be like drinking a double shot of espresso, so that you are wide awake, and then entering a sensory deprivation tank, in which you are completely isolated from your environment and even your own body. Then, imagine that your mind becomes completely quiet—while at the same time wide awake. With absolutely nothing appearing to your awareness, what do you know? You still know that you are aware.

These three methods are like nested Russian dolls. In mindfulness of breathing, attention is focused primarily on the breath, while introspectively noting and releasing involuntary thoughts and images when they arise. Meanwhile, you're also aware of being aware; you are confident that you are not unconscious. So awareness of awareness is inherent in mindfulness of breathing, as it is while being aware of anything else. When you move to settling the mind in its natural state, the outer Russian doll of awareness of the body falls away, and you focus on the mind alone. But this also entails awareness of awareness. Finally, the Russian doll of the space of the mind and its contents falls away, and you are left with the nucleus that was always present: awareness of awareness. This knowing has been reached by a process of subtraction. By releasing all the other kinds of knowing, you are left with only the knowing of your own awareness.

Śamatha can be described as cultivating a balance among three key characteristics. First is relaxation, which cannot be overemphasized in the modern world, so unlike ancient India or Tibet. Scientists studying the attention find that when people become very aroused and focused, using effort to sustain a high degree of attention, they soon become exhausted. Modern life is a cycle of alternating arousal and exhaustion. To break this cycle, you must learn how to cultivate a deepening sense of release, relaxation, and comfort in body and mind without losing the degree of clarity with which you began. Particularly in the supine position, it's as if you're inviting your body to fall asleep, and your respiration gradually settles in a rhythm as if you were asleep. Never losing the clarity of awareness, this is like falling asleep lucidly. Your body falls asleep, your senses eventually implode, and your mind falls asleep—but you keep the light of awareness on.

On the basis of such deep relaxation, the second balance is to cultivate stability. This means developing a continuity of attention that is free of excitation and lethargy, while never sacrificing the sense of ease and relaxation—the opposite of our habitually tight, focused effort. Attention is maintained continuously, with a deepening sense of ease that reinforces increasing stability.

With this stable foundation, the third balance is to refine and enhance the vividness and acuity of attention without undermining the stability of attention.

The key practices of mindfulness of breathing and settling the mind in its natural state can be very synergistic in balancing these three aspects. Mindfulness of breathing, especially in the supine position, develops relaxation and stability; and settling the mind in its natural state sharpens and refines the vividness of attention.

Düdjom Lingpa's practice of śamatha called *taking the impure mind as the path* means taking our own minds, with their mental afflictions, dualistic grasping, neuroses, and so forth, as the path. This simple method of śamatha entails withdrawing your attention from all five sensory fields and focusing single-pointedly on the domain of the mind: thoughts, memories, dreams, and so on, which are undetectable by the five physical senses and by all instruments of technology. Single-pointedly direct your attention to the domain of mental experience; and whatever arises, let it be. Whether mental afflictions (such as craving, hatred, and confusion), virtues, or nonvirtues arise, simply observe their nature and allow them to release themselves, without following after thoughts of the past or being drawn into thoughts about the future.

Here is a brief synopsis of the stages of this practice as given in the *Sharp Vajra of Conscious Awareness Tantra*. Entry into taking the impure mind as the path is defined by the experience of distinguishing between the stillness of awareness and the movements of the mind. Ordinarily when a thought arises, we have the sense of thinking it, and our attention is diverted to the *referent* of the thought. Similarly, when a desire arises, there is a cognitive fusion of awareness and the desire, so awareness is drawn to the object of desire. In such cases, our very sense of identity merges with these mental processes, with our attention riveted on the object of the thought, desire, or emotion. In this practice, we do our best to sustain the stillness of our awareness, and from this perspective of stillness and clarity we illuminate the thoughts, memories, desires, and so forth that arise in the mind. Distinguishing between the stillness of awareness and the comings and goings of the mind is the entry into the practice of taking the impure mind as the path.

Continuing in the practice, four types of mindfulness are experienced in sequence. First is *single-pointed mindfulness*, which occurs when you simultaneously experience the stillness of awareness and the movement of the mind. This is like watching images coming and going in a movie and hearing the soundtrack, while never reifying these appearances—that is, taking them to be inherently real things—or getting caught up in the drama.

As you grow more accustomed to letting your awareness rest in its own place—accompanied by a deepening sense of loose release and nongrasping, together with the clarity of awareness illuminating the space of the mind—you enter into an effortless flow of the simultaneous awareness of stillness and motion: this second stage is *manifest mindfulness*. Eruptions of memories, desires, and mental afflictions surge up periodically rather than continuously, and over time, your mind gradually settles in its natural state, like a blizzard in a snow globe that gradually dissipates and settles into transparency.

In the third stage of mindfulness, awareness of the body and the five senses withdraws into single-pointed awareness of the space of the mind, and you become oblivious to your body and environment. Prior to this stage, thoughts and other mental appearances become fewer and subtler, until finally they all dissolve and your ordinary mind and all its concomitant mental processes go dormant: this corresponds to *the absence of mindfulness*. Bear in mind that the terms translated as "mindfulness" in Pāli (*sati*), Sanskrit (*smṛti*), and Tibetan (*dran pa*) primarily connote recollection, or bearing in mind. Now you're not recalling or holding anything in mind; your coarse mind has gone dormant, as if you'd fallen into deep, dreamless sleep. But at the same time, your awareness is luminously clear. The coarse mental factor of mindfulness that allowed you to reach this state has also gone dormant; hence it is called *the absence of mindfulness*. When you are in this transitional state, you are aware only of the sheer vacuity of the space of the mind: this is the *substrate* (Skt. *ālaya*). The consciousness of this vacuity is the *substrate consciousness* (Skt. *ālayavijñāna*). Here is a twenty-first-century analogy: When your computer downloads and installs a software upgrade, it becomes non-operational for a short time before the new software is activated. Similarly, when your coarse mind dissolves into the substrate consciousness, the coarse mindfulness that brought you to this point has gone dormant, as if you had fainted—but you're wide awake. This is a brief, transitional phase, and it's important not to get stuck here, for if you do so for a prolonged period, your intelligence may atrophy like an unused muscle. This is like being lucid in a state of dreamless sleep, with your awareness absorbed in the sheer vacuity of the empty space of your mind. That space is full of potential, but for the time being, that potential remains dormant.

Finally, there arises the fourth type of mindfulness: *self-illuminating mindfulness*. This occurs when you invert your awareness upon itself and the substrate consciousness illuminates and knows itself. In the Pāli canon, the Buddha characterized this mind as brightly shining (Pāli *pabhassara*) and naturally pure (Pāli *pakati-parisuddha*). This subtle dimension of mental consciousness is experientially realized with the achievement of śamatha, corresponding to the threshold of the first *dhyāna*, or meditative stabilization. Resting in this state of consciousness you experience three distinctive qualities of awareness: it is blissful, luminous, and nonconceptual. Most important, this awareness is called *serviceable*; both your body and mind are infused with an unprecedented degree of pliancy,[18] so they are fit for use as you wish.

The Buddha explains the profound shift that takes place upon achieving this first dhyāna:

> Being thus detached from hedonic craving, detached from unwholesome states, one enters and remains in the first dhyāna, which is imbued with coarse investigation and subtle analysis, born of detachment, filled with delight and joy. And with this delight and joy born of detachment, one so suffuses, drenches, fills, and irradiates one's body that there is no spot in one's entire body that is untouched by this delight and joy born of detachment.[19]

A similar point is made in the Mahāyāna discourse known as the *Saṃdhinirmocanasūtra*:

> Lord, when a Bodhisattva directs his attention inwards, with the mind focused upon the mind, as long as physical pliancy and mental pliancy are not achieved, what is that mental activity called? Maitreya, this is not śamatha. It is said to be associated with an aspiration that is a facsimile of śamatha.[20]

Even when you emerge from meditation, this body-mind upgrade is yours to employ in your dealings with the world. It's a radical psychophysiological shift; although not irreversible, it can likely be sustained for the rest of your life. The five obscurations of hedonic craving, malice, laxity and dullness, excitation and anxiety, and afflictive uncertainty are largely dormant. There is an unprecedented pliancy and suppleness of both body and mind during formal meditation sessions and between them.

Such refinement of the body's energy system can be cultivated to some degree with controlled breathing and physical exercises such as *prāṇāyāma*, *chi gung*, and *tai chi*. The Buddha knew well the many ascetic disciplines of body and breath practiced in his time, but they are not taught in the Pāli canon; instead, he strongly emphasized the simple practice of mindfulness of breathing. This is a profound practice for settling the subtle body, the energetic body, in its natural state, and it is closely related to settling the mind in its natural state. The Buddha described the benefits of mindfulness of breathing with an analogy:

> Just as in the last month of the hot season, when a mass of dust and dirt has swirled up, a great rain cloud out of season disperses it and quells it on the spot, so too concentration by mindfulness of breathing, when developed and cultivated, is peaceful, sublime, an ambrosial dwelling, and it disperses and quells on the spot unwholesome states whenever they arise.[21]

In the practice of settling the mind, through the process of bringing full, clear awareness single-pointedly to the space of the mind and releasing all control over what appears there, you allow your mind to heal itself. This occurs simply by being gently aware of whatever arises, without the grasping of aversion or desire, and without identifying with thoughts.

Keep in mind that this will not always be a smooth ride! All your angels and demons will rise up to greet you or assault you, depending on how you conceptually designate them. But all the buddhas that appear cannot help you, and all the demons cannot hurt you. You are becoming lucid in the waking state. Like someone who is adept in lucid dreaming, you know that nothing can harm your mind, because nothing you are witnessing is truly existent: everything consists of empty appearances to your mind.

In parallel fashion, the practice of mindfulness of breathing, as the Buddha taught it, is a natural kind of prāṇāyāma. Instead of regulating the breath—as one would in many classical practices of prāṇāyāma—here we're allowing the entire system of the subtle body-and-mind to balance and heal itself. This practice is especially relevant in modern times, when so many of us hold chronic tensions and blockages in the body; if we don't know how to release them, they will block our meditative practice as well as our vital energy (Skt. *prāṇa*).

In mindfulness of breathing, even as we allow the respiration to settle in its natural rhythm, we bring this same quality of awareness (that we bring to the space of the mind, when settling the mind) to the space of the body. We observe the sensations associated with the fluctuations of vital energy, or prāṇa, which correspond to the rhythm of the respiration as they arise throughout the body, and simply let them be. At times the breath may be strong, erratic, or halting; it may be shallow or deep, fast or slow, regular or irregular. Just let it be. Allow the flow of respiration to gradually settle in its natural rhythm, while keeping your awareness still, resting in its own place. After some time, the fluctuations in the energy field of the body corresponding to the respiration will become gentle, subtle, and rhythmic; but don't force this—allow it to occur naturally. Your entire body-mind system settles into equilibrium, and for this to occur, your mind must also become quieter and subtler. Learn how to release control and influence at increasingly subtle levels. Avoid any sort of influence or modification of the breath. The corpse pose (Skt. *śavāsana*) is extremely valuable in this practice because it promotes total relaxation in both body and mind. The challenge is to avoid dullness and lethargy, maintaining the clarity of awareness.

Ordinarily when we know something, it's our conceptual mind that knows, and it knows within a conceptual framework. Nevertheless, all of us experience a state of nonconceptual awareness on a daily basis: deep, dreamless sleep. In nonlucid, dreamless sleep, the mind is nonconceptual and we have no explicit knowledge of anything at all. Even the most obvious fact of our experience—that we are asleep—is unknown to us.

In the practice of śamatha, we seek to cultivate an ongoing flow of explicit knowing that is simultaneously nonconceptual. Even if this knowing is not absolutely nonconceptual, it is not caught up in explicit thoughts. This capability for perceptual knowledge precedes any conceptual labeling or description. It accords precisely with the Buddha's teaching on mindfulness of breathing:

> Breathing in long, one knows, "I breathe in long." Breathing out long, one knows, "I breathe out long." Breathing in short, one knows, "I breathe in short." Breathing out short, one knows, "I breathe out short." One trains thus: "I shall breathe in, experiencing the whole body. I shall breathe out, experiencing the whole body. I shall breathe in, calming the composite of the body. I shall breathe out, calming the composite of the body." Thus, one trains.[22]

There's no need to apply words to this perception. In the early phases of such practice, the duration of the breath may vary considerably during a single session, but as the mind and body settle into a deeper state of equilibrium, the respiration becomes shallow. In my own experience, I have found that it settles into a frequency of fifteen breaths per minute, and over time, the amplitude, or volume, of the breath decreases. Some studies indicate that in deep sleep the respiration occurs at about fifteen breaths per minute, and Vajrayāna Buddhist sources claim that humans experience 21,600 breaths in a twenty-four-hour period, which turns out to be fifteen breaths per minute. It would be interesting to study these parallels more carefully with a combination of contemplative and scientific inquiry.

Scientific studies of lucid dreamers have revealed that the flow of the respiration of the dreamer within the dream corresponds to the flow of the respiration of the dreamer's physical body lying in bed. If, for example, the lucid dreamer holds her breath within the dream, the respiration of her physical body is also suspended for as long as she holds her breath within the dream. This means that by deliberately breathing long and short breaths within the dream, the dreamer can send messages by Morse code to researchers observing the duration of breaths of the dreamer's physical body. It also demonstrates that a lucid dreamer can be aware of the *rhythm* of her physical body's breathing even without being aware of any *tactile sensations* within that physical body. At an even deeper level of consciousness, meditators who are adept at becoming lucid while in dreamless sleep report that they are still able to mentally detect the *rhythm* of their respiration even though they are unaware of any *tactile sensations* within their body. This would imply that people who have achieved śamatha and are resting in the substrate consciousness may still be aware of the rhythm of their respiration, and such mindfulness of the respiration could continue even as one fully achieves the first dhyāna and beyond, with one's awareness immersed in the form realm. Such awareness of the respiration could continue until one achieves the fourth dhyāna, when the respiration ceases altogether for as long as one remains in that meditative state.

The Current Dark Age of Materialism

At the very beginning of his pith instructions in the *Vajra Essence*, prior to explaining how to take the impure mind as the path, Samantabhadra asks the visionary Bodhisattva Boundless Great Emptiness, "Among your body, speech, and mind, which is most important? Which is the main agent?" The bodhisattva explains in detail how the mind is primary, while the speech and body are derivative, concluding with the assertion, "It follows that these three are none other than the mind: they are ascertained to be the mind alone, and this is the best and highest understanding."[23] This statement echoes the opening verse of the *Dhammapada*, in which the Buddha declares: "All phenomena are preceded by the mind, issue forth from the mind, and consist of the mind."[24] A similar assertion is found in the Mahāyāna *Ratnamegha Sūtra*, also attributed to the Buddha: "All phenomena are preceded by the mind. When the mind is comprehended, all phenomena are comprehended. By bringing the mind under control, all things are brought under control."[25] Since Buddhist teachings pertain to the world of experience, "all phenomena" refers to appearances to consciousness rather than to a presumed independent, objective reality, as is usually thought to be observed by scientists.

The Buddhist view is in direct opposition to typical materialist beliefs that among the body, speech, and mind, the body is primary; and that all experiences are preceded by the brain, issue forth from the brain, and consist of the brain; and that when the brain is comprehended, all experiences are comprehended; and that by bringing the brain under control, all mental, verbal, and physical activities are brought under control. Judging by the many references to the mind in contemporary scientific and philosophical writings as well as the general media, we might easily assume that science has already solved the mind-body problem and that the nature and origins of consciousness are no longer mysteries. This is exactly the position taken by the influential philosopher John R. Searle, who declares that there is a simple solution to the mind-body problem, and "this solution has been available to any educated person since serious work began on the brain nearly a century ago, and, in a sense, we all know it to be true. Here it is: Mental phenomena are caused by neurophysiological processes in the brain and are themselves features of the brain."[26] Such scientific knowledge would have to be based on decisive discoveries revealing the necessary and sufficient causes of consciousness, and Searle maintains that this is indeed the case: "Causally we know that brain processes are sufficient for any mental state" and that "consciousness is entirely caused by the behavior of lower-level biological phenomena."[27] He further clarifies, "Consciousness is a system-level, biological feature in much the same way that digestion, or growth, or the secretion of bile are system-level, biological features."[28]

This belief, so clearly articulated by Searle, currently dominates modern academia, the scientific community, the medical establishment, government policy, and the general media worldwide. If scientists have indeed established empirical evidence that demonstrates beyond all reasonable doubt that all mental processes and states of consciousness are produced solely by the brain, they must be able to point to the specific discoveries—eminently worthy of a Nobel Prize—that reveal the necessary and sufficient causes for the emergence of consciousness in humans and in other life forms. But Searle himself acknowledges, "We would . . . need a much richer neurobiological theory of consciousness than anything we can now imagine to suppose that we could isolate necessary conditions of consciousness,"[29] and "If we had an adequate science of the brain, an account of the brain that would give causal explanations of consciousness in all its forms and varieties, and if we overcame our conceptual mistakes, no mind/body problem would remain."[30]

In other words, the hypothesis that the mind is nothing more than a function, or emergent property, of the brain and that consciousness is produced solely by the brain is an expression of faith, unsupported by conclusive empirical evidence. How could this conjecture be accepted so widely with virtually no challenges by scientists or science journalists, who seem to have abandoned the very notion of open-minded inquiry and investigative reporting when it comes to the materialistic reduction of the mind to the brain?

The roots of this anomaly can be traced back 150 years to the seminal writings of the eminent biologist Thomas H. Huxley (1825–95), who was extraordinarily effective in promoting that all scientific research, writing, and teaching should take place within the ideological and methodological constraints of materialism. For him, it was a matter of deep-rooted faith that science alone held the keys to unveiling all the mysteries of the universe. Regarding the relation between the body and mind, he declared, "I hold with the Materialist that the human body, like all living bodies, is a machine, all the operations of which will sooner or later be explained on physical principles. I believe that we shall sooner or later arrive at a mechanical equivalent of consciousness, just as we have arrived at a mechanical equivalent of heat."[31] In other words, his belief, like that of John Searle and many of his scientific and philosophical contemporaries, is based not on any available scientific evidence but rather on his confidence that future scientific research will confirm his metaphysical belief in materialism. Huxley affirms this point when he declares that "there can be little doubt that the further science advances, the more extensively and consistently will all the phenomena of nature be represented by materialistic formulae and symbols."[32] To him, the one true path to knowing the whole of reality was science alone, for "never has the attempt to set bounds to scientific inquiry and to the extension of scientific method, into every subject concerning which a proposition can be framed, proclaimed itself at once so fatuous and so impotent as now."[33]

Although theologians and philosophers have argued over their doctrines and speculations about the nature of the human soul, or consciousness, and the mind-body problem since the dawn of recorded history—without coming to any consensus—it was only in the late nineteenth century that an experimental science of the mind began to emerge. One of the most prominent pioneers of this new movement was the American psychologist William James (1842–1910), who defined this new branch of scientific inquiry: "Psychology is the Science of Mental Life, both of its phenomena and their conditions. The phenomena are such things as we call feelings, desires, cognitions, reasonings, decisions, and the like."[34]

This first generation of psychologists was faced with a dilemma: They could either follow the path of open-minded empiricism, as adopted by Galileo and Darwin, who thus triggered revolutions in the physical sciences and life sciences, or they could confine themselves to the ideological and methodological constraints of materialism, which had already come to dominate all other branches of science. Empiricism demands that one directly observe the phenomena of interest with unbiased, rigorous, sophisticated, precise methods that can be replicated by other suitably trained, open-minded researchers. On the other hand, scientific materialism entails the ideological assumption that all natural phenomena can be understood within the materialistic categories of space, time, matter, and energy; and it assumes that all such phenomena can be adequately explored using instruments of technology to make objective, physical, quantifiable measurements.

It must have been obvious to intelligent, educated people in late nineteenth-century Europe and America that subjectively experienced mental phenomena and states of consciousness could not be measured using the physical instruments of science, and that when observed introspectively, they displayed no physical characteristics. To any sensible person, this is compelling evidence that the mind is not physical. So the only way to explore the nature and origins of the nonphysical events of the mind would be by observing one's own mind—introspectively. While William James acknowledged the value of indirectly inferring facts about the mind by objectively examining its behavioral expressions and neural correlates, as a staunch advocate of radical empiricism, he insisted that when it comes to the scientific exploration of the mind, "Introspective Observation is what we have to rely on first and foremost and always. The word introspection need hardly be defined—it means, of course, the looking into our own minds and reporting what we there discover. Everyone agrees that we there discover states of consciousness."[35]

If one wishes to understand the relationship between any two phenomena, common sense dictates that one should carefully observe each of those phenomena individually, thus gaining a clear understanding of their individual natures and origins. Then one would simultaneously examine both phenomena together to see how they mutually interact. Mental phenomena—as distinct from their behavioral expressions and neural correlates—can be observed only by means of mental perception, or introspection. The body can also be observed introspectively—from the inside out, so to speak—and using this same faculty of introspection to carefully observe one's own psychological and somatic experiences, one can explore how the body and mind influence each other.

For those psychologists who embraced materialism, all scientific references to subjective mental states and to introspection posed a dire threat to their dogmatically held metaphysical doctrine. The materialist backlash to James's empiricism was vociferously promoted by the American behaviorist John B. Watson (1878–1958), who equated psychology with the study of objective, physical, quantitatively measurable human behavior. Arguing that psychology must "bury subjective subject matter [and] introspective method,"[36] he insisted that psychology must "never use the terms consciousness, mental states, mind, content, introspectively verifiable, imagery, and the like."[37] Thus the open-minded empiricism that had been embraced by all the great natural scientists of the preceding three centuries was abandoned in favor of allegiance to a metaphysical doctrine that valued unquestioning belief above experiential observation.

Over the past century, since the rise of behavioral reductionism, countless studies have been conducted on the influence of the body—particularly the brain—on the mind. But far less research has been conducted on the mind's influence on the body, for introspection has been largely excluded from the arsenal of methods scientists use to study mind-body interactions. Objective research has been confined to the study of brain activity and human behavior, while the direct observation of the mind and body from a first-person perspective has been marginalized. The implication of such lopsided research is that the immaterial mental processes are influenced by physical processes in the body, but those immaterial subjective experiences exert no causal influences on the body. As the Nobel prize-winning physicist Richard Feynman declared, "*There is nothing that living things do that cannot be understood from the point of view that they are made of atoms acting according to the laws of physics.*"[38] The Caltech physicist Sean Carroll concurs with this widespread view when he writes, "We are collections of atoms, operating independently of any immaterial spirits or influences, *and* we are thinking and feeling people who bring meaning into existence by the way we live our lives."[39]

Throughout *The Big Picture: On the Origins of Life, Meaning, and the Universe Itself,* Carroll repeatedly insists that the fundamental description of the world includes only atoms, forces, and the laws of physics. All references to "emergent properties" of these physical processes, including thinking and feeling people, mind, ethics, and the meaning of life, are simply "ways of talking" about the one true world of atoms and forces. This bifurcation of the universe into the "ultimate reality" of physical entities and the "conventional realities" of everything else is an expression of the evolutionary biologist Stephen J. Gould's theory of "nonoverlapping magisteria." This is the view that the domains of science and religion do not overlap: science deals with the world of objective facts, while the humanities in general, and religion in particular, are concerned with the world of subjective values.[40] In 1999 the National Academy of Sciences adopted a similar perspective, asserting that "scientists, like many others, are touched with awe at the order and complexity of nature. Indeed, many scientists are deeply religious. But science and religion occupy two separate realms of human experience. Demanding that they be combined detracts from the glory of each."[41]

The specific context of this statement is the relation between Creationism and science, and the authors of this position are quite right in affirming that this particular fundamentalist view can in no way be combined with scientific views. But conflating religious fundamentalism with religion is as misguided as conflating scientific materialism with science. There is nothing glorious in either the closed-minded dogmatism of religious fundamentalism or the equally closed-minded dogmatism of scientific materialism. The former is the bane of religion, while the latter is the bane of science. Scientific materialists can be just as adept at ignoring empirical facts that challenge their beliefs as religious fundamentalists can be at ignoring scientific discoveries that challenge their faith. And the more stridently one faction insists on its own exclusive grasp of reality, the more it triggers fanatical responses from the other side of this chasm between science and religion. Such dogmatic intransigence equally obscures the truths of spiritual and scientific inquiry—dumbing down religion and science in the process—to the point that growing numbers of people blindly embrace materialist values and ideological bias, thus unifying the dark sides of science and religion.

The glaring problem with this dualistic view of the nonoverlapping magisteria is that facts and values have *never* existed independently of each other, and the domains of science and religion have always overlapped, especially concerning the nature of the mind and human identity. No religious person in his right mind would accept the proposition that he should abandon all his religious beliefs regarding the natural world, and no advocate of science can reasonably claim that his views are untouched by nonscientific values. The worldview of scientific materialism tends to be intertwined with hedonic values and a consumer-driven way of life, with each of these three elements supporting the other two. There is no way that one's worldview and values can be disentangled, so the notion that combining genuine scientific inquiry and the nonmaterialist values of religion "detracts from the glory of each" is simply absurd.

Regarding the influence of our subjectively experienced intentions and decisions upon our behavior, Carroll comments, "To the extent that neuroscience becomes better and better at predicting what we will do without reference to our personal volition, it will be less and less appropriate to treat people as freely acting agents. Predestination will become part of our real world."[42] According to this worldview, subjectively experienced mental processes, being inert epiphenomena of the brain, should have no causal influence on the body. But this belief is undermined by the so-called placebo effect, which in fact should be called the "subject-expectancy effect," for its causal efficacy stems from subjective mental processes, including faith, trust, desire, and expectation. The one thing certain about placebo effects is that they are not effects of the placebo!

There is now compelling scientific evidence that the expectancy effect influences not only one's subjective experience, such as decreasing depression and pain, but also exerts measurable influences on the body that accord precisely with one's expectations. For example, studies have shown that when patients were given a placebo, this triggered the release of endogenous opioids, which lessened their pain.[43] In another study, patients with

Parkinson's disease were given a placebo injection, and their expectation that this would relieve their symptoms triggered a "substantial release of endogenous dopamine," which brought out the anticipated effect, "comparable to that of therapeutic doses of levodopa . . . or apomorphine."[44] Simply believing and expecting that the injected substance would relieve their symptoms triggered exactly the mechanisms in the brain that would bring this about, for a decrease in the production of endogenous dopamine contributes to the symptoms of Parkinson's disease.

The Harvard historian Anne Harrington poignantly wonders how "a person's belief in a sham treatment could send a message to his or her pituitary gland to release its own endogenous pharmaceuticals."[45] And Irving Kirsch, a leading researcher in this field, raises the all-important question that is so unsettling to materialists: Even if we assume that expectation is the fundamental factor, "a remaining question is how these expectancies then generate the corresponding responses."[46] Most scientists today treat subjective mental phenomena as products of nervous system activity, and in their view this obviates the mind-body mechanism problem of how subjective mind could act on the objective and physical body. But as we are cautioned by Patrick David Wall, a British neuroscientist described as the world's leading expert on pain, the explanations offered so far seem to be no more than "labelling an unknown process."[47]

The mind's influence on the body is ever present and is certainly not confined to expectation-driven effects, whether those occur positively, in the placebo effect, or negatively, in what is known as the nocebo effect. One area that has attracted scientific attention is neuroplasticity, in which it has been found that brain functions are influenced not only by biological factors influenced by the environment and physical behavior but also by attitudes, emotions, and mental training, including meditation. A provocative overview of this topic is presented in Sharon Begley's book *Train Your Mind, Change Your Brain: How a New Science Reveals Our Extraordinary Potential to Transform Ourselves*. This book was inspired by a meeting between a group of cognitive scientists and His Holiness the Dalai Lama, for which I had the honor of serving as co-interpreter. The Dalai Lama wrote in his foreword:

> We have reached a watershed, an intersection where Buddhism and modern science become mutually enriching, with huge practical potential for human well-being.

A great Tibetan teacher once remarked that one of the mind's most marvelous qualities is that it can be transformed. The research presented here confirms that such deliberate mental training can bring about observable changes in the human brain. The repercussions of this will not be confined merely to our knowledge of the mind: They have the potential to be of practical importance in our understanding of education, mental health, and the significance of ethics in our lives.[48]

Together with Galileo and Descartes, Francis Bacon (1561–1626) was highly influential in setting the course of the Scientific Revolution. He declared that the rise of experimental science was sanctioned by God Himself and presented biblical evidence in support of this view.[49] The gist of his argument was that science would help restore the dominion of man over nature that was lost through Adam's sin. He was also the chief promoter of the ideal of scientific and technological progress, based on the premise that knowledge is power, and when embodied in the form of new technological inventions and mechanical discoveries, it is the force that drives history.

Bacon identified four "idols" that stood in the way of such progress, using this word from the Greek *eidolon* ("image" or "phantom") to refer to a potential deception or source of misunderstanding, especially one that clouds or confuses our knowledge of the physical world.[50] The first of these consists of Idols of the Tribe, which are deceptive beliefs and perceptions inherent in the human mind. These include our senses, which are inherently dull and easily deceivable, which is why Bacon prescribes instruments and strict investigative methods to correct them. In Buddhist epistemology, these would be classified as expressions of "connate ignorance" and include the illusory nature of all appearances to the six senses, the errors of mistaking the impermanent to be permanent, the unsatisfying to be satisfying, that which is not the self to be the self, as well as the connate tendency to reify all phenomena, believing they exist in the way they appear.

Idols of the Cave are those that arise within the mind of the individual, which is symbolically depicted as a dark cave, which is variously modified by temperament, education, habit, environment, and accident. Thus an individual who dedicates his mind to some particular branch of learning becomes possessed by his own peculiar interest and interprets all other learning according to the colors of his own devotion. The beliefs of scientific materialism provide an example of the overreaching influence of the physical sciences into all aspects of how one views reality.

Idols of the Marketplace are errors arising from the false significance bestowed upon the commonly accepted usage of language. A contemporary example of this idol is the current substitution of "brain" for "mind" in scientific and popular accounts. Finally, Idols of the Theater manifest as false beliefs in the fields of religion, philosophy, and science, and because they are defended by people regarded as authorities, they are accepted without question by the general public. A contemporary example of this is the common belief that science alone holds equal authority over all aspects of nature, including the mind and consciousness. These latter three kinds of idols would be examples of what Buddhists call "acquired, or speculative, ignorance."

Inspired by Bacon's notion of Idols of the Tribe, the theoretical physicist David Finkelstein defines an *idol* as an unaffected partner in a coupling of two phenomena.[51] The idol is thus reified as an absolute. In accord with this definition, materialists regard the mind as taking a passive role relative to the brain. In this view, the objective, material reality of the brain is solely responsible for the generation of consciousness and all mental processes, and it is uninfluenced by these subjective phenomena. The brain thus becomes the idol in this coupling of mind and brain. Carroll accordingly claims, "There isn't that much difference between a human being and a robot. We are all just complicated collections of matter moving in patterns, obeying impersonal laws of physics."[52] More broadly speaking, in the natural world at large, objective, physical phenomena are presented as idols insofar as they influence subjective, nonphysical phenomena but are thought to be uninfluenced by them. As Finkelstein cogently argues, the entire history of physics shows how one presumed idol after another has been toppled by empirical research. The idols that have been made of the material world in general and the brain in particular are destined to follow the way of these many idols of the past.

It is a well-known psychological fact that we regard as real only those things that we attend to, while tending to dismiss as fantasy everything that we deliberately or unconsciously ignore. This point was clearly articulated by William James when he wrote:

> The subjects adhered to become real subjects, the attributes adhered to real attributes, the existence adhered to real existence; whilst the subjects disregarded become imaginary subjects, the

attributes disregarded erroneous attributes, and the existence disregarded an existence in no man's land, in the limbo "where footless fancies dwell." . . . Habitually and practically we do not *count* these disregarded things as existents at all . . . They are not even treated as appearances; they are treated as if they were mere waste, equivalent to nothing at all.[53]

In short, "Our belief and attention are the same fact. For the moment, what we attend to is reality."[54] In exact accordance with this principle, the most influential proponent of behaviorism, B. F. Skinner (1904–90), continued to argue forty years after the initial rise of behaviorism that since mental phenomena lack physical qualities, they have no existence whatsoever.[55]

The ideological and methodological agenda of the behaviorists sometimes looks more like a strategy for gaining power and influence rather than an open-minded scientific means of discovering the actual nature of the mind and consciousness, as evidenced by their dedication to cherished beliefs. Skinner makes this abundantly clear when he sets forth his proposal for the materialists' conquest of the mind: "To agree that what one feels or introspectively observes are conditions of one's own body is a step in the right direction. It is a step toward an analysis both of seeing and of seeing that one sees in purely physical terms. After substituting brain for mind, we can then move on to substituting person for brain and recast the analysis in line with the observed facts."[56] In reality, a historical analysis of the reasons for the rejection of introspection as a means to observing the mind shows that this was largely driven by the ideological and methodological dictates of materialism.[57] When observing one's thoughts, mental images, feelings, dreams, and all other subjectively experienced mental states and processes, it becomes obvious that none of them bear any physical attributes whatsoever. This can be disconcerting to those who dogmatically insist that everything in the natural world must be physical. They are forced to conclude either that there is more to the universe than material entities or that mental phenomena are not natural!

If what one feels or introspectively observes regarding one's mental states and processes are in fact physical conditions of the body, they should be physically observable. But they are not. To repeat, if mental phenomena are in fact physical, when one introspectively observes them, they should reveal physical qualities. But they do not. So Skinner takes the first step in his strategy by contradicting all third-person and first-person evidence pointing to the nonphysical nature of the mind. While Skinner uncritically substitutes the brain for the mind—without any compelling argument or empirical evidence—the neuroscientist Donald Hoffman refutes this simple-minded belief: "Now, Huxley knew that brain activity and conscious experiences are correlated, but he didn't know why. To the science of his day, it was a mystery. In the years since Huxley, science has learned a lot about brain activity, but the relationship between brain activity and conscious experiences is still a mystery."[58]

Skinner's justification for ignoring or discounting our first-person experience of mental phenomena seems to be that such observations violate the creed of materialism. If we systematically ignore a method of inquiry, according to the above principle articulated by William James, it should be only a matter of time before that method of inquiry is deemed nonexistent, or fundamentally misleading at best. This is precisely what has occurred for many contemporary researchers in psychology, neuroscience, and philosophy. For example, Alex Rosenberg, codirector of the Center for Social and Philosophical Implications of Neuroscience in the Duke Initiative for Science and Society, writes, "Empirical science has continued to build up an impressive body of evidence showing that introspection and consciousness are not reliable bases for self-knowledge. As sources of knowledge even about themselves, let alone anything else human, both are frequently and profoundly mistaken . . . We never have direct access to our thoughts . . . Self-consciousness has nothing else to work with but the same sensory data we use to figure out what other people are doing and are going to do . . . There is no first-person point of view . . . Our access to our own thoughts is just as indirect and fallible as our access to the thoughts of other people. We have no privileged access to our own minds. If our thoughts give the real meaning of our actions, our words, our lives, then we can't ever be sure what we say or do, or for that matter, what we think or why we think it."[59]

Since its origins roughly fifty years ago, modern neuroscience has not questioned the unverified hypothesis that all mental processes are purely biological in nature, and it sets itself the primary task of providing a comprehensive account of the mind based on this metaphysical assumption. Only evidence that supports this belief is deemed credible, while any evidence to the contrary is dismissed out of hand. This flagrant abandonment of unbiased scientific inquiry—the hallmark of all great scientific advances over the past four centuries—has been accepted without challenge by virtually all researchers in the field.[60] As the eminent neuropsychiatrist Eric R. Kandel unabashedly declares, "The task of modern neuroscience is as simple as it is formidable. Stripped of detail, its main aim is to provide an intellectually satisfying set of explanations in cellular and molecular terms of normal mentation: of perception, motor coordination, feeling, thought, and memory. In addition, neuroscientists would ultimately also like to account for the disorders of functions produced by neurological and psychiatric disease."[61]

Kandel elaborates on his final point of reducing all mental disorders to brain malfunctions as follows: "Our understanding of the biology of mental disorders has been slow in coming, but recent advances like these have shown us that mental disorders are biological in nature, that people are not responsible for having schizophrenia or depression, and that individual biology and genetics make significant contributions . . . The brain is a complex biological organ possessing immense computational capability: it constructs our sensory experience, regulates our thoughts and emotions, and controls our actions. It is responsible not only for relatively simple motor behaviors like running and eating, but also for complex acts that we consider quintessentially human, like thinking, speaking and creating works of art. Looked at from this perspective, our mind is a set of operations carried out by our brain. The same principle of unity applies to mental disorders."[62]

This approach dutifully follows the strategy set forth by Skinner of substituting "brain" for "mind" with regard to all human activities, and this sleight of hand has now become ubiquitous in the popular media. The mystery of the actual relationship between the mind and brain has been obscured by the relentless repetition of the unverified belief that the two are identical. In this way, available empirical evidence pertaining to the nature of mind, the mystery of consciousness, and the unknown relationship between the mind and brain are overshadowed by the falsehoods and groundless speculations of materialists, who undermine the integrity of open-minded scientific inquiry. The public has grown accustomed to seeing "brain" substitute even for personal pronouns such as "I" and "me." All too commonly, scientific writings and the popular press no longer report "I feel, I believe, my pain," but "the brain feels, the brain believes, the brain is subject to signals interpreted as painful." This substitution is even more momentous than the substitution of brain for mind, for speech about mind is still third-personal in its grammar, and therefore it *seems* innocuous to substitute one third-person discourse for another. But in fact, this substitution is a covert form of another substitution that is clearly incorrect: the substitution of a third-person discourse for a first-person discourse.

If the materialists' reduction of mental disorders to brain disorders were supported by the facts, then the great increase in knowledge about the brain and the discovery of many psychoactive drugs for the treatment of mental diseases over the past fifty years should have produced a significant decrease in the prevalence of mental disorders. While such drugs are effective in decreasing the symptoms of various mental disorders—with one out of six Americans regularly taking at least one drug to alleviate the symptoms of mental distress—drugs alone rarely heal the underlying causes. This is where counseling by a wise, compassionate, and experienced therapist comes in. Nevertheless, despite all the advances in drug therapy and talk therapy over the past fifty years, rates of depression have increased tenfold during this period, together with similar increases in other mental diseases such as general anxiety disorder, attention-deficit-hyperactivity disorder, post-traumatic stress disorder, and insomnia. The pseudo-scientific reduction of mental disease to brain disorders is especially influential in so-called developed countries, and it is in exactly those nations that the rise of mental disease is most prevalent. So it seems a plausible hypothesis that the materialist view that mental disorders are nothing more than brain disorders may even be exacerbating mental illness in the modern world.

The gist of the materialist substitution of brain for mind is that the biological organ of the brain is the actual agent of all our actions, and it operates solely in accord with the mindless, amoral laws of physics, chemistry, and biology. The immediate, but widely overlooked, implication of this assertion is that we are not morally responsible for any of our actions. We have no control over our brains, and, according to this view, as advocated by the psychologist Daniel M. Wegner, "It seems to each of us that we have conscious will. It seems we have selves. It seems we have minds. It seems we are agents. It seems we cause what we do ... it is sobering and ultimately accurate to call all this an illusion."[63] Although his materialist deconstruction of human agency, the self, and the mind appears to be similar to Buddhist views, as we shall see in the coming pages, this superficial resemblance obscures profound differences between these two views. In short, this mind-numbing reductionism is demoralizing, dehumanizing, and disempowering for every individual who has been brainwashed into believing it.

By excluding the mind and consciousness from their dystopian vision of the natural world, materialists have depicted not only human existence but also the entire process of natural evolution and the universe at large as meaningless. Worst of all, this existentially nihilistic view is falsely presented as scientific fact. When asked what he believes happens to our consciousness after death, the brilliant theoretical physicist Stephen Hawking, with almost unrivaled scientific authority, replied, "I think the brain is essentially a computer and consciousness is like a computer program. It will cease to run when the computer is turned off."[64] As for the nature of human existence in general, he writes, "The human race is just a chemical scum on a moderate-sized planet, orbiting around a very average star in the outer suburb of one among a hundred billion galaxies."[65] Based on years of research, Stephen Jay Gould concluded that "evolution is purposeless, nonprogressive, and materialistic."[66] And the Nobel Prize–winning physicist Steven Weinberg famously declared, "The more the universe seems comprehensible, the more it also seems pointless."[67] This widespread conflation of reductionist speculation with scientific fact may well be a major reason for the backlash of religious fundamentalists who reject the authority of science altogether. They would prefer to live in a world in which global climate change and natural evolution are myths rather than inhabit the nihilistic, meaningless world of scientific materialism. When the groundless speculations and falsehoods of scientific materialists are rejected in favor of the groundless speculations and falsehoods of religious fundamentalists and self-serving politicians, both science and religion are the first casualties, to the detriment of humanity and the ecosphere we share with all life on Earth.

At the very core of human nature is the undeniable fact of our own consciousness and our awareness of being conscious. But with the relentless denigration of first-person experience by materialists who claim to investigate the mind, even this most indisputable of all facts of our existence is thrown to the wind. Having ignored or at best marginalized our first-person experience of consciousness over the past century, some scientists have shown their readiness to reject its very existence. The Princeton neuroscientist Michael Graziano, for example, answers the question, "How does the brain go beyond processing information to become subjectively aware of information?" with this response: "It doesn't . . . there is no subjective impression; there is only information in a data-processing device."[68] The celebrated physicist Michio Kaku takes a slightly different tack by equating consciousness with mindless, physical reactivity: "Consciousness is the number of feedback loops required to create a model of your position in space, with relationship to other organisms, and finally in relationship to time. So think of the consciousness of a thermostat. I believe that even a lowly thermostat has one unit of consciousness. That is, it senses the temperature around it. And then we have a flower. A flower has maybe ten units of consciousness. It has to understand the temperature, the weather, humidity, where gravity is pointing."[69]

John Searle insightfully sums up the past century of such reductionism: "Earlier materialists argued that there aren't any such things as separate mental phenomena, because mental phenomena *are identical* with brain states. More recent materialists argue that there aren't any such things as separate mental phenomena, because they *are not identical* with brain states. I find this pattern very revealing, and what it reveals is an urge to get rid of mental phenomena at any cost."[70] This dismissal of first-person experience—while legitimizing only the observations made by scientists who religiously adhere to the tenets of materialism—is painfully reminiscent of the domination by entrenched authorities that has taken place during particular periods of history in many parts of the world, often given the appellation of a "Dark Age." Regarding the nature of the mind and consciousness, since the rise of scientific materialism over the past 150 years, modern society has been plunged into a new kind of dark age. Searle provides his own overview of this trend: "It would be difficult to exaggerate the disastrous effects that the failure to come to terms with the subjectivity of consciousness has had on the philosophical and psychological work of the past half century. In ways that are not at all obvious on the surface, much of the bankruptcy of most work in the philosophy of mind and a great deal of the sterility of academic psychology over the past fifty years . . . have come from a persistent failure to recognize and come to terms with the fact that the ontology of the mental is an irreducibly first-person ontology."[71] He sums up this point with the comment, "More than anything else, it is the neglect of consciousness that accounts for so much barrenness and sterility in psychology, the philosophy of mind, and cognitive science."[72]

Writing at the dawn of the new science of the mind, William James observed, "Psychology, indeed, is to-day hardly more than what physics was before Galileo, what chemistry was before Lavoisier. It is a mass of phenomenal description, gossip, and myth, including, however, real material enough to justify one in the hope that with judgment and good-will on the part of those interested, its study may be so organized even now as to become worthy of the name of natural science at no very distant day."[73] Sadly, this is truer now than it was when he wrote those words. The two materialist options of reducing the mind to the brain or denying its existence altogether present a false view not only of human existence but also of reality as a whole. One might study comprehensive accounts of the scientific knowledge of the universe at large and the evolution of life on our planet without finding any mention of the nature and origins of the mind and consciousness. Dominated by materialism, scientists have largely ignored the role of their own minds in scientific research and dismissed the role of consciousness in the universe. In his classic work *The Future of an Illusion*, Sigmund Freud declared, "The problem of a world constitution that takes no account of the mental apparatus by which we perceive it is an empty abstraction, of no practical interest."[74] The "world constitution" as depicted by modern science has no account of the nature and origins of the human mind or of consciousness in general. It is a view of a world in which consciousness is nonexistent or deemed so irrelevant that its exclusion is of no significance. But such a world exists only in the imagination of its believers.

The modern world is in desperate need of rescue from the clutches of reductionism, with its triadic juggernaut of materialism, hedonism, and consumerism, which is rapidly despoiling human civilization and the ecosphere. Ironically, we may look for inspiration to the one scientist who more than any other was responsible for the domination of science and human civilization by scientific materialism. This is none other than Thomas Huxley, who wrote, "Of all the miserable superstitions which have ever tended to vex and enslave mankind, this notion of the antagonism of science and religion is the most mischievous. True science and true religion are twin-sisters, and the separation of either from the other is sure to prove the death of both. Science prospers exactly in proportion as it is religious; and religion flourishes in exact proportion to the scientific depth and firmness of its basis."[75] To consider the possibility that religion may shed light on nonphysical realities that modern science has denied, perhaps we should look beyond the confines of Eurocentric civilization to wisdom traditions that have not been corrupted by the superstitions of materialism. As Einstein and fellow scientists implored Americans in 1946, facing the crisis to humanity from the devastating power of the atomic bomb, "A new type of thinking is essential if mankind is to survive and move toward higher levels."[76] It is here that Buddhism, which evolved outside the matrix of Eurocentric civilization—and which takes the mind as a central focus rather than dismissing it—may shed a bright light to help us fathom the mind in this dark age of materialism.

1. The Nature of the Mind

To achieve a consensual body of knowledge concerning the nature and origins of the mind that is comparable to scientific knowledge about many aspects of the objective, physical world, mental processes must be approached with the same spirit of unbiased empiricism that has inspired the past four hundred years of scientific inquiry. This means that mental phenomena should be observed with all the diligence and precision that Galileo and Darwin applied to physical and biological phenomena. William James recognized this fact in the late nineteenth century, but psychologists abandoned introspection, ostensibly because it failed to yield rigorous, replicable results. James was well aware of the challenges facing the first-person, scientific exploration of the mind, but he concluded that these were common to all kinds of observation: "introspection is difficult and fallible; and . . . the difficulty is simply that of all observation of whatever kind. . . . The only safeguard is in the final consensus of our farther knowledge about the thing in question, later views correcting earlier ones, until at last the harmony of a consistent system is reached."[77]

Nineteenth-century scientific attempts to use introspection to investigate the mind were primitive, faltering, with only rudimentary means for refining attention skills in general. The leading US researcher in this field was Edward B. Titchener (1867–1927), who created the largest doctoral program in the field of experimental psychology in the United States at the time, after becoming a professor at Cornell University. Having devoted his life to the development of introspective techniques, he observed that the main difficulties of introspection are "maintaining constant attention" and "avoiding bias," but a further difficulty is "to know what to look for."[78] But as we have noted previously, with the rise of behavioral psychology toward the beginning of the twentieth century, the direct observation and exploration of the mind by means of introspection was abandoned with the rise of behavioral psychologists, who simply decided to view the mind as nothing more than physical dispositions for behavior. From this time onward, the scientific study of the mind has been dominated by the ideological and methodological constraints of materialism. As we have seen, this approach gained further momentum with the rise of neuroscience in the 1960s, at which point experts in this field simply decided that the mind should be viewed as a biological function of the brain.

As we noted in the opening discussion on the śamatha practices of mindfulness of breathing, taking the impure mind as the path, and awareness of awareness, such advanced training in mental balance and concentration provides just the skills needed to engage in rigorous investigations of the mind and its role in nature. When the achievement of śamatha is conjoined with a range of practices of vipaśyanā, such research has illuminated four aspects of the mind's nature, based on replicable, empirical discoveries made by thousands of contemplatives throughout Asia. These are the phenomenological nature of consciousness, the essential nature of the mind, the ultimate nature of the mind, and the transcendent nature of consciousness that lies within the very ground of the whole of reality.

The Phenomenological Nature of Consciousness

While modern scientists and philosophers have proposed a wide range of definitions of consciousness, they have achieved no consensus, nor have they devised any scientific means of measuring consciousness. They have left us in the dark regarding the nature and origins of consciousness and its relationship to the body and the natural world at large. In the tradition of Buddhism originating in India and evolving further in Tibet for more than a millennium, contemplatives and scholars long ago identified two defining characteristics of consciousness: *luminosity*[79] and *cognizance*.[80] A definition of any entity is useful insofar as it enables one to identify that entity when it is observed and to distinguish it from all other entities. The Buddhist definition of consciousness satisfies these criteria, whereas the many notoriously diverse materialist definitions do not. The characteristic of *luminosity* (the Tibetan word for which may also be rendered as *clarity*) has a twofold meaning. The first is that consciousness is *clear* in the sense of being insubstantial, devoid of materiality. When observed directly, consciousness displays no physical qualities whatsoever—no mass, size, shape, velocity, or location—nor can it be measured or detected with any physical instrument. The second meaning is that consciousness *illuminates*, or *makes manifest*, all sensory and mental appearances. Were it not for consciousness, there would be no appearances of any kind. Consciousness enables us to experience visual shapes and colors, sounds, smells, tastes, and tactile sensations, as well as all mental processes, including thoughts, the arising of mental images, desires, emotions, dreams, and so on. The *cognizance* of consciousness refers to the experience of knowing and understanding the objects that appear to consciousness.

The obvious fact of the immateriality of consciousness has been fiercely resisted by materialists, who insist that the only things that exist are those that can be measured through physical means, namely, matter, energy, space, time, and their emergent properties. Over the past four hundred years, scientists have explored a vast array of physical entities, and without exception, their functions and emergent properties have also been found to have physical characteristics. But the materialists' assertion that the mind and consciousness are functions or emergent properties of the brain is an exceptional claim that is unsupported by compelling evidence. It is well known that mental and neural processes are correlated; however, as noted previously, the actual nature of those correlations remains as much as mystery as it was during Huxley's time. Indeed, he found ludicrous the very idea that states of consciousness could actually emerge from the activity of neurons: "How it is that any thing so remarkable as a state of consciousness comes about as a result of irritating nervous tissue, is just as unaccountable as the appearance of the Djin when Aladdin rubbed his lamp."[81]

Materialists would have us believe that there are only two options when considering the relation between the body and mind: either one adopts the mind-body dualism of Descartes, which is seen as having been discredited by contemporary science, or one accepts the view of materialistic monism, which is the metaphysical foundation for science promoted by Huxley. Both of these alternatives have proven sterile and unilluminating in terms of fathoming the nature and origins of the mind, so it is high time to escape the confines of this ideological straitjacket. Beyond the dichotomy of monism and dualism is the open expanse of a pluralistic universe, consisting of a wide range of phenomena that fall outside the categories of either mind or matter.[82] These include such nonphysical phenomena as meaningful information, appearances to consciousness, the mathematical laws of nature, and mathematical truths in general—along with justice, beauty, and human beings, who possess bodies and minds but are equivalent to neither.

Among the diverse phenomena that do not consist of states of matter *or* of mind, information is of particular interest, especially as modern civilization evolves beyond the industrial age to the information age. With the widespread use of personal computers and the Internet, we commonly refer to the amount of information stored in such systems; and since the brain is viewed as a biological computer, there is much talk of information being stored in brain circuits and processed by neurons and synapses. Many scientists and journalists go so far as to claim that individual neurons themselves "consciously" process and relay information to other parts of the brain, without being able to explain how the individual "consciousnesses" of a hundred billion neurons in the brain coalesce into the unitary stream of consciousness each of us experiences firsthand.

The philosopher John Searle challenges this naïve belief: "The information in the computer is in the eye of the beholder, it is not intrinsic to the computational system . . . The electrical state transitions of a computer are symbol manipulations only relative to the attachment of a symbolic interpretation by some designer, programmer or user."[83] In other words, meaningful, semantic *information* is not objectively present inside a computer in the same way that silicon chips are present. The information we say is stored in a computer exists *only in relation to the conscious agents* who create, program, and use computers. George F. R. Ellis further clarifies that bits of information "exist as nonmaterial effective entities, created and maintained through social interaction and teaching . . . Thus while they may be represented and understood in individual brains, their existence is not contained in any individual brain and they certainly are not equivalent to brain states. Rather the latter serve as just one of many possible forms of embodiment of these features."[84]

Consciousness—as the simple experience of being aware—is not an attribute of individual neurons or silicon chips, and there is no compelling evidence that such consciousness is an emergent property of the brain conceived as some kind of biological computer. The word "consciousness" has been used so often now in a loose and undefined figurative sense, in an almost playful effort to personify observed physical processes, that the scientific community sometimes seems to forget what it is we all experience as the fact of being conscious every day, which involves *being aware*. If we keep in mind such first-person experience, then it becomes readily evident that individual neurons just don't have the experience of being aware. Yet a belief in some imagined existence of a "consciousness" that could be an emergent property of matter has in many cases become an unquestioned assumption that precedes virtually all relevant scientific research while ignoring scientific evidence to the contrary.

The root of much modern confusion about the nature of information arises from the conflation of quantitative and qualitative information. Quantitative information, as defined by physicists, is the pattern of organization of matter and energy, which is inversely related to entropy. Qualitative, or semantic, information is meaningful in that it has a referent that is known by a conscious being.[85] Quantitative information is objectively measurable, whereas semantic information exists only relative to a conscious agent who is informed. The chemicals and electricity inside computers and brains have no referents. In and of themselves, they aren't *about* anything, and they don't *refer to* anything, any more than the letters "S T O P" refer to anything apart from their being understood by conscious agents who have agreed among themselves what this sequence of letters means. This point was clearly recognized seventy years ago by the MIT mathematician and philosopher Norbert Wiener (1894–1964): "The mechanical brain does not secrete thought 'as the liver does bile,' as the earlier materialists claimed, nor does it put it out in the form of energy, as the muscle puts out its activity. Information is information, not matter or energy. No materialism which does not admit this can survive at the present day."[86] Unfortunately, materialism has indeed survived to the present day, in part due to materialists' successful campaign to supplant this inconvenient truth with spurious conjectures.

Materialists tend to feel most at home in the mechanistic materialism that characterized physics during the closing decades of the nineteenth century. But cognitive scientists in particular have largely overlooked, misunderstood, or marginalized the revolutionary implications of quantum physics that emerged in the early twentieth century. As the physicists Časlav Brukner and Anton Zeilinger explain: "In classical physics a property of a system is a primary concept prior to and independent of observation and information is a secondary concept which measures our ignorance about properties of the system. In contrast in quantum physics the notion of the total information of the system emerges as a primary concept, independent of the particular complete set of complementary experimental procedures the observer might choose, and a property becomes a secondary concept, a specific representation of the information of the system that is created spontaneously in the measurement itself."[87]

Rather than viewing quantum systems as local, anomalous conditions created and protected from outside influences in physics laboratories, the eminent theoretical physicist John Archibald Wheeler (1911–2008), in collaboration with Bryce DeWitt, applied the principles of quantum physics to the universe as a whole, resulting in the field known as "quantum cosmology." One startling finding was that for the universe at large, time itself disappeared from the equations: the universe is frozen. Only when they introduced an "observer-participant," with a perceptual reference point in space-time, did time and a changing universe manifest. The evolution of the universe can occur only when a subjective consciousness declares his or her "now," thereby establishing both past and future relative to that present moment. But past and future exist only relative to this observer-participant; they are not absolutely existent.[88] This interpretation casts a fresh light on the so-called measurement problem in quantum physics, which has remained unsolved since it was first identified almost a century ago. According to Wheeler, for a measurement to take place, a true observation of the physical world must impart *meaningful information*, signifying a transition from the realm of mindless stuff to the realm of conscious knowledge. Rather than thinking of the universe as matter in motion, he proposed that one could regard it as information being processed, and this requires the participation of conscious observers who are aware of such information.

A major reason why scientists so widely believe that consciousness must emerge from matter stems from the current scientific understanding of the evolution of the cosmos as a whole. According to modern cosmology, the universe began with the emergence of matter and energy following the Big Bang, roughly 13.7 billion years ago; our planet formed about 5 billion years ago, and organic life first emerged roughly 3.5 billion years ago. Over the course of biological evolution on Earth, there is no physical record indicating the first emergence of conscious organisms, for the simple reason that consciousness is physically undetectable. But it is assumed that the first conscious organisms evolved from more primitive, less complex, unconscious organisms, so the emergence and development of higher and higher levels of consciousness in living organisms must be correlated with increasing degrees of complexity in their brains.

The logic of this argument appears to be irrefutable until one notes a simple fact that is almost universally overlooked by cosmologists and biologists: This entire narrative of the history of the universe and of life on Earth is based solely upon physical measurements. If you ask only physical questions and perform only physical measurements, the universe you conceive on this basis will contain only physical entities. If there were in fact nonphysical influences on the origin and evolution of the universe and living organisms, physicists and biologists would fail to discover them, as long as they limit themselves to the current methods of scientific inquiry. In short, the modern scientific view of the universe and humanity's place in it is materialistic for a simple reason: all observations that inform it are restricted to physical phenomena. The mind, consciousness, and all other nonphysical phenomena throughout the universe have been excluded from this reductionist worldview. Since the only world we know to exist is one in which the minds of conscious beings play the all-important role of *illuminating* and *knowing* the reality we inhabit, any projected universe that would consist solely of physical phenomena is a fantasy in the imaginations of those who have conceived it.

But if the universe that we experience exists only in relation to our experience of it, how could this be compatible with the known scientific facts concerning the evolution of the universe and life on Earth? John Wheeler offers a revolutionary solution to this conundrum. According to him, the universe consists of a "strange loop," in which physics gives rise to observers and observers give rise to at least part of physics. The conventional view of the relationship between observers and the objective world is that matter yields information, and information makes it possible for observers to be aware of matter by way of measurements. This can be depicted as a sequence: matter → information → observers. Wheeler, on the contrary, proposes that the presence of observers makes it possible for information to arise, for there is no information without someone who is informed. Matter is a category constructed out of information. Thus Wheeler inverts the sequence: observers → information → matter.[89]

This implies that the current scientific narrative of the history of the universe is not absolutely real and objective, existing prior to and independent of all measurements. Wheeler explains, "It is wrong to think of that past as 'already existing' in all detail. The 'past' is theory. The past has no existence except as it is recorded in the present. By deciding what questions our quantum registering equipment shall put in the present we have an undeniable choice in what we have the right to say about the past."[90] This implies that at the macrocosmic level, the universe is fundamentally an information-processing system, from which the appearance of matter emerges at a higher level of reality. At the microcosmic level, each sentient being is a conscious, information-processing system. In both cases, it is *semantic* information, and not objective, quantitative information, that is crucial. Thus, in quantum physics, the "materiocentric" view of the universe has been supplanted by an "empiricocentric" view; and this reframing is at least as far-reaching in its consequences as the reframing from a geocentric to a heliocentric view of humanity's place in the cosmos.

Brukner and Zeilinger caution that this hypothesis "does not imply that reality is no more than a pure subjective human construct."[91] On the basis of observations, scientists are able to conceive of objects with sets of properties that do not change across diverse modes of observation and description. They are "invariants" with respect to those observations. Predictions based on any such specific invariants may then be verified by any sufficiently trained observer, and as a result intersubjective agreement about the theories in question may be achieved; and this gives the impression that these invariant, mentally constructed objects exist at a level more fundamental than scientists' measurements and conceptual formulations.

Scientists or not, whenever we conceive of an entity, we think in terms of the entity as a "whole," which bears multiple parts and attributes. But which of these, if any, are objectively real and independent of our conceptual designation of them? William James suggests that "'Wholes' are not realities there, parts only are realities." Wholes are "not realized by any organ or any star, or experienced apart from the consciousness of an onlooker."[92] But as soon as we identify a part of any whole, that part itself is identified as having its own parts or attributes, in which case it, too, becomes a whole. Even the very notions of "part" and "whole" have no meaning independent of each other. To speak of a part that is unrelated to a whole is as meaningless as speaking of a whole with no parts. Yet if one exists only relative to the other, *they must both exist only relative to the mind that conceives of them.* James undermines his own assertion of the independent reality of parts when he cites the Scottish philosopher Edward Caird (1835–1908), who comments, "Isolate a thing from all its relations, and try to assert it by itself; you find that it has negated itself as well as its relations. The thing in itself is nothing."[93]

This principle of interdependence also applies to the relationships within the triad of semantic information, the informed consciousness, and the referent of the information; and this is key to understanding the implications of quantum cosmology. Remove any one of these three elements and the other two vanish simultaneously. That is, in the absence of semantic information, there can be nothing about which one is informed and no one who is informed about it. Likewise, if there is no conscious agent who is informed, there can be no flow of information and hence no reference to anything about which one might be informed. Finally, if there is no referent of the information, the categories "information" and "the consciousness that is informed" are devoid of meaning. This implies that consciousness lies at the very foundation of the known universe, and it is mutually interdependent with the information it perceives and the phenomena of which it is informed. Each of these three elements is devoid of existence in and of itself, for all three arise in mutual interdependence.

Much insight is to be gained from the analogy of the macrocosm of the universe to the microcosm of a human being. On this theme the Buddha declared, "It is in this fathom-long body with its perceptions and its mind that I describe the world, the origin of the world, the cessation of the world, and the way leading to the cessation of the world."[94] Rather than reducing human existence to an amalgam of matter and energy, it may be far more illuminating to regard ourselves primarily as conscious information-processing beings, who have conceived of the derivative constructs of matter and energy. We are not configurations of stardust, but rather the conscious creators of our known physical world, which we commonly conceive in the mentally constructed categories of matter, energy, and their emergent properties.

Waking up from the fantasy that only physically measurable phenomena exist, we may swiftly note that all the immediate contents of our sensory and mental experience are nonphysical. Appearances to our physical senses, such as colors and sounds, do not exist in the objective world, independently of our physical senses, nor do they exist inside our heads. All the information that we process about the world is devoid of any physical attributes, as noted previously. The physical world as it is imagined to exist independently of all nonphysical appearances and information can never be observed by anyone. This is not to say that the physical world doesn't exist, only that the physical world—as we observe it and make sense of it—doesn't exist independently of our observations and concepts.

This cutting-edge view of the interrelated nature of mind and matter, and more specifically the mind and body, finds a basis in even the earliest of Buddhist writings. For example, the Sri Lankan Buddhist monk and scholar Weragoda Sarada Maha Thero explains that the Pāli terms *nāma* and *rūpa*, sometimes translated as "mind" and "body," are in fact not two separate, inherently real entities that somehow interact with each other. Rather, they are two ways of looking at a unified experience. He suggests that *nāma* (lit. "naming") is experience seen subjectively as "the mental process of identifying an object." *Rūpa* ("appearing form") is experience seen objectively as "an entity that is perceived and conceived through the mental process of identification." *Manō*, often translated as "mind" or "mentation," refers to "the mental process of conceptualization, which integrates and makes meaning out of the different percepts brought in through the different senses." This meaningful total experience is viewed subjectively as the "identification of an entity" (*nāma*) and objectively as "the entity identified" (*rūpa*).[95]

The "mind-body problem" that has plagued Eurocentric civilization for centuries was created and has been perpetuated by a way of thinking that assumes that the mind and body exist as separate, inherently real entities that inexplicably interact with each other. Cartesian dualists have never been able to present a compelling explanation for how such interaction occurs, and materialist monists have pretended to solve the problem either by equating the mind with physical processes—without justification—or by dismissing the existence of the mind altogether. By challenging the metaphysical assumption that underlies this problem, Buddhists can show that the problem begins to unravel by itself.

The Essential Nature of the Mind

To understand what is meant in a Buddhist context by the "essential nature"[96] of the mind, we may contrast this with its "manifest nature."[97] The practice of *taking the impure mind as the path*, also called *settling the mind in its natural state*, which was introduced earlier, is a sophisticated method for examining the manifest nature of thoughts, memories, desires, emotions, and all manner of mental appearances. From the vantage point of the stillness of awareness, one may observe with an increasingly rigorous "internal objectivity" the circumstances by which mental events arise, how they are present once they have arisen, and how they vanish. In the classic Buddhist practice of closely applying mindfulness to the mind,[98] one also examines whether mental phenomena are stable or in constant flux, are veritable sources of well-being or fundamentally unsatisfying, and whether they are by their own nature "I" and "mine" or simply events arising in dependence upon prior causes and conditions. Moreover, a central theme in such investigations is to determine which mental factors play crucial roles in afflicting the mind and triggering harmful behavior and which give rise to a genuine sense of well-being for oneself and others. Specifically, one examines the ways in which craving, hostility, and delusion disrupt the equilibrium of the mind and generate unease, anxiety, and unhappiness.

The manifest nature of mind that is scrutinized in such practice does arise in dependence upon brain activity and physical stimuli from the body and environment, as well as on the basis of prior states of consciousness and mental processes. So this mind is strongly configured, or conditioned, by many environmental, physiological, and psychological factors that are uniquely human. In the practice of *settling the mind in its natural state*, one allows this flow of consciousness that is shaped by all such factors to "melt" into a progressively primal flow that is called the "essential nature of the mind." The relation between the manifest and essential nature of the mind may be likened to that between a specialized cell, such as a neuron, and a stem cell. Just as a stem cell is configured by biological factors to become any one of a wide variety of specialized cells, so this primal flow of consciousness, known as the *substrate consciousness*, is configured by mental and physical factors to become a wide range of human and nonhuman minds.

To review the method of settling the mind in its natural state: While resting in the stillness of awareness, withdraw the attention from all five domains of sensory experience, and focus single-pointedly on the domain of mental events, observing whatever thoughts arise, without following after those pertaining to the past, and without being drawn into thoughts about the future. Do not try to modify, block, or perpetuate any mental events that arise, but simply observe their nature, without letting your attention be drawn away to any referents of thoughts or images. Sustain the flow of mindfulness without being distracted by any objective appearances to your five physical senses, and without identifying with any subjective mental impulses or processes. Sustain the stillness of your awareness in the midst of the movements of the mind. As the Buddha Samantabhadra explains in the *Vajra Essence*, "Fluctuating thoughts do not cease; however, mindful awareness exposes them, so you don't get lost in them as usual. By applying yourself to this practice continuously at all times, both during and between meditation sessions, eventually all coarse and subtle thoughts will be calmed in the empty expanse of the essential nature of your mind. You will become still, in an unfluctuating state in which you experience bliss like the warmth of a fire, luminosity like the dawn, and nonconceptuality like an ocean unmoved by waves."[99]

The culmination of this process of settling the mind in its natural, or unconfigured, state occurs, as Samantabhadra comments, when:

> finally the ordinary mind of an ordinary being disappears, as it were. Consequently, compulsive thinking subsides and roving thoughts vanish into the space of awareness. You then slip into the vacuity of the substrate, in which self, others, and objects disappear. By clinging to the experiences of vacuity and luminosity while looking inward, the appearances of self, others, and objects vanish. This is the *substrate consciousness* . . . in truth you have come to the essential nature [of the mind].[100]

All sensory and mental appearances are illuminated, or made manifest, by this substrate consciousness, but it does not enter into, or cognitively fuse with, these appearances. They do not arise anywhere in physical space, but rather emerge from, are located in, and eventually dissolve back into the immaterial space of the substrate. The substrate is clearly ascertained when the mind has completely settled into its natural state, but you also enter into this state in deep, dreamless sleep, when you faint, and in the culminating phase of the dying process.

As noted above, the three salient characteristics of the substrate consciousness are bliss, luminosity, and nonconceptuality. When experienced from within the context of the ordinary mind, the three primary mental afflictions of craving, hostility, and delusion are seen to be highly toxic, disruptive influences on the mind. But when these same mental processes are viewed from the perspective of the substrate consciousness, one recognizes that their essential natures correspond respectively to bliss, luminosity, and nonconceptuality, from which each of those afflictions arises. As these primal qualities of the essential nature of the mind become conditioned and manifest in the ordinary human mind, they become afflictive, but their *essential* nature is not toxic in any way.

This raises the more general question of the causal origination of all states of consciousness and mental processes. In the mid-nineteenth century, the

German physicist Hermann von Helmholtz mathematically formalized the principle of the conservation of energy, which implies that in the world of nature, nothing ever arises from nothing, nor does something that exists ever transform into nothing, disappearing without a trace. All configurations of matter-energy emerge from prior configurations of matter-energy, and the same is true of configurations of space-time. This principle of conservation, which is a central pillar of modern physics, pertains to all the fundamental constituents of nature, so it is reasonable to ask: Does it also hold for the emergence and disappearance of consciousness?

We may consider three basic alternatives. First, if consciousness is non-physical, as indicated by all evidence, then the hypothesis that it emerges from a configuration of matter-energy would violate the physical principle of conservation of matter-energy, for this would entail something physical transforming into something not physical.

Second, if consciousness emerges from nothing, this would make it unlike anything else in the known world, while also defying common sense: How could nothing ever be influenced so that it transforms into something?

Third, if consciousness emerges from something nonphysical and it follows the same principle of conservation as matter-energy and space-time, then it must emerge from a prior configuration of consciousness, which is in fact the Buddhist view.

Of course, a fourth option is that consciousness is indeed physical, as so many materialists believe, at least those who don't deny its existence altogether. Evidence against this hypothesis is that it displays no physical characteristics when experienced directly, and it can't be measured with any physical instrument. States of consciousness in humans have been found to be correlated with brain states, and there is as much evidence that the brain influences the mind as there is that the mind influences the brain. But the mere fact that mental processes correspond to physical processes in the brain in no way logically implies that they are identical or that the mind is physical.

In the Buddhist analysis of causality, a clear distinction is drawn between a substantial cause[101] and a cooperative condition.[102] A substantial cause transforms into its effect and loses its own identity in the process, while a cooperative condition influences its effect without losing its identity in doing so. For example, a kernel of corn is a substantial cause of a stalk of corn, for the substance of the kernel transforms into the substance of the stalk, and in so doing, its identity as a kernel is lost as it becomes the stuff of the stalk. A farmer's decision to plant a field of corn, the tractor he uses to plow the field, and the workers who sow the crop all serve as cooperative conditions for the emergence of stalks of corn, but they do not transform into the crop. These two types of causality are prevalent in the field of physics as well. According to classical physics, when one billiard ball strikes another, it acts as a cooperative condition for the second ball to move, but it doesn't turn into that ball; and particles of matter influence fields and vice versa as cooperative conditions, but do not turn into them. According to Einstein's theory of relativity, space-time and mass-energy mutually influence each other as cooperative conditions without space-time turning into configurations of mass-energy or vice versa. Finally, in quantum physics, according to the Copenhagen Theory, the act of measurement causes a probability field to collapse, but it does not transform into that probability field or into the elementary particles or waves that arise relative to the measurement system.

Likewise, based on the above Buddhist analysis of the causation of human consciousness and the empirical discoveries of contemplatives who have recognized the substrate consciousness and its relation to the manifest nature of the human mind, the substantial cause of human consciousness has been identified as the substrate consciousness that transforms into it, and its cooperative conditions include many physical influences such as the formation of the human body and various environmental factors. In short, the physical body *conditions* human consciousness, as well as the whole range of human mental and sensory processes, but no state of consciousness or mental process ever directly *emerges* from the body or any other physical phenomenon.

At the same time, as we will see in the chapters to come, it can properly be said that states of consciousness strongly condition the way that a body will arise and appear for the person who consciously calls that body "mine." The relationship between subtle states of mind and the subtle physical energies with which they are correlated throughout one's lifetime is often explained with the analogy of a rider and his horse. Without the horse, the rider (a configured mind) has no ability to travel through space, no ability to engage with its objects of awareness in particular locations. But without the rider, the horse (the subtle energies, but one might also say the body in general) is blind, for physical matter in itself is not *aware*. The body is said to be the "support"[103] for a human life, while the mind is said to be that which is "supported."[104] Yet as in the analogy of a rider supported by a horse—or a house supported by the earth—this in no way suggests that the rider *emerged* from the horse, or that the house was produced by its foundation, as though the latter were the substantial cause of the former. Rather, just as a rider can get onto one horse, dismount, and get onto another one, but as long as he is riding, he is indeed "supported" by that horse, Buddhist contemplatives have understood that both the coarse and subtle levels of consciousness ride upon the physical support of a body for as long as a particular sentient being is alive. At death, however, this intimate interrelationship is severed, so that the mind no longer rides that particular configuration of subtle energies and coarse matter with which it had once identified. The subtle continuum of mental consciousness continues, and due to the driving force of karmic propensities, this substrate consciousness will eventually find a new "horse"—or more precisely, start influencing the formation of a new body. This in turn will take place only when the suitable cooperative conditions (parents, viable cells, etc.) have been assembled for consciousness to take birth on the basis of—but not produced by—a new physical support. Thus, the substantial cause for the consciousness of the new lifetime remains the substrate consciousness, even as its later continuation is now supported, or conditioned, by a new configuration of physical matter.

The substrate consciousness is known by various names within the Buddhist and other contemplative traditions. In the *Commentary on Bodhicitta*, attributed to the famed Nāgārjuna, it is stated:

> When iron approaches a magnet, it quickly spins into place.
> Although it has no mind, it appears as though it did.
> In the same way, the substrate consciousness has no true existence,
> yet when it comes [from a previous life] and goes [to the next]
> it moves just as though it were real.
> And so it takes hold of another lifetime in existence.[105]

In Mahāyāna Buddhism, especially as interpreted by the Tibetan master Jé Tsongkhapa (1357–1419), this foundational level of consciousness has also been called the "subtle mind" and the "subtle continuum of mental consciousness." In Theravāda Buddhism the same phenomenon is known as the *bhavaṅga*, or "ground of becoming," and the early Mahāsāṅghika school of Buddhism referred to this as a root- (Skt. *mūla*) consciousness that acts as a support (Skt. *āśraya*) for visual consciousness, etc., just as the root of a tree sustains the leaves, etc. The meditative level at which one has completely settled the mind in its natural state corresponds to the achievement of the proximate meditation, or threshold (Skt. *sāmantaka*) of the first dhyāna. Theravāda Buddhist contemplatives report that when one gains access to the first dhyāna, one experiences a naturally pure, unencumbered, luminous state of consciousness, which manifests when awareness is withdrawn from the physical senses and when the activities of the mind, such as discursive thoughts and images, have subsided. This happens naturally when one falls into dreamless sleep and in the last moment of one's life.[106] This dimension of consciousness is experienced as an undefiled state of the radiant mind that precedes mental activities (Pāli *javana*) and from which such movements of the mind arise. This is the essential nature of the mind that the Buddha referred to in his declaration:

> I know of no other single process which, thus developed and made much of, is pliable and workable as is this mind. Monks, the mind which is thus developed and made much of is pliable and workable. Monks, I know of no other single process so quick to change as is this mind . . . . Monks, this mind is luminous, but it is defiled by adventitious defilements. Monks, this mind is luminous, but it is free from adventitious defilements. [107]

The defilements are called "adventitious" because they are not intrinsic to the mind itself, but come and go. With their removal, the mind's intrinsic luminosity emerges—or, more precisely, becomes manifest. To unlock the power of this natural purity, the mind must be fully "awakened" by meditative training in samādhi, so that its radiant potential is fully activated. The Buddha further indicated that loving-kindness is an innate quality of the luminous mind, and it acts as a primal drive to develop and refine one's mind.[108] In a similar vein, the Buddha seems to be referring to this luminous[109] nature when he comments on the "sign of the mind,"[110] which is ascertained only when the five obscurations have been dispelled with the achievement of śamatha. This, he says, is an indispensable prerequisite for effectively engaging in the foundational vipaśyanā practices of the four applications of mindfulness.[111]

The Ultimate Nature of the Mind

Once the essential nature of the mind has been experientially identified, one is poised to explore the ultimate nature of the mind. Phenomenologically, contemplatives well trained in settling the mind in its natural state, by closely applying mindfulness to the mind, are able to observe how objective mental appearances emerge from and dissolve back into the substrate; and they can note how subjective mental processes emerge from and dissolve back into the flow of the substrate consciousness. But to identify the ultimate nature of mental events, we return to the question of the relation between the whole and parts, specifically, between mental events and their attributes.

Introspectively, contemplatives identify consciousness by way of its defining characteristics, namely, its luminosity and cognizance. But what is the nature of the "whole," consciousness, relative to its attributes, "luminosity" and "cognizance"? The same analysis can be applied to all mental processes, including desires, thoughts, emotions, and perceptions. Each mental process has its own qualities by which it is identified. Like all other phenomena, the mind is not identical to its attributes, but neither does it exist independently from them. Immediately after determining the primacy of the mind within the triad of the body, speech, and mind, in its discussion of establishing the mind as baseless and rootless, the *Vajra Essence* proceeds to analyze the mode of existence of the mind. First asking whether the mind has form, and upon determining that it does not, questions are then raised about the source and location of the mind. Does it arise from the physical elements or from space? Can its size be determined, and are the space of the mind and external space outside the body the same or different? The conclusion drawn is that the mind is of the very nature of space—its luminosity is indivisible from space itself—with no duality between external and internal space.

In the Mahāmudrā (the "Great Seal") and Dzokchen ("Great Perfection") traditions of Buddhism in particular, the ultimate mode of existence of the mind is analyzed in terms of the origin, location, and dissolution of the mind. Karma Chagmé (1613–78), a renowned master of both Mahāmudrā and Dzokchen, highlights the unique efficacy of first exploring the ultimate, or actual, nature of the mind as a means for subsequently fathoming the ultimate nature of all other phenomena. The training in probing into the origin, location, and dissolution of the mind, he asserts, "cuts through conceptual elaboration from within, so it is easy to learn, easy to understand, easy to know, and easy to realize. Cutting through conceptual elaboration from the outside is like wanting dried pine wood, and drying it by cutting off the pine needles and branches one by one. So that is difficult. In contrast, cutting through conceptual elaboration from within is easy, for it is like cutting the root of the pine tree so that the branches dry up naturally."[112]

The Tibetan Dzokchen master Lerab Lingpa (1856–1926), also known as Tertön Sogyal, summarizes how the mind's nature is ascertained as a result of such investigation: "Therefore, however much mere appearances that are empty of causes, consequences, and an essential nature may arise in the aspects of the birth, cessation, and abiding of a deceptive mind—or else in the aspects of its origin, location, and destination—from the very moment they arise, ultimately such movements and transformations have never existed. Recognition of that is known as *realization of the actual nature of the mind*."[113] His close disciple, Jé Tsultrim Zangpo (1884–1957), elaborates on this point:

> First of all, the creator of the whole of saṃsāra and nirvāṇa is this very mind of yours. This point is made in numerous sūtras and commentaries. So if you ascertain this mind of yours as being empty of true existence, simply by extending that reasoning you will ascertain all phenomena to be empty of true existence. Thus the guru will enable the disciple to discover how all phenomena depend on the mind, and consequently, how the mind takes a primary role within the context of the body, speech, and mind. Moreover, a person with sharp faculties who can determine that this mind, which plays such a dominant role, cannot be established as truly existing from its own side, as something really, substantially existent, is someone who can determine the absence of true existence even with subtle reasoning, simply by having been shown partial reasons for establishing that absence. For such a person, just by force of a revelation as to whether or not the mind has any color or shape, and just by force of being taught the reasons why the mind is devoid of any [true] origin, location, or destination, that person will proceed to establish the fact that the mind lacks true existence, by way of subtle reasoning that refutes a subtle object of negation. Thus, by the extraordinary power of relying on such reasoning, people with superior faculties are able to realize the emptiness of all phenomena.[114]

This concise mode of analysis regarding the origin, location, and destination of the mind is emphasized in the Mahāmudrā and Dzokchen traditions of contemplative inquiry as the most effective first step in realizing the emptiness of inherent nature of all phenomena. While Buddhism as a whole presents a wide variety of methods for refining one's attention skills by means of training in śamatha, the strong emphasis in Mahāmudrā and Dzokchen is the practice of settling the mind in its natural state, which is also known as *śamatha focused on the mind*. In contrast to the common approach of first studying Madhyamaka treatises on emptiness, based on the Perfection of Wisdom sūtras, and then turning to meditation, the great adepts of Mahāmudrā and Dzokchen encourage us first to achieve śamatha by focusing on the mind, and then to be introduced to the Madhyamaka view of emptiness and the Mahāmudrā and Dzokchen views regarding the transcendent nature of consciousness, known as the indwelling mind of clear light, primordial consciousness, or pristine awareness. When the many veils that obscure the essential nature of the mind have been gradually removed through the process of settling the mind in its natural state, the nature of conditioned consciousness is seen nakedly. While sustaining this immediate awareness of the essential nature of the mind, with relative ease one can recognize that it is devoid of its own intrinsic identity, one that could exist independently of the conceptual framework within which it is identified and demarcated from all other phenomena. As another close disciple of Lerab Lingpa named Lozang Do-ngak Chökyi Gyatso Chok (1903–57), also known as Dharmasāra, explains:

> When engaging in this kind of Mahāmudrā meditation, śamatha is achieved by focusing on the mind, such that one seeks the view on the basis of meditation. In dependence upon this śamatha, the mind is settled with the aspect of things as they are, once one has correctly determined the birth, cessation, and abiding of the mind as being without identity.[115]

All Buddhists refute the inherent existence of the "I," or personal identity, for the self is nowhere to be found among the five psycho-physical aggregates either individually or collectively, and it is not to be found apart from those aggregates. Of course, this does not mean that the self does not exist at all, as is sometimes erroneously claimed. For example, the Buddha declared, "It is by one's self that one purifies oneself," "there is such a thing as self-intiative,"[116] and "you must be a refuge unto yourself."[117] Theravāda Buddhists thus assert "personal identitylessness," but they generally leave unchallenged the assumption that the aggregates and all other phenomena exist truly, or independently, of any conceptual or verbal designation. From a Mahāyāna perspective, those following the Theravāda tradition are thus said to reject "phenomenal identitylessness."

However, there are sources in the Pāli canon that question the real existence of phenomena other than the self, suggesting that they, too, have a mere nominal existence. The Buddhist nun Vajirā, for example, declares that just as no "being" can be found among the aggregates, so can no chariot be found among its constituent parts. Both the self and a chariot (and by implication all other phenomena) exist only by convention.[118] Likewise, the arhat Nāgasena makes this same point, drawing on the analogy of a chariot and its parts, in his famous dialogue with King Menander.[119] Some might argue that the paucity of such references in the Pāli canon regarding the merely conventional nature of all phenomena means that one should not read too much into those passages. But the fact that these narratives are included in the canon suggests that they should not be overlooked, and they do provide a direct link to the teachings of the perfection of wisdom, which emphasize the empty nature of all phenomena, including the mind.

The Transcendent Nature of Consciousness

The realization of the emptiness of inherent nature of the mind is common to followers of Sūtrayana and Vajrayāna Buddhism. By engaging in Sūtrayāna methods of vipaśyanā, on the basis of achieving śamatha, one realizes the empty nature of the mind with respect to the subtle continuum of mental consciousness. But using the extraordinary skillful means of Vajrayāna, particularly those of Mahāmudrā and Dzokchen, one cuts through the conditioned nature of the substrate consciousness and realizes emptiness from the perspective of the transcendent nature of consciousness. The *Vajra Essence* explains:

> Previously, your intellect and mentation demarcated outer from inner and grasped at them as being distinct. Now, ascertaining that there is no outer or inner, you come upon the nature of great, all-pervasive openness, which is called *meditation free of the intellect and devoid of activity*. In such a meditative state, motionlessly rest your body without modifying it, like a corpse in a char-

nel ground. Let your voice rest unmodified, dispensing with all speech and recitations, as if your voice were a lute with its strings cut. Let your mind rest without modification, naturally releasing it in the state of primordial being, without altering it in any way. With these three, dispensing with activities of the body, speech, and mind, you settle in meditative equipoise that is devoid of activity. For that reason, this is called *meditative equipoise.*[120]

In *Buddhahood Without Meditation,* Düdjom Lingpa clarifies this point:

Although there is no outer or inner with respect to the ground of being and the mind, self-grasping simply superimposes boundaries between outer and inner, and it's no more than that. Just as water in its naturally fluid state freezes solid due to currents of cold wind, likewise the naturally fluid ground of being is thoroughly established as saṃsāra by nothing more than cords of self-grasping.

Recognizing how that is so, relinquish good, bad, and neutral bodily activities, and remain like a corpse in a charnel ground, doing nothing. Likewise, relinquish the three kinds of verbal activity and remain like a mute; and also relinquish the three kinds of mental activity and rest without modification, like the autumn sky free of the three contaminating conditions. This is called *meditative equipoise.* It is also called *transcendence of the intellect,* for by relinquishing the nine kinds of activity, activities are released without doing anything, and nothing is modified by the intellect. In the context of this vital point, you will acquire great confidence within yourself.[121]

In the modern popularization of Dzokchen meditation, many people are introduced to practices called "open presence," and some teachers misleadingly equate this with other meditative practices variously characterized as "mindfulness," "bare attention," "choiceless awareness," and "open monitoring." But authentic pith instructions make it perfectly clear that there can be no Dzokchen meditation divorced from Dzokchen view and conduct. This triad of view, meditation, and conduct are inextricably interrelated, so it is impossible to extract any one of these elements of practice from the other two. The practice of cutting through to original pristine awareness, often referred to as "open presence," entails first cutting through the substrate consciousness to pristine awareness and then sustaining this view of the Great Perfection from that perspective. This is possible only if one has realized the emptiness of inherent nature of consciousness, and that realization can be robustly sustained only if one has achieved śamatha.

In her commentary to Düdjom Lingpa's *Buddhahood Without Meditation*, the renowned female Dzokchen adept and treasure-revealer Sera Khandro Dewé Dorjé (1892–1940), spiritual partner of the eldest son of Düdjom Lingpa,[122] clearly illuminates the view, the meditation, the pristine awareness, and the appearances and mindsets of open presence:

> (1) Regarding the view of open presence, the great uniform pervasiveness of the view transcends intellectual grasping at signs, does not succumb to bias or extremes, and realizes unconditioned reality, which is like space. (2) Regarding the meditation of open presence, just as the water of the great ocean is the same above and below, whatever arises is none other than the nature of ultimate reality. Just as water is permeated by lucid clarity, in ultimate reality there is no saṃsāra or nirvāṇa, no joy or sorrow, and so forth, for you realize that everything dissolves into uniform pervasiveness as displays of clear light. (3) Regarding open presence in pristine awareness, just as the supreme mountain in the center of this world system is unmovable, pristine awareness transcends time, without wavering even for an instant from the nature of its own great luminosity. (4) Regarding open presence in appearances and mindsets, all appearing phenomena are naturally empty and self-illuminating. They are not apprehended by the intellect, not grasped by the mind, and not modified by awareness. Rather, they dissolve into great uniform pervasiveness, so they are liberated with no basis for acceptance or rejection, no distinction between luminosity and emptiness, and no room for doubt as to what they are."[123]

While resting in the substrate consciousness, in which thoughts and other activities of the ordinary mind have vanished, one examines the very nature of the mind in which thoughts have ceased, recognizing that it doesn't truly emerge from anywhere, is not truly located anywhere, and it doesn't truly depart to anywhere. It is inherently empty of any real origin, location, and destination. One then examines the nature of the awareness that has come to this realization, recognizing that there is no difference between the awareness *of which* one is aware and the awareness *with which* one is aware. The dichotomy of subject and object melts away. One then rests in open presence, with no striving, no effort, no modification, and no activity of any kind. All the activities of the conditioned mind of a sentient being are suspended, and one cuts through the substrate to realize the emptiness of the open expanse of the space-like nature of awareness. This is the view of the Great Perfection, in which one experiences the "one taste" of all phenomena of saṃsāra and nirvāṇa as equally pure expressions of pristine awareness. The empty essential nature of this awareness is called the *dharmakāya*, its manifest luminous nature is called the *sambhogakāya*, and its spontaneous expressions of limitless compassion are called *nirmāṇakāya*s. The indivisibility of these three embodiments of the transcendent mind of a buddha is called the *svabhāvikakāya*. The full realization of this transcendent nature of consciousness constitutes the perfect awakening of a buddha, the culmination of all Buddhist practice. One has now fully comprehended the transcendent nature of consciousness, the nature of the mind, and its role in the universe.

The Buddha admonished his followers to put his teachings to the test of reason and experience, rather than simply taking his words on faith: "Monks, just as the wise accept gold after testing it by heating, cutting, and rubbing it, so are my words to be accepted after examining them, but not out of respect [for me]."[124] So rather than regarding the preceding explanation of four aspects of the nature of the mind as matters of religious belief or philosophical speculation, those who are intrigued by this account and are committed to knowing the nature of the mind for themselves should regard this account as a set of hypotheses to be investigated with the utmost rigor. In other words, this account should be viewed as a presentation of Buddhist contemplative science of the mind. It can be tested by anyone with an open mind and sufficient dedication to put these hypotheses to the test of reason and experience, unlike the many materialist speculations about the nature and origins of the mind that are all too often misrepresented as scientific truths.

There are no explicit references in the Pāli canon regarding any unconditioned dimension of consciousness, and with the death of an arhat, the continua of all one's five aggregates, including mental consciousness, are said to cease forever. However, according to these canonical accounts, the Buddha refers to nirvāṇa as being "unborn, and deathless," and that it is "peaceful, blissful, auspicious" even beyond death. This implies that there must be a dimension of consciousness that persists after the death of an arhat, and it may be to this that the *Kevaddha Sutta* refers in the following passage:

> Where consciousness is signless, boundless, all-luminous,
> that's where earth, water, fire, and air have no basis.
> There both long and short, small and great, fair and foul—
> there "name and form" are wholly destroyed.
> With the cessation of consciousness this is all destroyed.[125]

Explanations of pristine awareness in the Great Perfection clearly parallel the teachings on buddha nature in the Mahāyāna canon, specifically those included in the third turning of the wheel of Dharma. The reality of an unconditioned dimension of consciousness is explicitly stated, for example, in the *Mahāparinirvāṇasūtra*, which states, "The Buddha-Nature of beings is eternal and unchanging." And the *Śrīmaladevisiṃhanāda Sūtra* similarly declares:

> The cessation of suffering is not the destruction of a phenomenon. Why? Because the dharmakāya of the Buddha is primordially existent; it is not made, not born, not exhausted, and not to be exhausted. It is permanent, reliable, completely pure by nature, completely liberated from all the sheaths of the mental afflictions... and so it is called the cessation of suffering. This is what is called the *tathāgatagarbha*, dharmakāya freed from the veils of the mental afflictions.

Thomas Huxley celebrated the rational and rigorous empirical nature of any true science, while warning all of humanity of the perils of being misled by closed-minded dogmas: "So far as any nation recognizes, or has recognized, the great truth, that every dictum, every belief, must be tested and tried to the uttermost, and swept ruthlessly away if it be not in accordance with right reason, so far is that nation prosperous and healthy; and so far as a nation has allowed itself to be hood-winked and fettered, and the free application of its intellect, as the criterion of all truth, restricted, so far is it sinking and rotten within."[126] If the reduction of the mind to the brain, the repudiation of the existence of consciousness itself, and the dismissal of introspective observation as a means to exploring the mind are valid, then one should be able to verify these assertions for oneself. And the same is true of the above account of the nature of the mind as it is understood in Buddhism, and more specifically in the tradition of the Great Perfection. Huxley makes this same point when he declares, "Every man can, if he pleases, apply to the sources of all scientific knowledge directly, and verify for himself the conclusions of others. In science, faith is based solely on the assent of the intellect; and the most complete submission to ascertained truth is wholly voluntary, because it is accompanied by perfect freedom, nay, by every encouragement, to test and try that truth to the uttermost."[127]

In his autobiography, Düdjom Lingpa records a visionary dream he experienced in the mid-1850s in which he was given a conch shell and asked to blow it in each of the four directions. The conch's sound roared forth to the west, more so than the other directions, signifying that disciples compatible with him lived in cities to the west. In that direction, he was told, his renown would spread, and he would have as many disciples as the rays of the sun.[128] In his foreword to *Düdjom Lingpa's Visions of the Great Perfection*, Sogyal Rinpoché writes: "Thirteen of Düdjom Lingpa's disciples attained the rainbow body, and in his prophecies Düdjom Lingpa was told that a hundred might even attain the great transference rainbow body. As Düdjom Rinpoché wrote, 'In this precious lineage of ours, this is not just ancient history. For today, just as in the past, there are those who through the paths of *trekchö* [cutting through to the original purity of pristine awareness] and *tögal* [direct crossing over to spontaneous actualization] have attained the final realization and have dissolved their gross material bodies into rainbow bodies of radiant light.'"[129] Düdjom Lingpa's visionary teachings on the Great Perfection repeatedly state that they were intended for people in the future, and there is strong evidence that this future is now, when the need to fathom the nature and potentials of the mind is greater than ever.

The *Vajra Essence* concludes with these words from Samantabhadra:

> In earlier times, the teachings of the Great Perfection shone like the sun. When sublime, supreme teachers explained them to people with good karma and fortune, first they would gain certainty by way of the view. Then they would identify pristine

awareness and dispel their flaws by means of meditation. And finally, by practicing, remaining in the conduct of inactivity, they all became siddhas and made manifest the state of omniscient enlightenment. This is the unsurpassed quality of the profound path of the *Vajra Essence*.

Nowadays however, people may meditate while having no experience or familiarity with the view, but identifying merely the natural luminosity of consciousness; they do not go beyond the ordinary, and they never achieve the fruition of omniscient enlightenment. Some teachers are expert at oral explanations, but they cannot reveal the path of liberation, so it is impossible for them to bring much benefit to the minds of others.

Thus, teachers who can explain it are gradually becoming more and more rare, and there is no one who is practicing. As a result, the teachings of the Great Perfection are lost to the point that they are becoming like a drawing of a butter lamp. This tantra has been revealed because of the dependently originated circumstances of the physical worlds and their sentient inhabitants in times such as this.

Like the sun briefly appearing through a break in the clouds, this will not remain for long. Why? Because there are no teachers who know how to explain it, and there are few people who have the karma, prayers, and fortune to receive it. Thus, just as it has emerged from absolute space, it will reabsorb back into it.[130]

2. Revealing Your Own Face as the Sharp Vajra of Vipaśyanā

We turn now to a presentation of vipaśyanā in the Dzokchen tradition, revealed in a pure vision to Düdjom Lingpa, who claimed he had no human teacher. Nevertheless, the following explanation is representative of classic discussions of this topic in ancient and modern meditation manuals in the Dzokchen and Mahāmudrā traditions in India and Tibet. Such contemplative inquiry enables one to "see one's own face," which is to say, perceive the ultimate nature of one's own mind, which has been there all along—hidden in plain sight. In Düdjom Lingpa's commentary to the *Sharp Vajra of Consciousness Awareness Tantra*, compiled by Pema Tashi, the "sharp vajra" is defined as primordially present, supreme wisdom, indivisible from emptiness, which has been invisible in the past but is revealed by the power of sublime pith instructions so that "it manifests and is seen, as if waking up from sleep."[131] To place these instructions in context, it is important to study the preceding section of the *Vajra Essence*, included in my book *Stilling the Mind*, which highlights the indispensability of achieving śamatha if one is to fully benefit from the vipaśyanā practices explained here.

In Düdjom Lingpa's pure vision, the bodhisattvas who surround the Teacher, Samantabhadra, are not historical figures but archetypal personifications of the faculties of Düdjom Lingpa's own mind: illusory displays of primordial consciousness. One such bodhisattva is called Faculty of Luminosity, and he represents something that each one of us is experiencing right now. The fact that anything at all appears to us is due to the aspect of luminosity, which is intrinsic to awareness itself. For example, as you read this page, photons emitted from it strike your eyes and catalyze a sequence of electrochemical events culminating in your visual cortex, but it is the faculty of luminosity of your mental awareness that illuminates these appearances in a meaningful way.

The dialogue begins between the Bodhisattva Faculty of Luminosity and the Bhagavān, Samantabhadra, who personifies Düdjom Lingpa's own primordial consciousness.

> **Then Bodhisattva Faculty of Luminosity rose from his seat and addressed the Bhagavān: "O Teacher, Bhagavān, Omnipresent Lord and Immutable Sovereign, please listen and consider me. Is the state of primordial, self-emergent liberation achieved solely by cultivating an inconceivable, ineffable, clear awareness, or not? If it is, how is this achieved? If not, what is the point of cultivating it? What kinds of good qualities arise? Please explain this for the sake of your disciples."**

It's imperative to recognize that this is not a dialogue between Düdjom Lingpa's mind and someone radically other than him; it's not a human conversing with some other independently existent supernatural being. This emanation of Samantabhadra, manifesting as Padmasambhava, is an archetypal personification of primordial consciousness, which is equally present in buddhas, Düdjom Lingpa, yourself, and all sentient beings. He's having a conversation with himself, as we all do quite naturally, in which his faculty of luminosity is addressing his primordial consciousness: "Is the state of primordial, self-emergent liberation achieved solely by cultivating an inconceivable, ineffable, clear awareness, or not?"

Primordial means it's always present and not something to be achieved in the future. It is also called *self-emergent*, which doesn't mean that it literally emerges from itself by a process of self-creation, but rather that it is naturally present and does not arise in dependence on any other causes. This state of liberation is already present in all of us, right now. It's not something to be achieved at another time—it's either realized or it remains veiled. Can you realize this natural liberation simply by cultivating or sustaining an inconceivable, ineffable, clear awareness, or not? Is this sufficient? Is simply resting in an ongoing flow of clear, nonconceptual awareness enough to attain liberation? If so, how is it achieved; and if not, what is the point of cultivating such a quality of awareness? Finally, if one cultivates this awareness, what good qualities arise?

> The Teacher replied, "O Faculty of Luminosity, listen and bear in mind what I say, and I shall fully explain this to you. Even though you achieve stability in this profound path free of conceptual elaboration in the state of conscious awareness, if the dharmakāya, primordial consciousness that is present in the ground of being, is not realized, as soon as you pass away from this life, you will be forcefully propelled to the form and formless realms."

Here we must read carefully, because as is often the case in Buddhist literature, one term, such as *rigpa*, can be used to refer to very different phenomena. In Buddhist psychology, the Tibetan term *rigpa*, or Sanskrit *vidyā*, simply means "knowing" or "cognition." But in the context of the Great Perfection, it refers to the ultimate dimension of consciousness, pristine awareness, which is primordially pure, beyond time and space. One term can refer to either the relative level or the ultimate level.

When the Teacher replies that even if you achieve stability and long-term continuity of abiding in conscious awareness, free of conceptual elaboration, he's referring to the substrate consciousness. For someone whose entire experience has been of the ordinary, coarse mind, the substrate consciousness is beyond the range of conscious experience. Talking about it would be like discussing chocolate without ever having tasted it. Someone who is born colorblind can discuss various wavelengths of light, but the actual experience of color is unimaginable for that person. This inconceivability is relative to one's experience. Similarly, the attainment of śamatha, with a direct realization of the substrate consciousness, is inconceivable to anyone who lacks this experience; there is no way to articulate it so that another person might know what this state is like. Even with great eloquence and a vast vocabulary, someone who has experienced it can only convey a vague facsimile in words to someone who has not. For them, it's ineffable. This is an important point to recognize when scientists with little or no meditative experience try to understand meditation solely by studying the brain activity and behavior of meditators and interrogating them about their first-person experiences. Their understanding of meditation is bound to be as limited as the understanding of mathematics that might be gained by researchers with no mathematical training who limit their methods of inquiry to surveying mathematicians and studying their brains and behavior.

Bear in mind that when resting in the flow of the substrate consciousness, one of its three fundamental qualities is nonconceptuality. Even if you have a direct, perceptual taste of the substrate consciousness, merely attempting to describe it in words takes you a step away from the experience itself; it's inconceivable even for you. The Teacher's response is that even if you rest for hours in such an inconceivable state of clear, conscious awareness, but you have not realized the transcendent dimension—the ever-present primordial consciousness of the dharmakāya—you will be forcefully propelled to the form and formless reams following this life.

In the preceding section of the *Vajra Essence*, the Teacher states that if you have achieved śamatha and dwell in the substrate consciousness, and if you are particularly drawn to the quality of bliss, then this karma will propel you to rebirth as a god in the desire realm. If you're strongly attracted to the luminous quality of the substrate consciousness, this karma will propel you into the form realm. Finally, if you're attached to the profound nonconceptuality and serenity of the substrate consciousness, this karma will propel you into the formless realm. In any case, you will not transcend saṃsāra.[132]

The substrate consciousness is very intriguing because, unlike the ordinary human mind, it does not belong to the desire realm. When one achieves śamatha, awareness crosses the threshold from the desire realm to the form realm. But the substrate consciousness is not located in the form realm either, nor is it located in any other realm, higher or lower. As mentioned previously, this is like a human stem cell, which hasn't yet developed into any of the diverse cell types in the human body, although it may eventually become any of them. The substrate consciousness is a stem consciousness, propelled by karma, which may eventually become configured as a consciousness in any of the three realms of mundane existence.

Here the Teacher is drawing a clear distinction between two ineffable, inconceivable, clear states of consciousness: the substrate consciousness and primordial consciousness. Similar adjectives are used to describe them, but they must not be conflated. One is firmly entrenched in saṃsāra, and the other is naturally liberated. In Tibet, many yogins over the centuries have come to rest in the substrate consciousness and mistaken this for pristine awareness. Similarly, in the Theravāda tradition, there have been yogins who have experienced the "ground of becoming" (Pāli *bhavaṅga*), which corresponds to the substrate consciousness, and mistakenly concluded that this was nirvāṇa. Such confusion is common to all Buddhist traditions, so great clarity is required to avoid it. This is not our goal of liberation, but merely a pleasant time-out in saṃsāra—a seductive trap, albeit a necessary stage on the journey to liberation.

> But with that alone it is impossible to achieve the omniscient state of buddhahood. Once you have identified this path for the first time, if the dharmakāya—primordial consciousness that is present in the ground—is then ascertained through the power of intense meditation, this is the path wisdom and the creative power of primordial consciousness.

By merely resting in the substrate consciousness, it is impossible to achieve the omniscient state of buddhahood. When you're resting in the substrate consciousness, you're simply aware of your own individual substrate. But when you cut through the substrate consciousness to the dharmakāya, this pervades all space and time. Once you have identified the path of the dharmakāya, or pristine awareness, for the first time, through the power of intense meditation, when the primordial consciousness that is present in the ground of being is ascertained, this is the path wisdom and the creative power of primordial consciousness. We shall soon see the type of intense meditation that is required.

> Here are the excellent qualities that result from this: Just as there is no space that is different from the space inside a pot and no water that is different from the water that fills a cup, likewise, there is no path other than this path of manifest, conscious awareness. Even if you wander downward in impure saṃsāra, this is constructed by the stream of consciousness. And upward, with the virtuous karma of fine merit, even if you generate deities and practice meditation and recitation, this is accomplished with the stream of consciousness. And even if you practice transforming the channels, bindus,

and vital energies into displays of the three vajras, it is the
stream of consciousness that liberates you. Moreover, it is
this alone made manifest that is the originally pure ground—
self-emergent, lucid, clear, nondual primordial consciousness.

Here are the excellent qualities that result from cutting through the substrate
consciousness to pristine awareness. Just as the space outside and inside a pot
are the same, and water is the same wherever it appears, there is no path
other than this path of manifest, conscious awareness. Even if you wander
downward, impure saṃsāra is constructed by the stream of consciousness.
The substrate consciousness flows through all the three realms of existence,
and whatever practice you engage in will be performed with this substrate
consciousness until you cut through it to primordial consciousness.

The substrate is the space of your own mind, in which all dream and waking appearances arise. These appearances may be influenced by the physical
forces associated with neurons, photons, and sound waves, but they actually
occur nowhere else but in the space of awareness: the substrate. If your karma
propels you downward into a lower form of existence, all those appearances
will be generated by seeds already existing in your substrate. Likewise, if your
awareness is lifted upward with the virtuous karma of fine merit, and you
generate deities and practice meditation and recitation, this is accomplished
with the stream of consciousness. In generation-stage practices of devotion,
refuge, guru yoga, and visualizing *yidams* and bodhisattvas, all these appearances are generated by your substrate consciousness and appear in your substrate. The stream of consciousness is the common denominator, no matter
where you go in saṃsāra. If you practice completion-stage transmutations of
the impure channels (Skt. *nāḍī*), vital essences (Skt. *bindu*), and vital energies (Skt. *prāṇa*) into pure displays of body, speech, and mind—the three
vajras—it is the stream of consciousness that liberates you. Moreover, it is
the unveiling of this alone that manifests as the originally pure ground—
self-emergent, lucid, clear, nondual primordial consciousness. This is why
the Buddha indicated that it is this "brightly shining mind" that leads one to
develop one's mind meditatively, in the pursuit of liberation.[133]

Here the description is quite subtle. The term *conscious awareness* is being
used to refer both to the substrate consciousness and to primordial consciousness, just as the term *awareness* (Tib. *rig pa*) refers in different contexts
to both ordinary awareness and pristine awareness. The key distinction is

Wisdom Publications

Please fill out and return this card if you would like to receive our catalogue and special offers. The postage is already paid!

Name

Address

City / State / Zip / Country

Email

Sign up for our newsletter and special offers at wisdompubs.org

Wisdom Publications is a non-profit charitable organization.

Wisdom

that primordial consciousness is referred to with the additional phrase *this alone made manifest*, which means that the substrate consciousness is not something fundamentally different from primordial consciousness. In the classic analogy, the conditioned consciousness of a sentient being, including the substrate consciousness, is likened to ice, whereas primordial consciousness is like ice that has melted into water. The ordinary mind is frozen by grasping, while primordial consciousness is fluid and free of all grasping.

When you realize the ultimate nature of the substrate consciousness, you see that it is none other than primordial consciousness. This is true not only of the substrate consciousness but of all coarse states of mind, including mental virtues and afflictions. For example, when anger arises, the dualistic mind experiences it as a disruptive mental affliction, giving rise to conflict and unhappiness. But if one can peer directly into the essential nature of anger, free of grasping, one sees it as nothing other than mirror-like primordial consciousness, one of the five facets of pristine awareness. The manifestation or unveiling of the substrate consciousness reveals it to be self-emergent, naturally present, and not arising in dependence on prior causes and conditions. It is lucid, radiant, and transparent; it is clear, or luminous; and it is nondual, with no absolute separation between subject and object.

What is the most direct route for cutting through the substrate consciousness to pristine awareness? When resting in the substrate consciousness, invert your awareness upon itself. In this self-knowing awareness, release all grasping to the bliss, luminosity, and nonconceptuality of the substrate consciousness, which are conditioned experiences arising from causes and conditions. Release all preference for the immensely satisfying bliss and exhilarating luminosity of the substrate consciousness, which are also conditioned. Release all clinging to the serene silence of nonconceptuality of this dimension of consciousness, wherein thoughts have only temporarily subsided, for this is only relative nonconceptuality. The bliss of primordial consciousness is immutable. The luminosity of primordial consciousness is beyond time and changeless. And while the substrate consciousness is relatively nonconceptual, primordial consciousness absolutely transcends all thought and language.

> In general, whatever yāna you enter, there is no entrance other
> than the stream of ever-present primordial consciousness.
> Even when ordinary, deluded beings chant many prayers and

count mantras with a virtuous motivation, such practices are taught for the sake of the stream of the ground consciousness. Therefore, since the stream of consciousness is what accumulates all karma, this manifest consciousness itself is unrivaled by any tainted virtue.

Whether you enter the spiritual vehicle (Skt. *yāna*) of Śrāvakayāna, Bodhisattvayāna, or Vajrayāna, there is no entrance other than the stream of ever-present primordial consciousness. Even here, where the Teacher refers to the substrate consciousness, which is the ground of saṃsāra, it is primordial in the sense of having no beginning. There was no point in time when a fresh substrate consciousness first arose. It is a continuously flowing stream. All everyday practices, such as chanting prayers and counting mantras with a virtuous motivation, are taught for the sake of cultivating and liberating the stream of the ground consciousness. This stream of the substrate consciousness, which is what accumulates all karma, is sometimes translated as the *storehouse consciousness*, and it carries imprints, memories, and karmic propensities from lifetime to lifetime. The point is to ascertain this stream of consciousness and then to reveal its ultimate nature. This is cutting through the frozen configurations of consciousness to melted, manifest primordial consciousness, which is unrivaled by any tainted virtue.

Primordial consciousness is a dimension of consciousness from which wisdom and virtue spontaneously emerge, in a nondual way, free of grasping. This is beautifully demonstrated in many stories of the great masters of the Zen and Chan traditions, whether in the martial arts, archery, flower arrangement, or the tea ceremony, in which something manifests spontaneously that is perfectly appropriate for the present moment. These spontaneous displays are not premeditated, conceptual, or tainted by dualistic grasping. They are effulgences from this deepest ground, and they are unrivalled by any virtue that is tainted by grasping to subject and object. All practices that involve dualistic grasping, such as cultivating loving-kindness and relative bodhicitta, meditating on impermanence, and so forth, are tainted virtues, practiced for the sake of manifesting the true nature of the stream of consciousness that was always there, as primordial consciousness.

Moreover, the difference between practicing a mere technique *pertaining* to the stream of consciousness on the one hand and actually *manifesting* consciousness on the other is like the difference between the sky and the earth. That being the case, all extraordinary sublime qualities are wholly present in this act of making consciousness manifest.

All practices in the stages of generation and completion utilize the stream of consciousness to freshly realize, achieve, or cultivate certain qualities, such as the six perfections. But the practice of the Great Perfection does not seek to attain or cultivate qualities, freedoms, or virtues that you don't already possess. Instead of using consciousness to achieve something, the point is to reveal the ultimate nature of consciousness that you have been using all along. By doing so, you tap into the wellspring of all untainted, spontaneous virtue, wisdom, and compassion. All extraordinary sublime qualities are simultaneously and wholly present in this act of making consciousness manifest.

O son of the family, ever-present primordial consciousness is this: When the mind of a sentient being, which is by nature clear light, does not objectify any appearances or mindsets, but makes them manifest, this very act of revealing is the external radiance of wisdom. The nature of what makes things manifest is the inner glow of wisdom. The tremendous significance of this distinction is like that of the dawn appearing in the sky.

This paragraph is a quintessential pointing-out instruction, enabling you to identify the primordial consciousness that is your innermost nature. Right now, in your own experience, there is an awareness of being aware. The practices of mindfulness of breathing, settling the mind in its natural state, and awareness of awareness progressively remove the outer layers of appearances and mindsets until this awareness is all that remains. Likewise, when we peel away all grasping—including grasping at our own awareness—that which was already there, the innermost Russian doll, is pristine awareness. Its nature is primordially still and immutable; it transcends all conceptual frameworks, illuminates all appearances, and regards appearances and mindsets as nondual. All appearances and mindsets are seen to be nothing other than the external radiance or sheen of wisdom. These manifestations are the external radiance of wisdom, and their nature is the inner glow of wisdom. If the external manifestation were a light bulb, the inner glow would be the light of the filament inside the bulb.

> If people with superior faculties and perseverance apply themselves continuously and single-pointedly to practice without distraction, the power of discerning primordial consciousness will ultimately blaze forth. As a result, the sublime qualities of the view and meditation of the clear light Great Perfection, which is ultimate reality, the very nature of suchness, will truly manifest; and those people will become enlightened in the original, primordial ground of Samantabhadra.

The Sanskrit language in which this Dharma was first formulated is quite interesting, with cognate terms appearing in English and the other Indo-European languages. Referring to the clear light Great Perfection, the Sanskrit term translated here as *ultimate reality* is *dharmatā*, which is also called *suchness* (Skt. *tathatā*). You are probably familiar with the term *śūnyatā*, or *emptiness*. The Sanskrit adjective *śūnya* means *empty*, and adding the suffix *tā* signifies that which makes something empty: the noun *emptiness*. Likewise, *dharma* simply means *phenomenon*, whether it's the mind or a galaxy; and *dharmatā* signifies that which makes something a phenomenon, its phenomenon-ness, which I've translated as *ultimate reality*.

What is the ultimate reality of all phenomena? All appearances arise from emptiness and dissolve back into emptiness. They do not exist apart from emptiness. Emptiness is form, and form is emptiness. This theme runs through all the Mahāyāna Buddhist teachings. In the Pāli canon, the Buddha states that "if there were no unborn, unbecome, unmade, unconditioned, no release from what is born, come to be, made, and conditioned would be discerned here, but because there is an unborn (etc.) a release from what is born (etc.) is discerned here."[134] In this passage, the "unborn, unbecome, unmade, unconditioned" refer to nirvāṇa, and the "born, come to be, made, and conditioned" refer to saṃsāra. Physicists are delighted to have recently discovered the Higgs boson, the "god particle," which gives all other particles in the universe their mass. It's a big responsibility! But how is it possible for the Higgs boson to exist? If there were no emptiness, there could be no Higgs boson either. Emptiness is the ultimate reality of everything in the universe, from Higgs bosons to galactic clusters to sentient beings.

Then we have *tathatā*, translated as *suchness*, where *tatha* simply means *that*, and *tathatā* means *that-ness*. The Zen kōan meditations are intended to reveal this dimension of reality. In fact, the terms *dharmatā, tathatā, nirvāṇa*, and *śūnyatā* are synonymous and refer to the same ultimate reality, as does the term *dharmadhātu*, the absolute space of phenomena.

Another Sanskrit term that is a counterpart of *dharmatā* is *cittatā*. The term *citta* is generally translated as *mind, cittatā* has the meaning of *mind-ness*, and I translate this term as the *ultimate nature of the mind*. What makes your mind a mind? Its primordial consciousness, or pristine awareness. Without primordial consciousness, there could be no conditioned consciousness. Without water, there could be no snowflakes. The two terms *dharmatā* and *cittatā* are closely linked, with the former corresponding to the ultimate nature of phenomena and the latter to the ultimate nature of the mind, and these two facets of reality are primordially nondual.

> Even individuals who are not of that sort may identify this crucial point, wherein unstructured, self-emergent consciousness becomes manifest without meditation, and they may achieve a little stability in it. Since all the other physical and verbal virtues accumulated throughout a galaxy would not come close even to a hundredth, a thousandth, a ten-thousandth, or a hundred-thousandth the merit of this, such people are bound to achieve long-lasting stability in the peak of mundane existence.

Even individuals who lack supreme faculties may identify this crucially important dimension of consciousness. It is unstructured, unconfigured, and not created by causes and conditions. It is self-emergent and naturally present. It manifests without meditation or doing anything in particular, when you are simply present and allow it to manifest. Such people may achieve a little stability in this, sustaining it for some time. The virtue of *manifesting* the very nature of awareness itself is said to exceed by many orders of magnitude the virtue of ordinary practices that merely *pertain* to the stream of consciousness. People who do practice sustaining this unstructured awareness, yet who are caught up in striving to achieve temporary effects based on causes, will indeed create an enormous amount of virtue, but are still limited to achieving long-lasting stability within a form or formless realm—they will not go beyond the peak of mundane existence, where they are still caught in saṃsāra. The key point is that one must ascertain this unstructured awareness as being the dharmakāya itself—primordial consciousness that is present in the ground—or else the mere practice of sustaining awareness, without realizing its ultimate nature, will not be enough to result in omniscient buddhahood. This is a general statement concerning the various practices of all traditions: their final goal is to know the ultimate nature of awareness.

✢ ✢ ✢ ✢ ✢ ✢ ✢ ✢

The Teacher has answered the question of whether liberation can be achieved by cultivating a state of inconceivable, ineffable, clear awareness. The answer is that simply resting in the substrate consciousness is not enough—this will only perpetuate your existence in saṃsāra. However, if you meditate intensively and cut through to the primordial consciousness of the dharmakāya, you will be free.

What is the practical method for doing so? It is not necessary to adopt any particular view or belief system to practice śamatha. Apart from maintaining an ethical lifestyle and arousing an authentic motivation, there is no single worldview that uniquely accords with the practice and achievement of śamatha. Padmasambhava makes it clear that the practice of awareness of awareness may be sufficient not only to achieve śamatha, but for the very gifted it may also be sufficient to cut through to pristine awareness.[135] Padmasambhava in his visionary manifestation as the Lake-Born Vajra also says that if those with superior faculties simply rest their awareness with no object, merging their mind with space, for a period of twenty days, this may allow them to cut through to pristine awareness.[136] However, if neither of these methods works for ascertaining the dharmakāya, then you must devote yourself to the practices of śamatha, vipaśyanā, and the Great Perfection.

There is no Great Perfection meditation independent of the view, for Great Perfection meditation is nothing more than resting in the Great Perfection view: perceiving reality from the perspective of pristine awareness. One way or another, you must cut through your ordinary, conditioned mind to pristine awareness, and then you view reality from the perspective of pristine awareness. This is why Great Perfection meditation is sometimes called *nonmeditation*. There is nothing to meditate upon, nothing to strive for, nothing to be modified, and nothing to accomplish. While engaging in nonmeditation, you do nothing to activate the conditioned mind of a sentient being. This is resting in pristine awareness, in Tibetan *rig pa chok shak*, which is the practice I translate as the *open presence in pristine awareness*. If you have not cut through the substrate consciousness to pristine awareness, but merely rest in a shallow facsimile of "open presence," you are simply dwelling passively in your inactive, dualistic mind. Instead of resting in the view of the Great Perfection, you are just treading water in the vast ocean of saṃsāra.

You can't simply rest in pristine awareness without identifying it. It's like dreaming of relaxing in the comfort of your Tesla, cruising through traffic on Autopilot. If you don't have a Tesla, you can't do it. Great Perfection meditation entails resting without any objectification whatsoever. There is no reification or grasping to any subject or object. Resting in the present, there is no distraction, and pristine awareness manifests. As you view reality from this perspective, all phenomena are seen as creative expressions or displays of pristine awareness, empty of inherent existence.

In generation-stage practices, you employ your insight into the emptiness of inherent nature of all phenomena. Sustaining this view of emptiness, you imagine all forms as displays of the nirmāṇakāya, all sounds as emanations of the sambhogakāya, and all mental events as displays of dharmakāya. You imagine your own body as the body of a buddha, your speech as the speech of a buddha, and your mind as the mind of a buddha.

In practicing the Great Perfection, you don't imagine anything at all. All phenomena are perceived as spontaneously arising displays of pristine awareness. But even a Great Perfection practitioner must eventually end the formal meditation session and engage in the activities of daily life. The Great Perfection conduct, or way of life, means behaving as if you are in the midst of a lucid dream. In a lucid dream, rather than identifying with the subject and objects in the dreamscape, you view this experience from the perspective that all these phenomena are equal as displays of your own substrate consciousness. From the perspective of one who is awake, all dream phenomena homogenously consist of empty appearances. But from the perspective of one who is ultimately awake, even the phenomena of the so-called waking state are no more than a dream from the perspective of pristine awareness. To familiarize yourself with this perspective, as you engage in activities throughout the day, you learn to sustain lucidity continuously in the waking state. You neither reify your own identity as a "self" nor anyone else as radically "other." There is no hope or fear, craving or aversion. This is not easy! If you lack even a conceptual understanding of the view of the Great Perfection and of emptiness, yet attempt to lead your life in accordance with the conduct of the Great Perfection, you may call your meditation the practice of open presence, but it's not even close. It's the meditation of a marmot, serenely warming itself on a rock on a sunny day.

To draw an analogy, if one visits a traditional Tibetan doctor, one's pulse and urine will be analyzed and herbal pills will be prescribed, generally to be taken two or three times per day. The doctor will also recommend that one eat certain foods and avoid others. Compared to the tiny herbal pills, one's daily food consumption is orders of magnitude larger. If one takes the pills but ignores the dietary recommendations, there is not likely to be any benefit. The unhealthy food one consumes will outweigh the potential benefits of the herbal medicine. Likewise, even if one practices a semblance of Great Perfection meditation, but in between sessions resumes one's ordinary habits of reification and unwholesome behavior, one will derive little benefit from the meditation. It is delusional to think that one is practicing the essence of meditation while maintaining a lifestyle and view of reality that are not deeply integrated with it. Until one has turned away from the worldview of materialism, the values of hedonism, and the way of life of consumerism, one has not taken even the first step on the path of the Great Perfection, regardless of how much one may have engaged in the traditional preliminary practices of Dzokchen or attempted resting in a sterile facsimile of open presence.

Once again, the Teacher is affirming that you can indeed be naturally liberated by resting in clear awareness—but only if you are successful in cutting through to the immutable, ineffable, inconceivable primordial consciousness of the dharmakāya. By the power of this realization, you will naturally perceive all phenomena as creative displays of pristine awareness, and thus you will realize that all phenomena are empty of inherent nature. The transition is like being in a nonlucid dream when something suddenly catalyzes a shift in your view of the dream—you cease viewing it from the perspective of the dreaming subject and view it from the perspective of being awake. Kōan meditations are meant to catalyze such a shift in perspective. Likewise, in the Tibetan tradition, pointing-out instructions are designed to induce a sudden shift to a radically new perspective: the view of pristine awareness.

By resting in pristine awareness and perceiving all phenomena as displays of pristine awareness, all appearances and mindsets are naturally seen to be empty of inherent nature.

Imagine that you're in a nonlucid dream, but you've heard some wonderful teachings about emptiness, and they have carried over into your dream state. As you investigate phenomena in your nonlucid dream, you begin to realize the emptiness of inherent nature of everything in the dream. Although all phenomena seem to appear, when you investigate them one by one, you discover that they're only empty appearances. Likewise, you may realize that even though your own self seems to appear, it is actually nowhere to be found, and over time you realize the emptiness of all objective and subjective phenomena. Subsequent to your meditations while in this nonlucid dream, between formal meditation sessions, you may view everything as dreamlike. Nevertheless, you are still dreaming without knowing it. Now if you imagine someone else who is awake and clairvoyant and peeking in on your nonlucid dream, he or she would find it ludicrous that you declared everything to be "dreamlike." One may realize emptiness without realizing pristine awareness, but the realization of pristine awareness necessarily entails the realization of emptiness.

This opening section has described the most direct route to liberation: realizing pristine awareness. Based on this, you will then discover your own primordial liberation. Until you are able to do this, you should meditate on emptiness, with the sound basis of the cultivation of śamatha.

3. Revealing the Ground Dharmakāya

Determining the Identitylessness of Persons as Subjects

Again Bodhisattva Faculty of Luminosity asked, "O Teacher, Bhagavān, Omnipresent Lord and Immutable Sovereign, please listen and consider me. If taking the mind and consciousness as the path does not result in the fruitional state of liberation or enlightenment, no matter how much one meditates in that way, please show us a way to directly identify for ourselves the originally pure Great Perfection, sovereign awareness free of extremes, without having to resort to such a long and difficult path that yields various joys and sorrows but no accomplishment of that result. Reveal to us the stages of the path free of hardships, and give us profound teachings to prevent us from falling into error."

He replied, "O son of the family, the great, universal ground of all yānas is profound emptiness. I shall explain the way to determine the reality of profound emptiness, so listen well! The basis for the delusion of all beings in the three realms is ignorance about one's self alone. Examine the basis and root of its origin, location, and destination."

If the practices of the preceding section—first taking the ordinary mind as the path, and observing your thoughts, desires, and emotions, until the ordinary mind gradually dissolves into the substrate consciousness, which has no ethnicity, gender, personal history, or species identity, and then taking consciousness as the path, and resting in the substrate consciousness itself—do not result in liberation, no matter how much you practice, then here is the crucial question: How can we directly identify for ourselves the originally pure Great Perfection, our own sovereign awareness, free of the eight extremes of conceptual elaboration? For it is unborn and unceasing, neither existent nor nonexistent, neither coming nor going, and neither singular nor plural. It transcends all the categories of the conceptual mind.

Compared to the Great Perfection, everything else is a long and difficult path. Everything else entails utilizing consciousness to strive for some things while seeking to avoid other things, but the path of the Great Perfection entails releasing all that obscures our own pristine awareness rather than trying to acquire qualities that we don't already have. For this reason, the path of the Great Perfection is said to be effortless, while all other paths are effortful. As long as you are still involved in striving to attain something that you don't have, you are bound to overlook the treasures that are already present within your own being, hidden in plain sight.

The Teacher replies that the way to realize the Great Perfection is to realize emptiness, which is the common ground of all yānas, from the Śrāvakayāna to the Great Perfection. Here is an enormously important statement: The basis for the delusion of all beings in the desire, form, and formless realms is ignorance about one's self alone: the so-called "I." From the Great Perfection perspective, the Buddha's second noble truth, of the origins of suffering, can be summarized in one sentence. Suffering results from two causes: mistaking that which is not "I" as being "I," and failing to recognize who you really are. Not knowing is ignorance, the root of saṃsāra. Grasping at that which is not "I" or "mine," including this body and mind, as being "I" or "mine" is delusion.

Similarly, in a nonlucid dream, ignorance is not knowing that it's a dream; and the resultant reification of everything in the dream as existing from its own side is delusion. Out of delusion flow the mental afflictions of craving, hostility, and all the miseries of the world. Once this illness has been diagnosed, the treatment is straightforward: Stop all delusional activity stemming from craving and hostility. Stop reifying external objects and yourself as being truly existent. Realize who you actually are—and wake up! This is the entire path of the Great Perfection, but it's not as easy as it sounds. There is only one fundamental difference between buddhas and sentient beings: buddhas know who they are and sentient beings don't.

By what method is this to be accomplished? The Teacher's answer is that you must examine the basis and root of the origin, location, and destination of your very own self: the referent of your sense of "I." Whence does it emerge, where does it abide, and where does it finally go? Here are the quintessential questions of vipaśyanā on the nature of the self: From where did you originate? Where are you right now? And where will you go to from here?

In his teachings on vipaśyanā within the context of the six *bardos*, or transitional phases, Padmasambhava comments:

> According to the custom of some teaching traditions, you are first introduced to the view, and upon that basis you seek the meditative state. This makes it difficult to identify awareness. In the tradition presented here, you first establish the meditative state, then on that basis you are introduced to the view. This profound point makes it impossible for you not to identify awareness. Therefore, first settle your mind in its natural state, then bring forth genuine śamatha in your mind-stream, and reveal the nature of awareness.[137]

Similarly, Lozang Chökyi Gyaltsen (1570–1662), the Fourth Panchen Lama and tutor of the Fifth Dalai Lama (1617–82), also refers to these two approaches, saying, "Of the two approaches of seeking to meditate on the basis of the view and seeking the view on the basis of meditation, the following accords with the latter approach."[138] When contemplative traditions become institutionalized, they tend to emphasize the study of theory before practice. Unfortunately, in some cases actual practice is deferred indefinitely. In this teaching, we will be following Padmasambhava's approach of developing the theory of the view based upon the practice of meditation, specifically, the preliminary achievement of śamatha.

Elsewhere, Düdjom Lingpa gives the example of entering into deep, dreamless sleep, in which the substrate consciousness dissolves into the substrate. The essential nature of the substrate is unawareness (Skt. *avidyā*). There is consciousness, but it is only implicit, and nothing is explicitly known. It's like a gas stove with all the burners turned off, but the pilot light is lit. When you're deep asleep and someone shakes you, saying, "Wake up!"

it's like turning on a burner, which instantly bursts into flame. If there were no pilot light of consciousness in deep sleep, you couldn't be awakened at all—you'd be dead.

As you emerge from deep sleep, in a natural progression, the substrate consciousness emerges from the substrate. Its nature is not human, but a mere luminous, cognizant awareness that illuminates the space of the substrate. Then, with the stirring of karma and habitual propensities, a mental factor called *afflictive mentation* (Skt. *kliṣṭamanas*) manifests. This is also called the "I-maker" (Skt. *ahaṃkāra*); it's the primitive, preconceptual sense of being right here—and being separate from the space of awareness, which is perceived as being something other, over there. This primal level of self-grasping is common to every sentient being, down to the smallest insect. Out of this emerges *mentation* (Skt. *manas*), by which one distinguishes and differentiates appearances; it arises together with appearances. Upon the basis of these appearances, conceptualization arises: "Here is this, and there is that." Discrete appearances are identified, objectified, and isolated from context. Finally, these appearances are labeled, verbalized, and reified. And from this basis emerges all mental activity, including the mental afflictions of craving and hostility.

Returning to the question of where the "I" has come from, this theory holds that the appearance of a self emerges from the substrate consciousness. While the illusory sense of really being someone certainly does arise, Padmasambhava challenges us to investigate whether this sense actually corresponds to anything in reality or whether it is merely an empty appearance, having no existence apart from the luminosity of our own awareness.

> If you investigate the root and basis whereby this "I" first arises: The basis is that pervasive, surrounding space to which a stream of consciousness grasps as though it were a self. No appearance or state of mind exists, even as they are not established as anything other than mere appearances. So the source from which they emerge is empty.

The stream of consciousness here means the substrate consciousness, and the surrounding space means the substrate, which I perceive as "my space." Is this space intrinsically mine, or merely imputed to be so? All objective appearances, along with the states of mind with which we engage appearances, do not truly exist; they are all empty appearances, like illusions and rainbows. When Padmasambhava says that all appearances and mindsets do not exist, he is speaking from the perspective of one who has awakened to his own buddha nature.

For example, in the context of a nonlucid dream, someone you encounter may appear to be truly existent and interact with you just like an actual person in the waking state. Such a person is causally effective, and as long as you remain unaware that this is a dream, you don't question his or her reality. But once you've awakened and you remember encountering this person in the dream, it's perfectly clear that he or she didn't exist at all, any more than *you* did as the person appearing in the dream. Likewise, from the perspective of one who is awakened, all the appearances and states of mind that we experience do not exist at all. They are not established as anything other than mere appearances, like rainbows and mirages. The don't really come from anywhere, so their source is empty. Out of emptiness, a wide array of appearances emerges, and despite their emptiness of existing from their own side, they causally interact with each other.

> **To investigate its location in the interim: The head is called the *head*, and it is not given the name "I." Likewise, hair is *hair* and not the "I." The eyes are *eyes* and not the "I." The ears are *ears* and not the "I." The nose is the *nose* and not the "I." The tongue is the *tongue* and not the "I." The teeth are *teeth* and not the "I." The shoulder blades are *shoulder blades* and not the "I." The upper arms are *upper arms* and not the "I." The lower arms are *lower arms* and not the "I." The palms, the backs of the hands, and the fingers are not the "I." The spine is not the "I." The ribs are not the "I." The lungs and heart are not the "I." The liver and its lining are not the "I." The small intestine, spleen, and kidneys are not the "I." The thighs, hips, calves, ankles, and all the finger and toe joints each have their own names, and they are not the "I." The skin, fat, flesh, blood, lymph, ligaments, tendons, and body hair all have their own names, and they are not established as the "I."**

Next, investigate the location of this so-called self, the entity you call "I," in the interim between its arising and disappearance. We can approach this topic from a modern perspective, quite different from Tibetan views of 150 years ago. As discussed previously, there is a widespread belief today, in the scientific community as well as in the popular media, that is articulated by the neuroscientist Antonio Damasio: "I think of human beings as brains with large bodies on their backs."[139] Instead of regarding individual people as the agents of their actions, the brain is now commonly referred to as the agent of all our physical, verbal, and mental activities. If this view is correct, then the "I" is located within the skull. End of discussion.

But how compelling is the evidence that human identity itself is equivalent to the brain? There is plenty of evidence that brain activities and mental activities are closely correlated. For example, neuroscientists can cause a specific memory to arise in the mind of a conscious human being when they stimulate a tiny collection of neurons with microelectrodes. Diverse regions of the brain are associated with a wide array of mental states and processes, and damage to those regions often results in the correlated subjective experience being impaired or eliminated altogether. This much is clear.

While there is definitive evidence that a wide range of subjective experiences arises in dependence upon movements and changes within brain tissue, it does not logically follow that mental phenomena must be *equivalent to* their correlated neural processes. As the neuroscientist Cristof Koch questions, "Are they really one and the same thing, viewed from different perspectives? The characters of brain states and of phenomenal states appear too different to be completely reducible to each other."[140] And the celebrated neuroscientist V. S. Ramachandra declares, "Consciousness is inherently subjective, it does not exist in the physical world."[141] When we objectively observe brain states, they exhibit none of the characteristics of mental states, and when we subjectively observe mental states, they display none of the characteristics of brain activity. So the burden of proof lies with those who believe the two are identical, despite all evidence to the contrary. Moreover, as mentioned previously, all the emergent properties of physical phenomena known throughout the universe are themselves physical and therefore detectable with physical systems of measurement. But mental phenomena themselves, as opposed to their neural correlates and behavioral expressions, are not physically measurable. So the claim that mental phenomena are emergent properties of brain activity is a claim that takes exception to the evidence. In accordance with the scientific principle that "exceptional claims require exceptional evidence," those who believe this claim should provide exceptional evidence to support it.

Neuroscientists who study the brains of subjects with scientific instruments, including EEG and fMRI, are completely blind to subjective experience itself. For that they must ask the subjects they are studying for first-person reports of their experiences. It is indisputable that influencing the brain can influence subjective experience, whether due to a head injury or alcohol consumption. Likewise, it has also been known for a long time that thoughts, desires, and emotions influence brain functions and other physiological processes. The causal interactions between mind, brain, and body are observable, but the notion that the self or else the mind is nothing other than the brain is mere speculation based on inconclusive evidence, however widely this belief is misrepresented as scientific fact.

Inquiry into the location of a self can be conducted introspectively and analytically. In his discussion of śamatha without signs, Padmasambhava offers this guidance:

> Having nothing on which to meditate, and without any modification or adulteration, place your attention simply without wavering, in its own natural state, its natural limpidity, its own character, just as it is. Remain in clarity, and rest the mind so that it is loose and free. Alternate between observing who is concentrating inwardly and who is releasing. If it is the mind, ask: "What is that very agent that releases the mind and concentrates the mind?" Steadily observe yourself, and then release again. By so doing, fine stability will arise, and you may even identify pristine awareness.[142]

When you seek to observe yourself introspectively, you may well have a sense of being located inside your head. But when you closely examine this experience of your own identity, it proves elusive, and all you actually perceive are empty appearances, none of which are *you*.

When we analyze the conjecture that the self is located in the brain and may really be equivalent to it, we might look to scientific studies that call into question such widespread beliefs. We begin with the study conducted in 2009 by Dr. Lars Muckli, a researcher from the Center for Cognitive

Neuroimaging at the University of Glasgow, in which MRI scans of a ten-year-old German girl's brain showed clearly that she had only one brain hemisphere. Her right brain hemisphere stopped developing early in the womb. So if we take Antonio Damasio's statement at face value, and begin to believe that a human being is a brain with a large body on its back, then someone with half a brain should be half a human, right? But Dr. Muckli commented, "Despite lacking one hemisphere, the girl has normal psychological function and is perfectly capable of living a normal and fulfilling life. She is witty, charming and intelligent."[143] Evidently this girl is a whole human despite the fact that she has only half a brain!

Even more dramatic are studies of individuals suffering from hydrocephalus, which results in large portions of their craniums being filled with cerebrospinal fluid. The British neurologist John Lorber studied such cases since the mid-1960s and documented over six hundred scans of people with hydrocephalus. Among the most serious cases, where the cranial cavity was 95 percent filled with cerebrospinal fluid, many were severely disabled—but half had IQs greater than 100.[144] While many neurologists, including Lorber, attribute this remarkable finding to the brain's redundancy and its ability to reassign functions, others are skeptical. For instance, Patrick Wall, professor of anatomy at University College, London, states, "To talk of redundancy is a cop-out to get round something you don't understand."[145] Although such studies do not provide conclusive evidence overthrowing the reductionist status quo, at the very least, such findings should call into question any simplistic equation of the brain with what it means to be a person or what it means to have a mind.

Returning now to our text, as we introspectively and analytically examine our own bodies in search of a real and singular location for our own personal identity, it becomes increasingly clear that such a locus is nowhere to be found. Nevertheless, when we look into a mirror, we identify strongly with this appearance as being a reflection of "me."

> If the "I" were located in the lower part of the body, there would be no pain if the head and the upper limbs were amputated, so it is not present there. If it were located in the upper body, there would be no pain if the lower portions of the body such as the legs were harmed. If it were located inside, there would be no reason why scraping off outer body hair and skin would cause searing pain.

Consider whether it is located in the body. When all your clothes, jewelry, food, wealth, and possessions are taken away and used by someone else, misery and intolerable attachment and hostility arise, so the "I" is not located within your body. If it were located in external objects, all physical worlds and their sentient inhabitants could be apprehended as being mine, but in fact all things have their own names, and they are not the "I."

If the sense of "I" and "mine" were confined to the body, we should not be upset if our external possessions were damaged or stolen. But when our cellphone is scratched or our car is dented, we feel bad. While we may identify with all kinds of external objects, they are not by nature "I" or "mine," for each one has its own label, and they are not "I." The body, mind, and all other things we identify with are "mine" only insofar as we project this label upon them. But none of these things are by their own nature "I" or "mine."

All phenomena of the physical worlds and their inhabitants other than the "I" seem to exist separately. Nevertheless, whether in a dream, the waking state, or the hereafter, the self and other appearances always appear like a body and its shadow, like liquid and moisture, and like fire and heat. So the "I" dominates all the physical worlds and their sentient inhabitants, but the "I" is not located anywhere.

We habitually view the world and its inhabitants as being "out there," while we ourselves are "in here." We grasp at appearances as something "other" and reify them as being absolutely separate, while we reify ourselves as being absolutely here. In every state of consciousness, including the transitional phase between lives, the appearances of the self and of other objects always coexist. As soon as there is the sense that "I am," there are corresponding appearances that are other than "I." Whenever appearances are perceived as "other," there is necessarily a sense of "I am." Self and other always go together; subject and object are mutually interdependent. In the absence of one of them, the other is nowhere to be found, which indicates that neither is inherently existent.

When it comes to our thoughts, in what way are they really "ours"? If we are tormented by an endless stream of uncontrollable, angry, contemptuous thoughts, we may feel terribly guilty for having such thoughts. Just because we have witnessed such thoughts, must we own them, or identify with them? Sometimes thoughts simply happen.

The sense of self or "I" saturates and dominates all our experience, in which the entire world is bifurcated into that which is "I" and "mine" and that which is not. Nevertheless, if we diligently search for it, this "I" is nowhere to be found. It is empty of location. How can something be so influential if it doesn't truly exist?

Despite the fact that a self doesn't really exist in the way we think it does, our grasping at such a self has consequences. This is an utterly crucial point within all Buddhist yānas. If we grasp at our identity as a sentient being, we identify with our mental afflictions and not with our buddha nature. Where exactly is this pathetic sentient being who is caught in the suffering of saṃsāra? If this being is nowhere to be found, why do we take ourselves so seriously? Are we like a child afraid of a monster in the closet? Turn on the light and we see that there's no monster to fear. Likewise, grasping at the true existence of a self is causally efficacious, even though such a self is not really there.

The Dzokchen explanation of the second noble truth says that we suffer because we grasp at that which is not "I" as being "I." In a nonlucid dream, when we grasp at our dream body and identify with it, our dream body is nothing more than empty appearances. But our grasping to these appearances as "me" and to other appearances as "not me" is the root cause of all delusion, craving, and hostility. Every nonlucid dream is like being locked in an insane asylum for believing you are Napoleon, or Cleopatra, or a dog. Even if you don't yet know who or what you are, the first step is to recognize what you are not. You aren't what you think, because the "I" you habitually identify with is nowhere to be found.

> Finally, to investigate and analyze where it goes: All possible worlds serve as the basis for and have the essential nature of the great trickster that is the "I," so its destination is empty of itself. All three realms arise as apparitions of grasping at the "I," so it has nowhere else to go. That which goes did not arise, and it is not located anywhere, which implies that it has no objective existence.

Recall that when the sense of "I" first arises from the substrate consciousness, it arises in opposition to the space of the substrate. We may then identify that space as "mine," and the scope of space that we identify as "mine" can be as large as we like: my country, my planet, my galaxy. The entire universe and its inhabitants can be the basis of "my space." But nothing there is by its own nature either "I" or "mine." Even though it all acts as the basis for the "I," it is empty of "I" and "mine." The three realms of desire, form, and formlessness arise as apparitions of grasping at the "I," so it has nowhere else to go that could somehow escape beyond the scope of these displays.

This is a fascinating point! As mentioned above, the Great Perfection explains that the substrate gives rise to the substrate consciousness, from which the sense of self arises, from which arise mentation, conceptualization, and all appearances. For any appearances to arise, there must first be a congealing sense of "I am." The three realms appear only relative to this sense of self, and they have no existence independent of it. When the sense of "I" dissolves, it has nowhere to go, because the three realms are merely its displays. What is it that goes? That which goes did not arise, and it is not located anywhere, which implies that it has no objective existence, no object to which it refers.

This summarizes the entire approach of vipaśyanā, Mahāmudrā, and the Great Perfection in carrying out an investigation to discover the origination, presence, and dissolution of all phenomena, beginning with the supposed self. Thus every phenomenon is determined to be empty of origination, empty of location, and empty of destination.

> Again Faculty of Luminosity asked, "So if it is certain that the origin, location, and destination of the 'I' do not exist and are not established as real, how do you account for the continuity from one appearance to the next? Teacher, please explain!"

We all have a strong sense of continuity in our lives. I remember what I had for breakfast, who I spent time with last year, and where I lived as a child. There's a common thread running through all my experiences: me, myself, and I. How can we explain this continuity if a self is nowhere to be found?

> He replied, "O son of the family, after the consciousness that grasps at the 'I' has manifested, the 'I' and mine emerge

from their own space, and they disappear back into their own space. They alternately emerge from and withdraw into the expanse of an ethically neutral, vacuous ground. Thus, dream phenomena, phenomena in the waking state, and all the phenomena of the three realms arise as mere appearances without existence. So know that the places where they go and the ones who go there are not established as being real."

The ethically neutral, vacuous ground from which the sense of "I" and "mine" emerges is the substrate. All phenomena in the three realms, in dreams, and in the waking state arise as mere appearances without true, independent existence. What do we mean when we say that something truly exists? We mean that it exists prior to and independent of our conceptual designation of it. We may see a mirage and even photograph it, but is it really there? When we investigate, we determine it to be nothing but an empty appearance. All phenomena appear to move within the space of awareness, the domain of the substrate. When we travel from one place to another, there is a sense of movement, but it's no more real than the sense of movement when watching a movie of riding on a roller coaster. These are simply empty appearances arising.

> Again Bodhisattva Faculty of Luminosity asked, "O Teacher, Bhagavān, when grasping at the 'I' vanishes into the space of awareness, isn't its continuum severed? Teacher, please explain!"
>
> He replied, "O son of the family, even when the appearances and mindsets of grasping at the 'I' vanish into the space of awareness, that ethically neutral state in which the good qualities of the ground are not manifest acts as the cause of self-grasping. So it is just this unimpeded continuum of holding the 'I' to have the identity of being a self—the causal ignorance—that is called *grasping at the identity of a person*."

Even when the ordinary mind dissolves into the substrate consciousness, which dissolves into the substrate—for example, when you fall deep asleep, faint, or become comatose, and you are unaware of anything—all the seeds for habitual propensities are present in the substrate, ready to germinate once again. An angry, hot-tempered person who has been unconscious for days will emerge from his coma with habitual tendencies for anger intact. From the Buddhist perspective, when such a person dies, he will be reborn manifesting the same habits for anger in his next life, since the propensities for our mental habits are "stored" not in the brain but in the substrate. This explanation seriously challenges the widespread, materialist view of the mind, brain, and human identity.

✤ ✤ ✤ ✤ ✤ ✤ ✤

In the preceding section of the *Vajra Essence*, which describes śamatha, Padmasambhava makes it clear that the achievement of this dissolution of the coarse mind into the substrate consciousness is an indispensable basis for entering the path by way of vipaśyanā. He comments that even in Tibet of 150 years ago, relatively few yogins actually achieved śamatha; most were satisfied with a lesser degree of stability and eager to advance to more advanced Vajrayāna practices. They didn't penetrate deeply enough to fathom the substrate consciousness. He asserts that if you wish to derive the full insight of vipaśyanā and the later stages of the path, śamatha is a necessary foundation. This makes sense, because by overcoming excitation and laxity completely, the mind becomes serviceable, supple, stable, and clear—which is very useful.

Imagine resting in the sheer vacuity of the substrate, the space of the mind, as in deep, dreamless sleep. This state corresponds to the first of the twelve links of dependent origination: unawareness, or ignorance (Skt. *avidyā*). As mentioned previously, the symmetry of this state is broken by karmic imprints, or energies, which correspond to the second of the twelve links: mental formations (Skt. *saṃskāra*). These movements serve as cooperative conditions for the emergence of the substrate consciousness from the dormant awareness of the substrate, which corresponds to the third link: consciousness (Skt. *vijñāna*). Then, as you gradually move toward waking consciousness, you can observe how afflictive mentation arises, separating a primal sense of "self" from the space of which you are aware; this is the beginning of the bifurcation of subject and object. The next phase of engagement in the ordinary world is the occurrence of a multitude of appearances as a result of the emergence, first of subtle mentation, and then coarse mentation. In early Buddhism, this phase corresponds to the emergence of the fourth link: name-and-form (Skt. *nāma-rūpa*). This results in a clear differentiation of diverse objective appearances, corresponding to the fifth link: the six sense bases (Skt. *ṣaḍāyatana*), which appear as separate from one's subjective awareness of them. When mentation (Skt. *manas*) becomes activated, it differentiates objective appearances from subjective names. As you continue to emerge from samādhi, the higher cognitive faculties are aroused, along with memory, conceptualization, and language. And finally, out of this conceptual nexus emerge outside, inside, matter, mind, and all phenomena. The subsequent links of contact (Skt. *sparśa*), feeling (Skt. *vedanā*), craving (Skt. *tṛṣṇā*), and close identification (Skt. *upādāna*) gradually emerge in due course.

Once you have achieved śamatha, with the dissolution of ordinary mind into the substrate consciousness, you can observe this process directly as you emerge from samādhi, along with the reverse sequence as you enter samādhi once again. It becomes perfectly clear that all sensory and mental appearances, including dreams, occur only in the space of the mind, here called the substrate. All these appearances are illuminated, or manifested, by the substrate consciousness. Likewise, this same sequence occurs at conception, when one's consciousness as it was during the prior "transitional process of becoming" dissolves into the substrate, which is then catalyzed by karmic energies and their concomitant mental factors. Thus the process begins again. From one lifetime to the next, the links of contact, feeling, craving, and close identification trigger the subsequent links of becoming (Skt. *bhava*), birth (Skt. *jāti*), and aging and death (Skt. *jarāmaraṇa*). We then see the parallels of this process as it takes place when taking birth, when waking from deep sleep, and when lucidly emerging from the substrate consciousness after having achieved śamatha.

With the insight gained from achieving actual śamatha, it becomes clear that all phenomena perceived by awareness are simply appearances, which are not material or physical. In a dream, all the colors, sounds, smells, and so on, that arise objectively, as well as the thoughts and emotions that arise subjectively, have no physical existence whatsoever. Moreover, dreams do not exist in any physical location. The images that appear during a dream are not located inside the frontal cortex or the brainstem. And this is equally true for all sensory and mental appearances during the waking state.

This is not to suggest that everything you perceive exists only in your mind. The atoms in the walls of your room are not figments of your imagination, and they will persist whether or not anyone is looking at them. The walls have physical attributes, but the *colors* you see when photons are absorbed and reemitted from those walls do not exist anywhere—not in the atoms, the photons, your retina, or your visual cortex. The colors you perceive, in dependence on your visual faculties, arise only in the space of the mind, which has no physical attributes and no location.

If I snap my fingers, energetic waves propagate through the air. But the sound you hear is not located in those waves or in your auditory cortex; it has no physical location. All we experience via the rest of the six senses, including odors, tastes, tactile sensations, and thoughts, consists of nonphysical appearances occurring in the space of awareness, or the substrate. They are not physical, and they are also not identical to the mind that perceives them; they are *appearances perceived by awareness*. Appearances do not exist independently of the awareness of them, and the awareness of appearances does not exist independently of the appearances either.

Within this flow of the experience of name-and-form, with appearances and mentation arising together, the conceptual mind separates mind from matter, subject from object, and particle from field. But none of these distinctions were preexisting or have any inherent existence; they are not perceived but conceived. In short, the fundamental division between mind and matter, or body and mind, is not simply a given; we conceive it based on appearances, which, like information, are neither physical nor mental.

Determining the Identitylessness of Phenomena as Objects

The next section of the text investigates the emptiness of all phenomena as objects, beginning with your own body. This analysis is conducted in the same way as the examination of the emptiness of a self. The body is no more truly existent than is the self: both are equally empty. This is not easy to understand conceptually, and it's far more difficult to realize experientially. It is possible to gain a degree of realization of emptiness without having achieved śamatha, but this achievement makes it possible to sustain that realization so that it eradicates mental afflictions irreversibly.

As an alternative to the demands of such an elaborate, analytical approach, you might prefer a step-wise, radically empirical route to realizing emptiness in the waking state, by which you first realize the emptiness of dreams. This still requires a lot of work, and it entails a great deal of meditation, beginning with the achievement of śamatha. Once you've achieved it, however, the power of your samādhi and the clarity and stability of your awareness naturally spill over into your dreaming consciousness, which becomes equally stable and clear. It is then easy to recognize when you are dreaming, and you have lucid dreams. You can even fall asleep consciously, going directly from the waking state into lucid, dreamless sleep, and from there into lucid dreaming.

Now you can venture into dream yoga, the perfect laboratory for investigating the nature and creative potential of consciousness itself. Every aspect of a lucid dream is a display of mind, and it is evident that nothing is physical. In this laboratory, you can investigate the lack of inherent nature of everything in the dream—which you already know, being lucid—and you can also conduct some interesting experiments by transforming and emanating the contents of your dreams. Anything you imagine can be actualized within the dream: changing people into dogs, making big things small, turning one into many, and shifting your own shape at will. You see that not only are phenomena empty of inherent nature, but that their manifestations are directly related to your conceptual designations of them. For example, you might wish to have a conversation with Albert Einstein in your dream, knowing that he's dead. By simply wishing it, you can experience it, while knowing perfectly well that the Albert Einstein in your dream is a free creation of your own mind, arising from your substrate.

Bear in mind that in a nonlucid dream, you believe that everything you perceive truly exists. Because you don't fathom the empty nature of your dream appearances, what you wish for in the dream is not likely to come to pass. But in a lucid dream, everything is completely malleable. There is nothing to resist the whims of your imagination. Such profound realizations in the dream state are like a dress rehearsal, which will give your investigations into the empty nature of waking reality a tremendous boost. The dream and waking states are not the same, but they are very similar. If you realize that the emptiness of phenomena that you realize in the dream state is equally true in the waking state, you may be able to transform phenomena in the waking state as easily as in a lucid dream.

There are two other traditional approaches to realizing the emptiness of your own body. One approach is to *directly perceive* the sensations corresponding to the elements of earth, water, fire, and air within the space of your body and to realize that they do not constitute the body, individually or collectively. These subjective sensations don't belong to the body, they do not actually exist within the physical space of the body, and the body is not in them. No inherently existent body can be found among these tactile sensations.

The second approach, the one followed in our text, is to *analyze* the anatomical parts of the body, one by one, recognizing that they are not equivalent to the body, either individually or collectively. Such an analysis is also presented in the Buddha's teachings, as included in the Pāli canon, on the close application of mindfulness to the body, but in that context, it is to demonstrate that there is nothing in the body that corresponds to a self. In the present discussion, we apply such analysis to show that no part of the body is equivalent to what we call "the body." We will examine the common designations for the body and its various parts, including skin, bones, blood, and internal organs, because this is what we generally consider to be the real body. But is this body real or not? The same mode of analyzing parts that we applied in the search for a self will now be applied in the search for a real body.

Here's a subtle point: When you conceive of something, like "my head," which has many parts, what comes to mind is a single image, a fixed concept. For example, when you see a child whom you haven't seen in a year, you will likely remark, "How you've grown!" Your idea of this child is a static one, so you may be surprised when a constantly changing reality fails to match your static image. Our concepts of everything are relatively static in this way. We tend to reify whatever we apprehend, assuming that there really is something "out there" directly corresponding to our fixed concept. We firmly hold on to unchanging ideas of things and fail to see the evidence that things are constantly changing. This is true not only for outer phenomena but also for our own bodies, minds, and selves.

Remember that we aren't questioning the conventional existence of our bodies and their many components. We are investigating whether any underlying entity exists that is independent of our conceptual designations but corresponds to them, bearing the external attributes we actually observe. The nonexistence of such an independent entity is precisely what vipaśyanā meditation is intended to demonstrate. There is no preexisting entity of the "head" to which we attach this name.

> Faculty of Luminosity asked, "Teacher, Bhagavān, how are external objects empty? Teacher, please explain!"
>
> He replied, "Let's investigate how, when you grasp at the identities of the phenomena that proliferate when apprehended by the 'I,' all these names, things, and signs are not established as being real. First, let's determine how the names

of the body are empty by investigating the basis of designation
for each name."

Grasping at the identities of phenomena means reifying them. A crucial
point in this regard is to distinguish between a name and its basis of designation. For example, suppose you see a friend approaching in the street and
you exclaim, "Look, it's Jim!" What is the basis upon which you have made
the designation of that name? Assuming you didn't recognize his clothing, it
was probably his face, and perhaps no more than the color of a patch of skin,
a silhouette of hair, or the shape of the eyes. A face is not a person; it's the
basis of your designation "Jim." Likewise, a face is not a body, but it may serve
as the basis of designation for a body. The general principle is that the basis
of designation and the name designated upon it are never the same thing.

> To examine what is called the *head*: hair is *hair* and not the
> head. The eyes are *eyes* and not the head. The ears are *ears* and
> not the head. The nose is the *nose* and not the head, and the
> tongue is the *tongue* and not the head. Likewise, the skin,
> flesh, bones, blood, lymph, ligaments, and so on all appear as
> having their own individual names, so they are not established
> as the head.

These constituent parts of the head, as well as the brain, constitute the basis
of the designation *head*, but they are not equivalent to the head. Still, if all
the components of a head are present, we instinctively assume that the head
is, too, as our interlocutor objects:

> Faculty of Luminosity asked, "Teacher, Bhagavān, if you
> reduce the head to its components like that, it is not estab-
> lished as being real, but their assembly is still called the *head*,
> isn't it?"

We think of it as a recipe: brain and skull, flesh and blood, skin and hair
make a head.

> He replied, "Son of the family, observe that in general there
> are many cases in which the collection of those components is

not designated as a *head*. If you ground someone's head into particles and then collected them and showed them to others, they would not call them a *head*. Even if those particles were moistened and formed into a sphere, it would not be called a *head*."

This unbaked meatloaf of ground head would not fool anyone into thinking it was a head. It's simply not true that an assembly of its parts is the same as a head.

"If your head that appears in a dream, your head that appears during the waking state, your head that appears in the past, and your head that appears in the future were all identical, whatever sores, swellings, goiters, moles, and warts you possessed would have to appear on all those occasions. But they don't."

If there were only one real head, and all these appearances under various conditions were its reflections, like an actor playing various roles, there should be some consistency among them. But these diverse appearances you call "head" are not the same at all.

"If each of those heads were different, either you would have to get rid of all the prior heads, or it would become evident that they were never established as real."

If instead you imagined that there were multiple, different, real heads that appear in your dreams, the waking state, the past, and the future, then you should be able to account for each head's disappearance when the next head takes over. Or you can realize that all these heads arise only relative to their cognitive frameworks—of waking perception, dreams, remembrances, or fantasies—and none of them has an inherent nature.

Now we consider a functional definition. The Tibetan word pronounced as *go*, translated as "head," can refer to anything on top of something else. Besides referring to the top of the body, it can refer to the top or beginning of other things, just as we might refer to the head of the class or the head of a staircase.

> "If you say something is called the *head* because it is seen to
> be on top, you should analyze the upper and lower regions of
> space. Thus, by investigating how the front, back, upper, and
> lower regions of space exist, you will determine that the head
> is not established as any of them."

Your cognitive frame of reference makes all the difference, because all such designations are relative ones. There is no inherently existent head, or top, of anything. Whether it's the head of a person, a staircase, or a class of students, it becomes a head only by the process of being so labeled.

In London's Hyde Park, a long tradition of free public speech, debate, and protest has its home in Speakers' Corner, where anyone so inclined is free to mount a soapbox and expound to passersby. Many years ago, I heard of a man whose message was to proclaim, "I want you all to know, I have no head. It's perfectly obvious that I have shoulders, arms, a body, and legs, but no head." This man presented himself as a kind of radical empiricist, refusing to affirm the existence of something he couldn't see. And he couldn't see his own head, only reflections or photographs of it.

Along similar lines, in his book *Concepts of Modern Mathematics*, Ian Stewart tells the story of an astronomer, a physicist, and a mathematician who were taking a holiday in Scotland. "Glancing from a train window, they observed a black sheep in the middle of a field. 'How interesting,' observed the astronomer, 'all Scottish sheep are black!' To which the physicist responded, 'No, no! *Some* Scottish sheep are black!' The mathematician gazed heavenward in supplication, and then intoned, 'In Scotland there exists at least one field, containing at least one sheep, *at least one side of which is black.*'"[146] What might happen if we were to take such care in noticing the process by which we designate labels and draw conclusions based on always-partial evidence? It wouldn't mean we would not have heads, but perhaps we might not tie our identity so tightly into what we think is there: whether smart or dull, beautiful or ugly, a mass of meaningless gray matter or a suitable vehicle for a mind that can transcend itself to realize ultimate truths.

> Likewise, upon what is the *eye* designated? Not all fluid
> spheres are known by the name *eye*. The skin, blood, fat,
> channels, and muscles are not given the name *eye*. As in the
> previous case, the eye does not exist as their assembly either.

> If you think that a fluid sphere that sees forms is called the
> *eye*, observe whether that which sees forms at all times—in the
> past, future, and present, while dreaming, and in the waking
> state—is this fluid sphere that exists now. The manifestations
> of your own appearances are due to primordially present con-
> sciousness rather than this present fluid sphere. Even if you
> held a hundred million eyeballs in your hand and made them
> look in the same direction, they would not see form.

When you are dreaming, even though your physical eyes are closed, your
dream eyes may see a vast panorama—but these are empty appearances. The
point here is that your ability to see colors and forms fundamentally depends
on consciousness, and although in most cases the sensory consciousness relies
on outer forms to trigger it, the physical sense organs of the eyes may not be
required in all cognitive frameworks.

One of the most interesting attested examples in this regard concerns
near-death experiences in which patients have allegedly seen and heard
events in the operating room while they were temporarily brain dead, and
their subsequent reports of what they witnessed have been corroborated by
medical staff who were present. Such patients commonly report that their
out-of-body perceptual experiences are far more vivid than anything they
experienced previously, and their memories of these experiences remain crys-
tal clear for years afterward.[147]

There is no scientific explanation for how a person whose cerebral cortex
is flatlined could see objectively verifiable colors in a room shared with normal, conscious human beings without photons striking that person's own
eyes and activating the visual cortex. Moreover, the possibility of extrasensory perception is incompatible with the beliefs of materialism, and this may
account for the fact that so many cognitive scientists ignore the evidence
of such examples. But such a dogmatism, which ignores empirical evidence
simply because it is incompatible with one's beliefs, is contrary to the highest
ideals of scientific inquiry. As Richard Feynman writes:

> It is only through refined measurements and careful experi-
> mentation that we can have a wider vision. And then we see
> unexpected things: we see things that are far from what we
> would guess—far from what we could have imagined. . . . If

science is to progress, what we need is the ability to experiment, honesty in reporting results—the results must be reported without somebody saying what they would like the results to have been . . . . One of the ways of stopping science would be only to do experiments in the region where you know the law. But experimenters search most diligently, and with the greatest effort, in exactly those places where it seems most likely that we can prove our theories wrong. In other words we are trying to prove ourselves wrong as quickly as possible, because only in that way can we find progress.[148]

According to the Buddha himself and many generations of later Buddhist contemplatives who have perceived such things directly, following death, the perceptions of beings in the intermediate period are no longer constrained by the physical senses, so they experience various kinds of extrasensory perceptions that living people can normally achieve only if they have achieved śamatha. While brain activity enables our mental and sensory faculties in terms of the operations of the "coarse mind" that arises in dependence upon the brain as its cooperative condition, the "subtle mind" that carries on from one lifetime to another has a much broader range of extrasensory perception that is not conditioned or limited by the human brain. Some contemplatives discover this in the course of dying lucidly and later report on it by drawing on their recollection of having passed through the transitional process of becoming after a previous lifetime. Other contemplatives, by fathoming both their substrate consciousness and pristine awareness while still alive, directly perceive the nature of the various transitional processes without actually dying. In this regard, the great Indian Buddhist scholar and contemplative Atiśa (982–1054) wrote in his classic *Lamp for the Path to Enlightenment*:

> Just as a bird with undeveloped wings cannot fly in the sky, those without the power of extrasensory perception cannot work for the good of living beings. The merit gained in a single day by someone with extrasensory perception cannot be gained even in a hundred lifetimes by one without extrasensory perception. . . . Without the achievement of śamatha extrasensory perception will not arise. Therefore, make repeated effort to accomplish śamatha.[149]

Have we yet fathomed what a range of perceptual faculties we might gain once the mind is no longer limited by its close association with and attachment to the physical senses of this particular configuration of body and mind? Once the mind has dissolved into the substrate consciousness, it is no longer tied to the particular location of the physical senses that function on the basis of the configurations of cells we tend to call "my body." If in even a single case it is possible for valid perception of a shared world to arise without being correlated to the electrical activity of certain parts of a brain, and if contemplatives of the past have indeed reported many types of veridical perception not based on the range of the normal sense faculties of a human body, then what infinite possibilities might there be for perception beyond the confines of the human body as we know it? The arguments here have not yet proven any of this to be the case beyond a shadow of a doubt, but recognizing that the eyes are not *in themselves* what see forms—as the example of a bunch of disconnected eyes held in the hand demonstrates *ad absurdum*—is already a giant leap in the direction of understanding that valid perception of form might not require eyes at all.

> Likewise, as for the *ears*, since the flesh, skin, channels, muscles, blood, lymph, and cavities each have their own names and not the name *ear*, what is called the *ear*? If you say something is called the *ear* because it hears sounds, check whether that which hears sounds at all times, during and after this life, while dreaming and while awake, is the ear. By doing so, you will find that it is mental consciousness that hears, and not the form of the present ear. Even if you held countless attentive ears in your hands, they would not hear sounds. So the ear has never been established as something real.

Like the eyes, the ears are designated based upon various components, but the ears are not the same as their parts. If the basis of designation were identical to the designated object, it would be inherently existent and independent of being so labeled. It's a subtle but crucial distinction. Alternately, if you define an ear functionally, as that which hears sounds, then your ears in a dream would qualify in the same way as your physical ears. But your dream ears have no substantial reality, and so it is only your mental consciousness that hears in the dream and in the intermediate period. The physical ear itself does not hear, and this suggests that in some cases you can hear without physical ears. Saying that the ear has never been established as real means that it is not an independent entity that existed prior to being so designated. An ear comes into existence in dependence upon our conceptual designation. Without this labeling, and the function in relation to which it is applied, there would be no ear.

> Similarly, by investigating and analyzing the name and actual characteristics of the *nose*, you find that the flesh, bones, blood, lymph, channels, muscles, and cavities all have their own different names, so they are not established as the *nose*, nor is it established as their assembly.
>
> If you think that that which smells odors is called the *nose* and that odors are sensed through this orifice, consider that this orifice is not needed in the dream state or in the bodies of other lifetimes. Consciousness in the intermediate period detects odors as well. Therefore, since mental consciousness has no nose, the nose certainly has no objective existence.
>
> Likewise, the *tongue* is not established as any of the individual components of the flesh, blood, skin, channels, and muscles; nor is the name *tongue* given to their assembly. If you assert that that which experiences tastes is the tongue, check out whether or not it is this very tongue that experiences tastes in the dream state, the intermediate period, and in the bodies of other lifetimes. Then it will become clear to you.
>
> By investigating the so-called body in terms of the skin, fat, flesh, blood, marrow, bones, and all the channels and muscles, you will find that the body is not established as being real. If they were all reduced to minute particles and then massed together, the name of *body* would not apply. Even if they were moistened and formed into a lump, that would not be a *body*. If you say that that which experiences tactile sensations is designated as the *body*, check out what experiences tactile sensations while in a dream and the intermediate period. By doing so, you will see that it is mental consciousness itself, and since the name *body* is not applied to the mind, the body does not exist.

Thus, examining the olfaction of the nose, the gustation of the tongue, and the tactile sensations of the body in the same way, analyzing structurally and functionally, we find that these sense organs have no existence independent of our designations. The sensory experiences we commonly associate with these organs are always dependent on mental consciousness, while the physical senses are under certain circumstances optional, as in the experience of dreams.

Three aspects form the crux of each of these examples—the basis of designation, the act of designating, and the designated object—and they are mutually interdependent. Without any one, the other two cannot exist. This shows that none of them has inherent existence. Saying that the body doesn't exist means that this designated composite object doesn't exist independently of the act of designating and its basis of designation.

In reifying something, we exempt it from any such interdependency. We deem it to be truly existent, independent of any designation by any name, for anyone. Shakespeare's Juliet in a sense reifies Romeo's true existence in dismissing his surname: "What's in a name? That which we call a rose / By any other name would smell as sweet." I remember when I was a boy, our family went out for dinner to a fine restaurant. I ordered spaghetti with Bolognese sauce. For some reason that I never understood, this perfectly good spaghetti smelled to me like vomit. I couldn't get that fixed idea out of my mind, and I burst out laughing. Even though I knew it wasn't vomit-flavored spaghetti, I still couldn't bring myself to eat it! Moral of the story: that which we call "spaghetti," when called by another name, such as "vomit," does not necessarily smell as savory.

The great bard highlighted the significance of names and thoughts when Hamlet, in his exchange with Guildenstern and Rosencrantz, famously remarks, "Why, then, 'tis none to you; for there is nothing / either good or bad, but thinking makes it so." From Hamlet's perspective, Denmark is a prison, but for his companions, it is no more so than the world at large. According to the general Buddhist view, the whole of saṃsāra, with its myriad pleasant and miserable realms, is a prison. But from the perspective of pristine awareness, all of saṃsāra and nirvāṇa is equally suffused by the primordial purity of the Great Perfection.

Reification comes naturally. It enables a quick distinction between friend and foe when there's no time to waste: Snakes are dangerous! When the mental afflictions of hatred, desire, and ignorance are activated, reification is always at their root. It powers our feelings of anger, attraction, or ambivalence toward the reified object of our attention, allowing us to ignore the interdependencies of the situation and our role in it: One may abhor all snakes because they are dangerous, even the innocent garter snake! Indeed, a classical illustration of the effects of reification is the case in which one becomes frightened upon mistaking a bit of rope for a snake.

> Moreover, upon investigating the location of the so-called arm, you will recognize that the shoulder is not the arm, nor are the upper arm, the forearm, or the palm and fingers the arm. So I say, "Identify what the arm is and tell me." You may claim that whatever performs the functions of the arm is called the *arm*. But then, if you examine the appearance of an arm that performs the functions of an arm in a dream, and all such appearances in the intermediate period, and ask of them, "Is this it?" you will find that it is not. Rather, you will determine that they are merely appearances to the mind. So the arm is not established except as something imputed by the mind.
>
> Moreover, upon examining the *shoulder*, you will see that the flesh is not the shoulder, nor are the bones, channels, or muscles. It is not established as any of those individual components, and it is not the assembly of the particles to which they can be reduced, even if you were to moisten them and form them into a lump. Likewise, carefully examining all the *joints* proves that the basis of designation of that name has no objective existence.

In each case, there is no independently preexisting thing that serves as the basis of designation for the name. Something can only become a basis of designation by agreement, or convention.

The distinctions being made here might appear to be merely semantic, but there is more to them than wordplay. The way of viewing reality that is being challenged here is called *metaphysical realism*, which is held to be true by many scientists and philosophers but rejected by others. This is the view that (1) the world consists of mind-independent objects, (2) there is exactly one true and complete description of the way the world is, and (3) truth involves the correspondence between an independently existent world and a description of it. A metaphysical realist asserts that what's "out there" is really there, independent of any observer, no matter what you call it.[150]

The most practical inquiry, particularly for a beginner, is to probe into the emptiness of "I am." The independent, objective reality of physical objects like a house or our body appears to be so obvious that it's hard to call it into question. But of course, this is exactly how we feel about physical objects in a nonlucid dream—which is one reason why it doesn't occur to us that we are dreaming. Dream objects really seem to be there. Unlike mirages or rainbows, we can interact with dream objects in all the expected ways. When we shake hands in a dream, the handshake may feel hard or soft, but we can feel another hand in ours that is usually quite convincing. Even in a lucid dream, appearances may be as realistic as in waking experience. Nevertheless, the actual nature of the dream is completely incompatible with the appearances of the dreamscape. In both waking and dream states, phenomena appear to exist truly from their own sides. But this is deceptive, because all appearances arise only relative to a cognitive framework. They do not represent an independent reality.

> Furthermore, to what do you give the name *person* for the appearance of a person over there? The head is not a person. The five sense faculties are not a person. The name *person* is not established upon flesh, blood, bones, marrow, channels, muscles, major and minor limbs, or consciousness.

When we identify someone, it is usually on the basis of that person's head and face. If we only see other parts of the body, we are less likely to recognize the person, while a face is highly recognizable. It may be the basis of designation for a person, but a head or face is not a person. Once again, the basis of designation is never the same as the object that is designated upon it. A person may be designated upon the five sensory faculties or other parts of anatomy, but none of these constitutes a person. The mind, which is invisible to others, can be a basis of designation of a person, but it is not equivalent to a human being.

A fundamental premise in the Buddhist teachings is that whenever a mental affliction arises, such as craving, hostility, jealousy, or pride, it is always directed toward an object that is being reified and grasped as having its own inherent nature. For example, in many modern societies feelings of low self-esteem are commonplace, and they can mutate into self-contempt. This mental affliction is an expression of aversion that is only nominally different, by virtue of being directed against yourself. When you succumb to low self-esteem, its object is your own reified self. If you search for this self, you will not find it anywhere. It's as if you had authored a novel with a fictional character—whom you despise—and you are tormented because you identify with your hated creation.

When we conceive of any object, whether it's a thing, a person, or our own self, the act of conceptualization functions like a knife to carve away everything that is not that object. The conceived object is isolated from its context and the network of interrelations from which it arose. Harmless conceptualization can be useful in ordinary conversation: if we ask for water, we won't be given coffee instead. The problem comes from reifying the conceived object as having true, inherent existence that is independent of context.

Here is an interesting experiment to conduct in your daily engagement with the world: When you observe the arising of a mental affliction, such as aversion for someone, examine closely the basis of designation for the object of this mental affliction. When your object is reified, you might assert, "That man is evil," as if he consisted of pure, homogenized evil, with no other ingredients. If this were true, everyone should be able to recognize it about him; but of course they don't, and the man's loved ones might strongly disagree. Carefully investigate the actual basis of designation for this object of your aversion. Is it his face, body, mind, beliefs, or behavior? In so doing, you begin to deconstruct the reified object of your aversion. Instead of an independently existent person, you can see his actual context, including the causes and conditions that gave rise to his relative existence, his diverse roles relative to different people and situations, and his disparate array of characteristics. The actual person is in a continuous state of flux—just like yourself—with many qualities arising and passing from moment to moment. He is influenced by his changing environment, and he influences it in return. But the reified concept of him is a caricature, frozen in time, a straw man serving as the object of a mental affliction.

When we reify another person, whether with attachment or aversion, there is nothing independently preexisting that serves as the basis of designation for the person. Something can become a basis of designation only by consensual agreement, or convention. When does a human person come into existence? Few would call an unfertilized egg a "sentient being," nor do we think of sperm cells as sentient beings. During the nine months following conception, scientifically it is difficult, if not impossible, to know whether there is a separate sentient being in the mother's womb, and all the more difficult to know when that sentient being becomes a human person. But everyone would agree that a newborn baby is one. Our judgments might depend on ethical concerns, legal implications, medical criteria, and religious beliefs, making them highly personal. Each of us may have our own unverifiable views regarding the time of origin of a human being in a mother's womb, but then we mustn't overlook the fact that when there *is* a conscious creature in the womb, with a mind separate from the mother's, it has its own perspective on this matter, too!

The same dependencies characterize the reverse process. Something gradually decays, losing parts and functions, until at some point, within a specific conceptual framework, it ceases to be called what it once was. The designation is modified or withdrawn altogether. Accidents and disease can destroy many of a person's parts and functions—hair, skin, teeth, knees, hips, limbs, and eyes; thought, memory, speech, vision, and mobility—and regardless of whether doctors are able to compensate for these losses or not, everyone will agree that the person still exists, as long as he or she is alive. After death, people may continue to refer to the *deceased person* for a while, but eventually the body will be called a *corpse*; and even that label will no longer apply when only bones or ashes remain.

In the Buddhist tradition of contemplative inquiry, if one wishes to experientially explore the beginning and end of human life, again one must first achieve śamatha, for this enables one to explore the continuum of the substrate consciousness that precedes birth as a human and carries on after death. The ability to lucidly observe one's mind dissolve into the substrate consciousness while settling the mind in its natural state well prepares one for observing a very similar dissolution during the dying process. While resting in the stillness of awareness, one watches one's physical senses shut down as they withdraw into the continuum of mental consciousness, and following the cessation of one's respiration, one gradually witnesses the final disappearance of the last vestiges of one's human mental faculties as one comes to rest in the remaining substrate consciousness. For those who have never lucidly experienced the substrate consciousness, the final stage of the dying process entails falling unconscious as one's mind dissolves into the substrate. This is the point of death. One's human life has now come to an end in what is called the "dark near-attainment." But this is not the end, and the eternalist belief that one now "rests in peace" forever as well as the nihilist belief that one is now completely annihilated are both mere speculations unsupported by empirical evidence or compelling logic. The major drawback of being dead is that it doesn't last.

Padmasambhava explains that people may remain unconscious in that state of being dead for as long as three days. During this time, your body no longer functions as a human body, and your human mind has dissolved into its source, the substrate. So, without a human body or a human mind, you are no longer a human being. You've gone primal: an undifferentiated sentient being, designated on the basis of your substrate. During this phase—whether it last minutes or days, your body does not decompose, for it is still held by your subtle continuum of mental consciousness. If, by the power of your previous achievement of śamatha, you have passed through the entire dying process lucidly, you may also experience death lucidly. If a human life is likened to a novel, then this is like reading the narrative all the way to the end, whereas a person who simply passes out when coming to the final dissolution of the human mind is like a person who falls asleep when coming to the final page of the book. How sad to have missed out on the ending!

Although your human existence has terminated at that point, there is more to death than meets the eye. Following the dissolution of human consciousness into the substrate, pristine awareness spontaneously manifests, and who those have realized this dimension of consciousness through such practices as Mahāmudrā and Dzokchen are well prepared to recognize it again as it manifests as the "clear light of death." Padmasambhava explains:

> Following that is the dissolution of the dark attainment into the clear light. As an analogy, just as the space inside a jar is united with the space outside, without even a speck of any appearance of a self, a radiant, clear expanse arises like all-pervasive space, free of contamination—like dawn breaking in the sky. At this time, people who are already very familiar with ground pristine awareness by means of cutting through and who have acquired confidence in this will recognize the meeting of the pristine awareness in which they have previously trained—which is like a familiar person— and the clear light that emerges later on. There they must hold their own ground, like a king sitting upon his throne.[151]

Accomplished contemplatives may lucidly dwell in this clear light of death for many days on end, during which their bodies do not decompose, for it is still imbued with the radiance of pristine awareness. During this time, even their substrate consciousness has melted into its primordial ground, so there is no sentient being there, at least not from their perspective. They've gone primordial. For those who have no experience of pristine awareness, it will arise and pass swiftly without being noted, and as soon as the subtlest dimension of awareness departs from the body, it begins to decompose. Padmasambhava's teachings on the six transitional processes explains the next phase, known as the transitional process of ultimate reality.[152] Following that is the commonly known "intermediate state," or transitional process of becoming. The optimal preparation for maintaining lucidity during this phase is the practice of dream yoga, for the illusory experiences throughout this process are remarkably similar to those in a dream.[153]

When this transitional process comes to an end and is followed by a human rebirth, the consciousness of the transmigrating being dissolves into the substrate, and from this emerges once again the substrate consciousness as it enters into the union of the egg and sperm of one's new parents. This is the point at which the fertilized egg becomes conscious, and there is now a separate sentient being in the mother's womb. During the early phases of human gestation, Buddhist contemplatives refer to this being as "becoming human."[154] It is not yet human, but it is in the process of becoming so. In dependence upon the gradual formation of the brain and nervous system, the subtle continuum of mental consciousness becomes differentiated into the different modes of sensory awareness, and the unique faculties of the human mind likewise emerge from that continuum. As explained earlier, the substantial cause of these modes of human consciousness is the preceding substrate consciousness, and the changes taking place in the formation of the human body serve as cooperative conditions for the emergence of the human mind. I don't know of any precise point in this development at which the being that is becoming human actually becomes human. This, once again, is a matter of conceptual designation, and it depends on one's definition of what it means to be human. This entire cycle of birth and death can be lucidly explored by those with sufficient contemplative insight, but for everyone else, the beginning and end of life remain shrouded in mystery.

Meanwhile, medical abilities to thwart death, including cardiopulmonary bypass and advanced surgical techniques to repair once-fatal injuries, have led to increasing numbers of published accounts of near-death experiences (NDEs). A number of Western scientists have studied the phenomenon and developed explanatory hypotheses.[155] While most such reports are retrospective and offer little more than anecdotal evidence, several prospective studies of cardiac-arrest survivors have been conducted. Bruce Greyson, of the Division of Perceptual Studies at the University of Virginia and one of the world's leading experts in this field, developed a scale for quantifying the core elements of NDE reports, with cognitive, affective, paranormal, and transcendental features.[156] These often include aspects such as peacefulness and bliss, an out-of-body experience (OBE), traversing a dark tunnel toward a light, a panoramic life review, and meeting deceased relatives and spiritual beings in another realm. Survivors frequently report significant and lasting changes in their outlook on life, including reduced fear of death, reduced materialism, and increased spirituality. They also report frustration and inability to convey their profound and ineffable insights to others—along with a strong urge to do so, despite often being dismissed as hallucinatory or insane.

The term *near-death experience* dates only to 1975, but close encounters with death have been reported throughout human cultures, with common elements as well as culturally specific ones. In Tibet, rather than being dismissed or ridiculed, such experiences are valued for their spiritual potency. In his translation of *The Tibetan Book of the Dead*, Robert Thurman contrasts the Western focus on material conquest of the outer world with the Tibetan focus on spiritual conquest of the inner frontiers of consciousness. While Westerners have dismissed the significance of death, he calls the Tibetan concern for death "the ultimate example of the inwardly directed rationality of the modern Tibetan mind."[157] This drive to explore and understand the reality of death resulted in narrative accounts that became a Tibetan literary genre by the sixteenth century.[158] One who has returned from the bardo of death is called a *delog*,[159] and is often consulted for spiritual as well as worldly advice. A famous example who became a spiritual authority was Dawa Drolma, the mother of Chagdud Tulku Rinpoché, who published her detailed diary. He reports that "for five full days she lay cold, breathless, and devoid of any vital signs, while her consciousness moved freely into other realms."[160] Her reawakening was witnessed by a prominent lama, and she revealed secrets that convinced others of the authenticity of her visions of the bardo. Following the advice of her personal deity, White Tara, she shared her vivid experiences of the karmic results of virtue and vice, teaching others to make correct moral choices by paying careful attention to cause and effect.

Scientific materialism holds that a human person truly exists, as a complex assembly of matter, which has evolved into a body with a nervous system that gives rise to consciousness—an epiphenomenon that is simply extinguished at death. Buddhism holds that there is no truly existent person, body, life, death, or consciousness—all conditioned phenomena are seen as arising interdependently, according to cause and effect. And the principal dancer in this spectacle is not insentient matter but sentience itself.

✢ ✢ ✢ ✢ ✢ ✢ ✢

We continue with our determination of the identitylessness of phenomena as objects, now turning to those that are other than the human body. Thus we consider an ordinary house, which could represent any constructed object.

> Likewise, what is the basis of designation for a so-called house? The clay is not a house. As for the stones, they are called *stones*, not *house*. Nor are pillars, rafters, beams, or the foundation called *house*, and even if they were piled together, the name *house* would not apply.

The various components of a house can serve as its basis of designation, but they are not the same as a house. We designate a *house* based on diverse criteria that are abstract, personal, and context-sensitive. For example, we may consider a mobile home to be a "trailer," and not a real house, but after visiting our friend's new triple-wide "manufactured home," we might revise our criteria.

The interdependent nature of designated objects becomes particularly clear when something physical like a house is being built. At first, with only bare land, everyone would agree that there is no house on the land. When a foundation has been poured, a contractor might say that there is a house that is under construction. Once the walls and roof are up, most people would agree that there is a house, even if the interiors are incomplete. When plumbing, electrical, appliances, and finishing work are complete, the municipal inspector will verify that building codes have been satisfied, and the city will deem the structure a legally habitable house. Ultimately, the definition of the completed house that matters most to the owner and the builder will be spelled out in their contract, or costly disagreements might ensue. Precisely when did this house come into existence? It's simply a matter of agreement, and people utilize multiple agreements with very different criteria. But the Buddhist answer is that no house ever came into existence objectively. A *house* is merely a name, imputed onto a basis of designation, according to a particular human convention. It is a house because we say it is.

It's equally revealing to examine the opposite process, of destruction. Years ago, I watched news reports of a wildfire in the Sierra Nevada mountains of California that destroyed many homes. One couple was left with nothing but a hole in the ground and a stone chimney, and yet they pointed to it as their house, which they planned to restore. A burned-down house can still be a house in the eyes of the homeowner.

> Take another example: a cup. Its exterior is not the cup, nor is its interior, its mouth, or its base the cup, nor is the wood the cup. Neither its individual components nor their assembly exist objectively as its basis of designation.

When we reify a cup, we conceive of it as a single entity. But if we decompose it into its parts, none of them is a cup, nor is there a universally accepted way to assemble a cup from parts, as this traditional Tibetan construction of a cup suggests. In fact, we only designate a *cup* relative to the particular purpose we have in mind. A cup with holes in the bottom might be perfectly fine for holding pencils, yet unsuitable for drinking tea. Our hand can be a cup for drinking, or a sieve for rinsing cherries, or a paddle for spanking. We apply these different names to a single hand according to its use at any given moment, so the basis of the designation is not in our hand itself but in our momentary intention.

> Also in the case of a so-called mountain, earth is not a mountain, nor are grass or trees. Their assembly is not a mountain either, so the word *mountain* is empty.

There is nothing inherent in the basis of designation for a mountain that constitutes the mountain. This name is applied only according to changing conventions. A mountain in Minnesota is a hill in Colorado. Geologists, surveyors, and artists may have different criteria, but the definitions for a mountain are all relative ones: rising steeply or abruptly, higher than the surrounding land, bigger than a hill, high enough to be impressive or notable. Some draw the line between hill and mountain at 1,000 feet, others at 2,000 feet. The plot of the 1995 comedic film *The Englishman Who Went Up a Hill but Came Down a Mountain* revolves around the conflict between a surveyor's criteria and the people's feelings about their local "mountain." The US Geological Survey no longer offers official definitions for hills and mountains, ponds and lakes, or creeks and rivers due to the ambiguity of such terms.

> **To examine the basis of designation of a single stick, its tip is just a tip and not a stick. Its base is nothing other than its base, the wood is nothing other than wood, its burnt ashes are nothing more than ashes, and its pulverized particles are just particles and not a stick. So even that name simply vanishes, with no object to which it refers. And there is nothing beyond that.**

Even a simple wooden stick is only a designation that depends on context and convention. The same piece of wood might be a walking stick to an adult and a pole to a child. If one end is relatively pointed it might be a spear, or if relatively bulbous, a club. With your pocketknife you could transform this wood into a basis for the designation you prefer, while others may continue to see something entirely different.

But Düdjom Lingpa's revelation takes us a step further, here, to the question of what is there when an ordinary object, visible to the naked eye, is broken down into its component parts, so that even the basis one had been calling by a certain name can no longer be found. Once a stick has been burned to ashes, it does not even make sense to say "stick" any more. Yet even while the "stick" is intact, if one is carefully investigating to find a *real* basis of designation—as in all these examples—and one looks to its particles, one has to admit that there is no stick there either. This passage is reminiscent of a famous verse from Nāgārjuna's *Letter to a King: The Garland of Precious Jewels*:

> Since something with form is merely a name,
> then space, too, is nothing but a name.

How could there be form without elements?
So even the "mere name" itself does not exist.[161]

Tsongkhapa glosses Nāgārjuna's point as follows: "Thus it states that ultimately there is not even the mere name, and conventionally, apart from
being established by force of the convention of a name, there is nothing at
all. This is what it means to abide merely as labeled with a name."[162] It is interesting to note that Düdjom Lingpa's revelation from the Lake-Born Vajra
is in perfect harmony with Tsongkhapa on this and so many other points.

**Know that earth, water, fire, and air also do not exist in the
realm of gross particles, tiny particles, or minute partless particles.**

This statement is true according to modern physics. Nothing at the level of
molecules, atoms, or elementary particles is solid, fluid, hot, or cold. Such
features emerge only with larger assemblies of atoms. But in contrast to the
Buddhist explanation, the modern view, even within most scientific disciplines, is that atoms are absolutely real.

As we analyze phenomena in search of inherent existence, we might find
ourselves agreeing with the classical Buddhist school called Vaibhāṣika, a
philosophical system that differentiates ultimate realities from relative ones.
It asserts that something like a *stick* is a designation for a physical configuration of many tiny particles, which do really exist, while the stick exists only
relative to its conventional designation. Similarly, it asserts the real existence
of brief moments of cognition, such as an instant of visual perception of
blue or a flash of anger. Our conceptual labeling processes configure these
moments into experiences, which are only relatively true. But the Vaibhāṣika
view is that the tiniest physical atoms and briefest mental moments are real,
absolutely existent, and independent of our concepts and designations. The
physical world is composed of these atomic elements, and it's real as well.
Our conceptual overlays are merely relative.

While advocates of the Vaibhāṣika view asserted the equal reality of particles of matter and moments of cognizance, the materialist view, called "atomism," accepts the ultimate reality only of the former. In the West this view
traces back 2,500 years to Democritus, the pre-Socratic Greek philosopher
who asserted that all that exists consists of atoms and space. This view has

been accepted by many, but certainly not all, scientists since the rise of scientific materialism in the mid-nineteenth century: all that really exists consists of elementary particles and their emergent properties.

At the turn of the twentieth century, quantum physics appeared, and it challenged the notion that atoms possess absolutely objective existence. There are currently unsolved problems and controversies in this field, such as disagreement about the role of the observer and the nature of measurement. But there is unequivocal agreement that the world does not consist of tiny particles with definite mass, location, and momentum, existing independently and prior to our measurements. This became abundantly clear in the Mind and Life meeting that was held in 1997 with His Holiness the Dalai Lama and a group of leading physicists, including the cutting-edge Austrian experimentalist quoted earlier, Anton Zeilinger.[163] He explained to us that in his actual experiments attempting to isolate and measure the properties of a single elementary particle, it was nowhere to be found as an entity existing prior to and independent of the act of measurement. The attributes of an electron, such as its mass or velocity, arise only relative to the measurement of it; they aren't independent of it. From their own side, they are empty. Prior to the act of measurement, you can describe only a probability that some value will be observed. Such experiments demonstrate that there is no preexisting attribute awaiting your measurement—it doesn't already exist.

I was serving as interpreter for this discussion, which His Holiness listened to with great interest. When Anton said that when you look for an electron as it exists independently of measurement, you don't find it, His Holiness seemed quite pleased. He turned to Anton and said, "How could you know that without knowing Madhyamaka philosophy?"

"What's that?" Anton replied. His Holiness gave a brilliant synopsis of the essence of the Madhyamaka view, which is that all phenomena are empty of inherent nature, arising only as dependently related events. Anton, who has studied philosophy, listened to this explanation with interest. He then responded, "How could you possibly know that without knowing quantum mechanics?" He invited His Holiness to his laboratory in Austria to show him the experiments that had led him to these conclusions. His Holiness accepted immediately. The following spring, we had a glorious two-day meeting at Anton's labs in Innsbruck, followed by discussions about philosophy, physics, and Buddhism that continued as we walked about in the Tyrolean Alps. Those were two of the most memorable days of my life!

A central assertion of quantum mechanics, tracing back to its pioneer, Werner Heisenberg (1901–76), is that prior to the act of measurement, physicists can speak only of a field of possibilities. If you measure an attribute of electrons, for example, then information about that attribute is generated relative to your chosen question and methodology. But until you measure it, there is no preexisting absolute value for that attribute, some invariable truth just waiting to be discovered. The value you obtain arises only relative to your methods.

It's interesting that one of the Tibetan terms used to refer to the world is "sipa,"[164] which simply means "possibility," based on the view of cyclic existence as a range of possibilities. These are depicted in the "wheel of becoming," in which the English term "becoming" is another rendering of the Tibetan "sipa." There are many ways to make a measurement, whether with sophisticated instruments or only the naked senses. Merely looking to see if another person is present constitutes an act of measurement. In looking for a face or other appearances, your perceptions of colors, shapes, and motions let you conclude that a person is here or not. Is this person's presence or absence a preexisting fact, merely awaiting your measurement? As far as you're concerned, there is only a field of possibilities. Until you make your observation, which is enabled, guided, and constrained by your conceptual frameworks—such as the criteria for being a real person; the values you hold for diverse human characteristics, such as gender, age, height, beauty, and intelligence; and the space you currently occupy, be it a room, a car, or a soccer field—it is impossible to say whether a person is actually here or not. The answer is only true, for you, when you make your observation.

But we must not overlook the fact that the other person, like the cat in the physicist Erwin Schrödinger's famous thought experiment, has his or her own perspective on existence. He or she doesn't suddenly come into existence by catching my attention. When I take notice of someone, the person-relative-to-me comes into existence, while the person-relative-to-that-person was already there, from their perspective. But something without reference to the perspective of *any* conscious being never comes into or goes out of existence. Even my awareness of my own existence provides me with no information about myself independent of any observer. It is just one more perspective, in some ways as partial and prone to flaws as anyone else's awareness of me.

What this also implies is that there are as many physical worlds as there are sentient beings—human and otherwise—who inhabit them. All physical worlds exist only relative to the cognitive frameworks in which they are perceived and conceived. In an earlier work, I have called this view "ontological relativity."[165] Although this view implies that there are many worlds corresponding to the many cognitive frameworks of sentient beings, this is fundamentally different from the "many-worlds interpretation" of quantum mechanics, proposed in 1957 by Hugh Everett in his doctoral thesis, developed under his advisor, John Wheeler.[166] According to Everett, every act of measurement divides the quantum world into one more alternative classical world, all of them equally "real." The observer subjectively perceives only one classical world, but in reality, in all the unseen alternative worlds it is as if replicas of the observer exist, whose experiences provide each of them with a picture of precisely the world they believe they inhabit. This hypothesis is wonderfully imaginative but totally untestable; it is mere conjecture, with no possibility of ever being validated or invalidated. Nevertheless, over the past twenty years this idea has attracted growing attention and respect, so that today it is regarded as one of several mainstream interpretations of quantum theory.

Why has such an other-worldly, utterly speculative view become so fashionable among hardcore physicists? The answer may lie in the fact that most physicists nowadays adhere to the principles of metaphysical realism and materialism, and they have been educated to believe that consciousness has no significant role in the natural world. The many-worlds interpretation omits consciousness from the picture and reifies all the invisible worlds that would split off with each (supposedly) mindless measurement. Thus this view appears to be a desperate attempt to maintain the paradigms of metaphysical realism, determinism, and physicalism, yet with no possible evidence to support it. Nevertheless, it has many proponents, who cherish their metaphysical presuppositions over the ideals of empiricism that have inspired all the great breakthroughs in the history of science.

Until the twentieth century, most physicists believed that everything truly existed relative to God's perspective, regardless of whether any mere mortals were looking on. Hence the scientific quest, tracing back at least to Galileo, to view the universe from a God's-eye perspective. But with the deletion of God from the predominant modern scientific conception of the universe, the notion of an absolutely objective world existing independently of *anyone's* observations or conceptual frameworks becomes a groundless conjecture that is untestable. Whatever theory is devised based on observations and experiments, there is no way of comparing it to any reality as it would exist independently of any observations or measurements. Such a universe—prior to and independent of any observation—cannot be said to exist or not to exist, for the categories of "existence" and "nonexistence" are human creations, which we define. And there are many definitions of these categories among scientists, philosophers, and others. To apply these labels to something about which we can know nothing is a category error. At most, all that we can speak of is the possibility, or probability, of their existence, which is determined only when an observation is made. The "view from nowhere," as the philosopher Thomas Nagel calls it,[167] is devoid of subject and object, with no sentient beings and no physical universe to inhabit.

On the other hand, here's a classic Buddhist explanation of the differing perceptions available to five possible states of *conscious* being within the desire realm of saṃsāra: An ordinary glass of water, to a human being, is seen as water. To an animal, it's something to drink or to live in. To a *preta*—a type of being consumed by insatiable hunger and craving—it is seen as pus and blood. A hell being, dominated by the karmic results of past hatred and aggression, sees it as molten metal or lava. A god-like *deva* experiences it as the bliss of ambrosia. Each class of being perceives the liquid very differently, according to its sense faculties, karmic propensities, and conceptual frameworks. The basis that arises as a glass of water to a human encompasses all these possibilities, with no identity inherent in the liquid itself, independent of any observer.

When Werner Heisenberg and the other founders of quantum mechanics were making their discoveries, they reportedly felt that the very ground beneath them was giving way. This revolution meant that the universe is fundamentally different from what scientists had believed about it for centuries, because in some mysterious way, the role of the observer and the act of measurement are woven into the very fabric of the universe. Any notion of "naturalism" as a synonym of "physicalism" is a misnomer, for there's nothing natural about omitting the mind and consciousness from nature, or else reducing them to merely emergent properties of matter, without having any idea as to how inert matter and energy ever give rise to subjective experience.

Modern science and the Buddhadharma agree that our sensory appearances of the physical world are misleading and therefore illusory. Some physicists have abandoned the classical notion that there is some "underlying stuff" of the universe that exists independently of all observations and propose that mind and observations constitute the only reality.[168] The theoretical physicist Leonard Susskind has proposed that the world is best understood as a hologram.[169] Yet other leaders in their fields, including the physicists George Smoot and James Gates, the cosmologists Alan Guth and Max Tegmark, the technologists Elon Musk and Ray Kurzweil, the philosopher Nick Bostrom, and the artificial intelligence expert Marvin Minsky suggest that the universe may be a giant computer simulation, and we are living in a Matrix-style virtual world that we mistakenly think is really "out there."[170]

Long before those thinkers began speculating about who might have created this illusory matrix that we call "the universe"—whether it was God or beings with advanced intelligence dwelling in some other world—the Buddha presented a theory based on his own contemplative discoveries, which have been corroborated by generations of contemplatives after him. The hypothesis to be tested by open-minded seekers is whether each of the illusory worlds of saṃsāra, inhabited by all manner of sentient beings, is indeed created by the seeds of our own karmic actions, done in previous lifetimes and then ripened and impelled to fruition by our own self-grasping, or the reification of our own personal identities. These karmic imprints are said to be stored in our individual streams of consciousness, propelling us from one lifetime to another, each with its own corresponding physical environment. When the karma ripens as a human rebirth, we share many intersubjective appearances with our fellow humans, and to a lesser degree with other species and life forms. The ripening of one individual's karma may be experienced by that person alone, but the ripening of collective karma is experienced by everyone who sowed very similar karmic seeds. Such intersubjective corroboration of multiple first-person observations gives rise to the mistaken belief that the shared observations constitute a "third-person" view of reality that is absolutely objective. This creates an illusion that is exceedingly difficult to challenge, let alone dispel.

✢ ✢ ✢ ✢ ✢ ✢ ✢

Buddhism uses many examples, analogies, and metaphors to help us understand the illusory nature of reality, in which all phenomena appear to exist from their own side but are in fact empty of any inherent nature of their own. What follows is a list of ten classical analogies for illusion,[171] taught to illustrate that all phenomena lack inherent nature and arise only as dependently related events.

> The illusory nature of all kinds of names cannot even be established as an illusion, for it is nothing more than the mere name *illusion*.

Even when one has taken every sort of thing that can be named, and through analysis revealed that it is no more than an illusion, the very fact that such a merely labeled phenomenon is thus an illusion is not inherently existent as an illusion; "illusion" is no more than a label imputed upon a basis of designation.

> Insofar as there is no mirage in a *mirage*, it is nothing more than a mere name.

When we impute a name like *mirage*, our labeling process isolates it from everything that is not a mirage. But the mirage has not drawn its own borders and labeled itself, nor does it have its own intrinsic defining characteristics. It is not a preexisting phenomenon; it is merely an appearance, which is completely dependent on specific conditions, including a particular observer's perspective. While it appears to your visual perception and can even be photographed, there is no corresponding reality where the mirage appears to be. The closer you approach it, the more its illusory nature becomes apparent. It appears and has causal efficacy, but it isn't really there.

> Insofar as there is no dream in a *dream*, it is nothing more than a mere name.

If you say you had a dream and proceed to describe it, your synopsis is not the dream. You might struggle to express in words or pictures the events, feelings, and thoughts you remember, trying to capture their essence and storyline, but your narrative framework is not the dream. If you practice remembering and recording dreams, you will remember more dreams, with more details, and profound insight may arise, but it is not the dream. Even if you become lucid while dreaming, knowing that you're dreaming, the entire construct of the dream is your own simulation; knowing this is what gives a lucid dream its astonishing impact. But in every case, the dream has no existence of its own and is only a name you have assigned to a remembered experience.

Since there is no reflection established in a *reflection*, it is nothing more than a mere name.

A reflection in a mirror does not exist in the mirror or anywhere else. If you gaze at a mirror while standing six feet in front of its surface, your reflection can be seen and photographed as existing at a distance six feet *behind* the mirror. But of course, when you walk behind the mirror, nothing there corresponds to the image you perceived.

In a city of gandharvas there is nothing but a nominal *city of gandharvas*.

Gandharvas are described as celestial musicians of exceptional skill, subsisting only on fragrances and living in cities in the sky. They appear in dependence upon samādhi, with no independent existence of their own.

An echo has no objective existence apart from its mere name *echo*.

You identify an *echo* by hearing a sound a short time after hearing a similar, but not quite identical, sound. If you didn't hear the first sound, you wouldn't call the second one an echo, which shows that the echo has no inherent existence as an echo.

The moon in water is nothing more than the mere words *moon in water*.

A reflection in water of the moon, or of the planets and stars, is a frequently used analogy in Buddhist teachings, and it appears many times in the works of Düdjom Lingpa. A single moon in the sky may give rise to any number of water-moons, reflected in every lake, puddle, and dewdrop. Every individual, each possessing a bucket of water, sees his or her personal water-moon. If the water is clean and still, the reflection will be clear; if not, it will be distorted.

When you look at the reflection of the moon in water, its appears to you as if it were 240,000 miles beneath the surface of the water. Even though your eyes bring this image into focus as if viewing a "real" phenomenon at that distance, nothing there corresponds to your perception. It is an empty appearance, conceptually designated by the mind that apprehends it, and it has no existence apart from that illusory appearance and conceptual designation.

> **And a water bubble is not established as having any objective existence apart from the mere utterance of the words *water bubble*.**

A bubble of air in water is completely dependent on dynamic factors; and it inevitably rises to the surface, where it disappears without a trace.

> **And a hallucination, furthermore, is not established as having any objective existence apart from the mere name.**

Hallucinations, which in the Buddhist teachings may be caused by the effects of drugs, disease, or manipulation of the sense organs, are easily understood as having no inherent existence. During a Buddhism and science conference in Dharamsala, India, in 2009, presided over by His Holiness the Dalai Lama, the psychologist Anne Treisman commented that perception is a kind of externally guided hallucination. We create experience rather than "photographing it," she added, so psychologists regard subjective reports as data rather than as factual accounts. But if all perceptions are nothing more than hallucinations, then the very observations and measurements made by psychologists and other scientists must also be illusory. According to such Buddhist analysis as we see here, all appearances to the physical senses, images produced with the instruments of technology, and appearances to mental perception are illusory, for they appear to exist by their own nature but in fact arise only relative to the system of measurement by which they are observed and relative to the conceptual framework in which they are understood.

> **And an emanation cannot be established as existing apart from the mere utterance of the name.**

In this classical analogy, an illusionist who has mastered the power of emanation in samādhi can conjure up the appearance of an elephant, for example, and the spectators will actually see it. Similarly, a highly realized practitioner can guide a multitude of disciples all at the same time by manifesting a number of emanations equal to the number of disciples and in forms perfectly appropriate to each disciple's perceptions.

> Like the utterances of the sounds of those names, all the bases of designation of the names and words that are uttered for all kinds of appearing phenomena are nonexistent. They are emptiness, which itself is not established as being real. Recognize that emptiness has no objective existence, for it is none other than the expanse of space. These are pith instructions.

Other well-known analogies include an optical illusion, a rainbow, a flash of lightning, and the trunk of a plantain tree. These examples of illusion illustrate the nature of all other phenomena—all are empty of inherent existence, and all arise in dependence on causes, conditions, component parts, and in the end, upon names and designations.

Here is a final, crucial point: It is imperative not to reify emptiness itself, as if it were absolutely real. Nāgārjuna declares that if one grasps to emptiness as having inherent existence, one transforms the only medicine that can liberate us from saṃsāra into poison. Some Buddhist scholars translate the Sanskrit term *śūnyatā* as "voidness," but I find this misleading, for it suggests there's really something out there, lurking "behind" the veil of appearances, namely, something like "the void." The Sanskrit adjective *śūnya* simply means "empty," and the syllable *tā* transforms the adjective into an abstract noun, "emptiness." Appearances themselves are empty of inherent existence, and there is no emptiness apart from appearances. Neither the objective appearances of colors, sounds, and so on, nor the subjective appearances of thoughts, feelings, and so on, exist from their own side, and upon investigation we find that the demarcation between "subjective" and "objective" is purely nominal as well.

In a similar vein, Werner Heisenberg warned physicists against thinking that quantum wave functions comprise the basic stuff of reality, as if they truly exist out there, prior to and independent of the act of measurement. Niels Bohr, the grandfather of quantum mechanics, declared, "There is no quantum world. There is only an abstract physical description. It is wrong to think that the task of physics is to find out how nature is. Physics concerns what we can *say* about nature."[172]

In the documentary film *Probability and Uncertainty: The Quantum Mechanical View of Nature*, Richard Feynman declared, "I think I can safely say that nobody understands quantum mechanics,"[173] and this observation holds true to this day. Despite such warnings from these eminent quantum physicists, some scientists who cling to the tenets of metaphysical realism and materialism with almost religious zeal reify the quantum wave function as objectively real and physical, while reducing everything else to mere ways of talking.[174] But emptiness and the equations for quantum mechanics are themselves simply different ways of describing the nature of reality. These are *all* just ways of talking, so the referents of such terms as "quantum wave functions," "particles," and "forces" exist only relative to the conceptual frameworks in which they are designated. Their existence is only nominal, so it is a fundamental error to mistake the finger pointing at the moon for the moon itself. As the philosopher Hilary Putnam explains, "elements of what we call 'language' or 'mind' *penetrate so deeply into what we call 'reality' that the very project of representing ourselves as being 'mappers' of something 'language-independent' is fatally compromised from the very start.*"[175]

Coarse and Subtle Considerations for Determining Emptiness

These teachings on the emptiness of the external world are difficult to fathom, for two reasons deeply rooted in our experience: First, we perceive the world in a common, mutually verifiable way, which seems to prove the existence of an objective world. Second, things in the world around us apparently change according to their own rules, whether we are looking or not. The world we experience does not appear to be empty: it appears to be full of independent entities.

On top of these fundamental predispositions in our natural ways of perceiving, the past four hundred years of scientific development have focused almost exclusively on the outer world, where phenomena are objective, physical, and quantifiable. Scientific authority gives far less weight to phenomena that are merely subjective, mental, or qualitative. And as William James said, "For the moment, what we attend to is reality," and if scientists focus exclusively on objective, physical phenomena, only they will be come to be regarded as real. Modern society has a very strong bias in viewing the physical as real and the nonphysical as unreal. In current scientific practice, as we have seen, even the mind itself is typically investigated in terms of the objectively measurable, physical phenomena of behavior and brain activity. Subjective mental consciousness is dismissed as a mirage created by neurological circuits and network processes.

With such strong biases, we need remedial efforts to help restore equilibrium between the physical and mental aspects of life. For example, if we have a deeply rooted resentment for another person, we will see only his or her faults and fail to see any positive qualities. But by actively looking first for neutral qualities, and then for positive ones, we can gradually develop a more balanced attitude toward that person. Similarly, our imbalance between physical and mental phenomena can be corrected. The way to do this is by focusing on the mind, mental events, and consciousness itself. For many hundreds of years in Tibet, and before that for millennia in India, people have engaged in the intense practice of immersing awareness in purely mental phenomena over extended periods of time. And what they attended to came to be regarded as reality for them, but not to the exclusion of the outer, physical world.

How could you verify this empirically? You could thoroughly immerse your awareness in the mind itself, the śamatha practice that Padmasambhava calls *taking the mind as the path*, for eight to ten hours a day, accumulating 10,000 hours or so. One result would be that even in between formal practice sessions, you would increasingly see all phenomena as mere empty appearances arising to the mind. This doesn't require having realized emptiness. Düdjom Lingpa also calls this *taking appearances and awareness as the path*, because the result of practice is that everything naturally boils down to just two things: appearances and awareness.

Lerab Lingpa says that by settling the mind in its natural state, by taking the mind as the path, one comes to a "nonconceptual sense that nothing can harm your mind, regardless of whether or not thoughts have ceased."[176] He makes the interesting point here that one can be nonconceptually aware of concepts. This is possible by resting in a flow of nonconceptual awareness, without becoming fused with thoughts that arise. This is one of the central purposes of resting in the stillness of awareness in the midst of the movements of the mind. It is highly analogous to the result of becoming lucid in your dreams: When you know it's a dream, you know that nothing can harm you, no matter what appears. In order for these teachings on emptiness to help you to alleviate mental afflictions and decrease suffering, you should focus on observing and understanding the phenomena in your own mind during the waking state and, if you can, in the dream state as well. With extensive practice, all appearances will naturally be seen to arise only in the space of the mind, the substrate.

How can you avoid the error of nihilism when witnessing the fact that all appearances are creations of your own mind? If you conclude that you are the only sentient being in the universe, you have succumbed to solipsism. It's crucial to find the middle way here. There is an important difference between the dream and waking states. In a dream, there is only one sentient being, and everyone else who appears in the dream is a creation of one mind. If you kill someone in your dream, there is negative karma due to the motivation that has arisen at subtle layers of your consciousness, but no one else is harmed. In the waking state, you are interacting with many sentient beings, each one the center of their world, and your actions have actual karmic effects on others as well as yourself. From the waking perspective, we see that nothing in the dream was real. Similarly, from the perspective of pristine awareness, we see that nothing in waking experience is real either: everything is an array of empty appearances and causal interactions. It is deluded to confuse the dream state for the waking state. And likewise, it is deluded to conflate pristine awareness with ordinary consciousness.

> Again Bodhisattva Faculty of Luminosity asked, "O Teacher, Bhagavān, if all the deluded disciples, bound by clinging to true existence, cannot realize the ground, the nature of existence of ultimate reality, simply by recognizing the nonexistence of the basis of designation of a name, please, Teacher, reveal a way to determine the fundamental way in which things do not exist by way of coarse and subtle considerations."

In case the preceding explanation of the relationship between a designated object and its basis of designation has not led to insight into the empty nature of all phenomena, there are other approaches. The following teaching contrasts nonexistence with its alternative, which is permanence, as defined by seven vajra qualities.

He replied, "O Faculty of Luminosity, it is like this: When a tree trunk appears to you, consider whether it is permanent or utterly nonexistent."

We might all agree that a tree trunk is neither permanent nor utterly nonexistent, so why are we being asked to choose between these two options? Bear in mind that this is vipaśyanā presented from the perspective of Dzokchen. The best analogy is the insight of a lucid dreamer.

In the Pāli canon there is a wonderful story recounted in the *Doṇa Sutta*.[177] A wandering brāhmin ascetic named Doṇa saw footprints marked with a *dharmacakra*, a dharma wheel. One of the thirty-two major marks of a buddha is the appearance of thousand-spoked wheels embossed upon the palms of his or her hands and the soles of his or her feet. Doṇa was amazed, thinking that these footprints could not have been made by a human being. Like a hunter, he tracked them to the Buddha, who was seated cross-legged beneath a tree. The Buddha's confident and tranquil presence inspired Doṇa, who approached to ask who this great being might be. In those days, it was understood that devas, or gods, could appear in human form, and so this was Doṇa's first guess as to the identity of the astonishing being in front of him:

"Master, are you a deva?"
"No, brāhmin, I am not a deva."
"Are you a gandharva? A yakṣa? A human being?"
To each question the Buddha responded, "No."
"Then what sort of being are you?"
The Buddha answered, "I'm awake."

In Sanskrit, the word *buddha* simply means "one who is awake." The Buddha's parents were human, his wife and son were human, and yet he said he was not a human being. Was he refuting the obvious fact that he was a human being, albeit a highly unusual one? Rather, the Buddha answered, "I'm awake," from an entirely different perspective. Imagine yourself in the midst of a lucid dream, in which you are revealing your miraculous powers, such as walking on water, flying, or changing water into wine. People in your dream would notice your unusual abilities, and they might approach you to ask, "Are you a god?"

Being lucid in this dream, you would have to answer, "No."

Like the Buddha, you would also have to disagree with any other identity that the nonlucid observers in your dream might propose, for their imaginations are limited to familiar entities within the dream, which they take to be absolutely real. Anything they could conceive would be a false characterization of your actual status as a lucid dreamer, one who recognizes the actual nature of the dream from a perspective outside the parameters of the dream. You are nothing like any of the fictitious characters in your dream. But you could answer affirmatively, "I'm awake." From the perspective of a lucid dreamer, everything in the dream consists of empty appearances, and nothing exists from its own side. It is from this perspective that the Teacher in the above passage is asking whether a tree trunk is permanent or utterly nonexistent. Is it permanent, like the absolute space of phenomena, or utterly nonexistent, like a unicorn or the son of a barren woman?

The crucial point is that in the act of reifying a tree trunk or anything else, we not only conceptualize it but we also isolate and freeze it, as an unchanging, permanent entity. Is a tree trunk permanent or is it utterly nonexistent? In posing these two alternatives, the Teacher is highlighting the two extremes of substantialism and nihilism, with the middle way being what remains upon avoiding these two extremes. Anything that is truly permanent must possess seven vajra qualities, as the Teacher explains:

> The investigation and analysis go like this: If it were permanent, it would have to be invulnerable, indestructible, real, incorruptible, stable, unobstructable, and invincible. Since a gash occurs when it is chopped with an ax, it is vulnerable, and when it is chopped many times, it is destroyed. Since the one becomes many, it is false and not real; and since it can be stained with white and black dyes and powders, it is corruptible, not incorruptible. Since it is subject to change due to the seasons and other influences, it is not stable. Since there are objects that it cannot penetrate, it is obstructable. This wood can be demolished in any number of ways, so it is not invincible.

A tree trunk seems so massive and firmly embedded in the ground that it's easy to reify it as a real entity. But in this analysis, we chop it into progressively smaller chips, and we can see that there can be no objective demarcation between the tree trunk and wood chips. It only stops being a tree trunk when we withdraw the designation. Similarly, as a seed germinates, a sprout arises, and a sapling grows into a tree, there is no point at which we would all agree, based on purely objective evidence, that a tree trunk exists. Anything that comes into existence and ceases to exist like this was never really there at all—it is nonexistent from the perspective of one who has awakened to the illusory nature of phenomena.

Not having even one of the vajra qualities, it is proven not to exist.

The tree trunk we think is there, since it is found to lack any of the seven vajra qualities of permanent existence, does not really exist at all. The actual basis for designating a tree trunk is impermanent, a temporary collection of matter and energy, cells and molecules, which is constantly changing as the tree sprouts, grows, dies, rots, and disperses into the environment. There is nothing, from its own side, that corresponds to the designation *tree trunk*.

This insight constitutes the core of the Madhyamaka view. These teachings on vipaśyanā from the Dzokchen perspective are completely compatible with the Madhyamaka view of Nāgārjuna as interpreted by Candrakīrti, Śāntideva, Tsongkhapa, and other proponents of the Prāsaṅgika school of Buddhist philosophy. Nāgārjuna's writings offer a great many reasonings to help us penetrate to the reality of emptiness. The king of logical reasoning and the most powerful analysis is the method of dependent origination (Skt. *pratītyasamutpāda*). Because any phenomenon, like a tree trunk, arises in dependence on causes, conditions, and conceptual designations, it must therefore be empty. If you genuinely fathom the impermanence of any phenomenon—anything that arises from moment to moment, depends on causes and conditions, and eventually perishes and vanishes—this necessarily implies that it must also be empty of inherent nature.

This insight is completely contrary to our natural intuition. Ordinarily, if we are asked whether something in our environment is real or illusory, it's easy to verify that it's real by directly touching or seeing it, for example. If it's causally effective, in the way that a tree trunk that can support the weight of a hammock is, it must be real. From the Madhyamaka perspective, it's just the opposite. It's precisely because of impermanence and dependent origination—the fact of phenomena arising, influencing other phenomena, being influenced in return, and eventually being broken down, destroyed, and dispersed—that such phenomena must be empty of inherent existence. All conditioned phenomena are impermanent; they possess none of the seven vajra qualities of permanence.

If there were something independent of conceptual designation, causes, and conditions, then it would be permanent, or unchanging. So the question naturally arises, does anything have these seven qualities?

> Faculty of Luminosity asked, "O Teacher, Bhagavān, what is a vajra replete with all the seven vajra qualities? Please explain!"
>
> He replied, "O Faculty of Luminosity, referring to the existence of a deceptive,[178] material vajra is like referring to the son of a barren woman. A material vajra is shown to be made out of bone, and a stone vajra can be incinerated and thus destroyed. And iron vajras can be melted in fire. Not being truly existent, those deceptive vajras are destructible."

A conventional, material vajra, such as a cast metal object that may be employed in Vajrayāna practices, is a symbolic one. Here is what it symbolizes:

> The space vajra that appears everywhere (1) cannot be cut by anything else, such as weapons; (2) objects or circumstances cannot destroy it; (3) devoid of faults or contamination, it is the great basis for the proliferation of phenomenal existence, so it is real; (4) it cannot be corrupted by faults or virtues, so it is incorruptible; (5) it is free of change throughout the three times, so it is stable; (6) since it can penetrate everything to its emptiness, it is utterly unobstructable; and (7) it cannot be modified or changed by anything, so it is invincible.

The space vajra is nothing other than emptiness (Skt. *śūnyatā*), synonymous with the dharmadhātu, the absolute space of phenomena, which is indivisible from primordial consciousness. As the great basis for the appearance of phenomenal existence, it encompasses the whole of saṃsāra and nirvāṇa. This is the Dzokchen interpretation of what the Buddha meant by saying that if there were no nirvāṇa, or dharmadhātu, there would be no saṃsāra, or phenomenal existence, which arises from this great basis. Just as there can be no ultimate truth without a deceptive truth, no object without a subject, and no present without a past and a future, there can be no saṃsāra without nirvāṇa.

> This is the space vajra that appears everywhere. For those who hold it to exist autonomously, it is a deceptive vajra, and for those who perfectly and completely comprehend the way it fundamentally exists, as unadulterated liberation, it is the ultimate, indestructible vajra. If some other object replete with all seven vajra qualities were to exist, it would be permanent. But since there is no such thing, everything is definitely emptiness, which is not established in itself.

Once again this caveat appears: Even the ultimate nature of emptiness is not established in itself; it does not have inherent nature. Resist the temptation to reify emptiness.

> Thus, substances that appear as things, such as tree trunks, earth, stones, buildings, or household goods, may be pounded, broken, and ground up. By grinding them down to particles, they are reduced to powder. By pulverizing such particles to one-seventh of their size, they are reduced to minute particles, and by disintegrating these to one-seventh of their size, they are reduced until they have no spatial dimension. They are obliterated and vanish into the nature of space.

The above references to "particles" and "minute particles" pertain to categories of matter as conceived by Buddhist contemplatives and philosophers based on first-person experience, without the aid of technology. The elements of earth, water, fire, air, and space are also categories pertaining to the world of experience, and these have proven useful in traditional Tibetan medicine and Buddhist contemplative practice. Unlike the model of particles, atoms, and molecules presented in modern physics and chemistry, the particles and elements posited in Mahāyāna Buddhism are not held to exist in some objective world, independent of experience. They are instead viewed as fundamental units of matter and elementary features of the world of experience (Skt. *loka*).

> Moreover, the ashes of any substance that has been burned
> in fire naturally disappear into space, and something that
> appears to be the form of a living being totally vanishes once
> it has been killed and burned up. By examining and analyz-
> ing all phenomena that appear in this way, you find that they
> all vanish completely, and not a single thing is established as
> being truly existent. Intensive inquiry into this topic is essen-
> tial, so know this!

Modern science has described the structure of matter in much finer detail
and with greater sophistication than the explanation here, but the conclusion is the same. When you decompose matter into smaller and smaller constituents, there is nothing substantial to be found—only empty space, and
even that does not exist by its own, independent nature. For even space can
be divided into the constituent parts of its directions, and directions cannot
even be thought of except as interdependently related to one another.

In quantum field theory, which is the unification of Einstein's special relativity and quantum mechanics, empty space itself is described as having a
potential called the *zero-point energy*.[179] Imagine a thought experiment in
which you remove all thermal energy, mass, electromagnetic fields, and gravity from a volume of space; nothing is left but empty space, a vacuum. Does
this space have any energy of its own? It seems impossible, but there is energy
in empty space itself. If you calculate the energy density of empty space using
quantum field theory, the mathematical result is that the zero-point energy
has infinite density. How can we understand this?

Mainstream physicists depict this result as a vision of reality in which all
appearances of mass and energy in the universe exist as configurations of the
energy of empty space. From elementary particles up to galaxies, everything
emerges from empty space, exists as configurations of empty space, and eventually dissolves back into empty space. One theory for the origins of the Big
Bang is that something caused a fluctuation in the zero-point energy of the
vacuum, which resulted in the ongoing expansion of our entire universe.[180]

How All Phenomena Arise and Appear

> Faculty of Luminosity asked, "O Teacher, Bhagavān, if they
> are not established as being real but are unreal in that way,

from what do all phenomena arise and appear? May the
Teacher explain!"

Thus far, the emphasis has been on the empty aspect of phenomena. Now the
question is, how do they actually arise?

He replied, "O Faculty of Luminosity, grasping to an identity acts as the primary cause and conceptualization acts as
the contributing condition, due to which phenomena emerge
as mere appearances. When the initial moment of consciousness moves to an object, the appearance arises suddenly. With
the conceptual thought that something is being eliminated
and then the appearance of the idea that something has been
destroyed, it shifts or vanishes altogether. All phenomena are
mere appearances arising from dependently related events,
and nothing more. There is certainly nothing whatsoever that
is truly existent from its own side."

When waking consciousness emerges in progression from the substrate, first is
the substrate consciousness, followed by afflictive mentation, mentation, and
various appearances. Without the sense of self introduced by afflictive mentation, also called the "I-maker" (Skt. *ahaṃkāra*), no appearance can arise. This
causal grasping at identity occurs at a primeval level. The conceptualization
that follows is secondary. Through the combination of these two, the primary
cause[181] and the contributing condition,[182] all appearances manifest.

Take the example of a seed as the primary cause, with the contributing
conditions of soil, moisture, and sunlight; when cause and conditions com-
bine, a sprout appears. If either primary cause or secondary conditions are
absent, no sprout appears. According to the general Buddhist theory of
causality, nothing is ever produced by a single cause alone. There are always
contributing conditions.

Gen Lamrimpa, an extraordinary yogin with whom I lived for a year, said
that when you meditate on emptiness, as he had at great length, and you
gain some realization, then you may reach a point where all conceptualization collapses. This is not like practicing śamatha, with awareness completely
withdrawn from all appearances, or else as in falling asleep. In this case your
senses and awareness may be wide open; and yet when concepts collapse and

conceptual imputations cease, all appearances vanish. Without the contributing condition of conceptualization, appearances cannot arise. From the
perspective of one who is meditatively absorbed in the nonconceptual realization of emptiness, the phenomenal world of saṃsāra does not exist at all.
As the *Heart Sūtra* declares: "there are no visual forms, sounds, odors, tastes,
tactile sensations, or phenomena."

This contradicts our intuition. We imagine that an object really exists
from its own side, and that concepts and names have no bearing on its
appearance or disappearance. In fact, it's just the opposite. The phenomena
arise, remain, and disappear relative to the perceptions and conceptual designations of them.

The view presented here could not be further removed from the dominant materialistic view that consciousness and mind are simply properties of
the brain. The mainstream assumption is that consciousness, thought, and
mind emerge when assemblies of neurons in the brain interact dynamically.
The philosopher John Searle asserts that consciousness is "an emergent feature of certain systems of neurons in the same way that solidity and liquidity
are emergent features of systems of molecules."[183] As noted previously, even
Stephen Hawking, when asked about the nature of consciousness and what
happens at death, compared the brain to a computer with consciousness as
its software: when the brain dies, consciousness vanishes.

Mainstream science assiduously avoids the taboo of subjectivity, purport-
ing to rely exclusively upon third-party, independently verifiable data. The
science writer Alex Rosenberg promotes the view of "scientism" and lists
its first precept as "the conviction that the methods of science are the only
reliable ways to secure knowledge of anything."[184] Writing in the *New York
Times*, he describes counterintuitive experimental results in which subjects
are mistaken or inconsistent in reporting their motivations, cognitions, emotions, or sensations. As noted in the introduction, Rosenberg claims that it's
only an illusion that we know our own mind better than the minds of others,
whereas cognitive science and neuroscience provide "detailed understanding
of the mind." Since the mind can fool itself, it cannot be trusted: "introspection and consciousness are not reliable bases for self-knowledge."[185]

Those who believe, like Rosenberg, that all first-person experience, especially introspective experience, is illusory at best, will dismiss any evidence that
training in mindfulness and introspection reveals important truths about the
nature of the mind and its role in nature. They will have no use for contempla-

tive training and will refuse, on ideological or methodological grounds, to put contemplative discoveries to the test of first-person experience. Such an attitude is reminiscent of that of Giulio Libri, an opponent of Galileo who refused to look through Galileo's telescope for reasons based on Giovanni Baptista Della Porta's 1589 book *Natural Magic*, which argued that first-person visual experience was fraught with all manner of optical illusions. Of course, he was right. The visual images of the stars, sun, moon, and planets that Galileo observed through his telescope appeared to be out there in space. But in reality, they were produced in dependence upon Galileo's human visual cortex and were therefore anthropocentric images that existed nowhere outside his mind. But, happily, generations of astronomers since then have made numerous discoveries about the universe based precisely on the illusory appearances that arise in dependence on photons from distant objects and the lenses of telescopes, as well as the human brain and consciousness. So the term "illusory" can be taken at many different levels, some more or less productive for useful knowledge. But we should be careful what we dismiss as merely illusory, or we might forgo meaningful access to whole dimensions of reality in the process.

This was not the only reason that some of Galileo's contemporaries refused to look through a telescope. Among them was Cesare Cremonini, a friend of Galileo who explained his refusal with the words, "I do not wish to approve of claims about which I do not have any knowledge, and about things which I have not seen . . . and then to observe through those glasses gives me a headache. Enough! I do not want to hear anything more about this."[186] Cremonini was a professor of Aristotelian philosophy at the University of Padua, and according to this view the heavens were incorruptible, which would preclude the possibility of sunspots—one of the many unexpected phenomena Galileo discovered. Cremonini's reasons were thus ideological and ruled out Galileo's observations a priori, so he had no need for telescopes.

In a similar way, modern materialists categorically deny the value, or even the possibility, of introspection as a means to explore the mind, for it leads to the discovery of many phenomena that undermine their most cherished beliefs. Physicists who reject out of hand the possibility that consciousness may play a fundamental role in the universe have kept humanity in the dark regarding the role of the observer in the still-unsolved measurement problem of quantum physics; and cognitive scientists who refuse to question their uncorroborated belief that consciousness is nothing more than an emergent property of the brain have kept humanity in the dark regarding the still-unsolved mind-body problem. Such a perspective prefers to remain in ignorance and then obscure that ignorance with illusions of knowledge rather than question metaphysical assumptions and break new ground in understanding the role of the mind in nature. History may not repeat itself, but it certainly does replicate the same patterns of ideological closed-mindedness.

Whether in the philosophy of mind, neuroscience, or physics, with few exceptions, consciousness is accorded a relatively insignificant role in the universe as conceived by leaders in those fields. Western accounts of the mind generally rely upon Freud and Jung, while the Buddha and non-Western traditions go unmentioned.[187] The typical contemporary view, in which everything boils down to matter, treats consciousness as a trivial byproduct of material systems and forces.

In Buddhism, consciousness is central because all phenomena are realized to be mere appearances to consciousness that have no independent existence. The objects and subjects that are naïvely reified by ignorance are explained to be illusory appearances that simply arise due to causes and conditions. The same ten classical analogies of illusion that were discussed above to illustrate the empty nature of all phenomena are reprised here, where they are explained as appearances arising due to interdependent origination.

> For example, with the convergence of (1) the primary cause of another person's eyes, (2) the basis of radiant, clear space, and (3) the contributing conditions of conjuring substances, mantras, and an illusionist's mind, the dependently related event of an illusory apparition appears, even though it is non-existent.

A magician conjures up an illusory apparition in dependence upon the minds of the spectators and other conditions. Although it appears, it is non-existent, which may be verified by looking behind the stage or from another perspective.

In March 2014 I had the good fortune to serve briefly as interpreter for the eminent Bhutanese lama Gangteng Tulku Rinpoché at his home monastery of Gangteng Gönpa. He had just returned from visiting the monastery of one of his principal lamas, Jé Khenpo Rinpoché, and while there, he met a highly

advanced yogin who used the power of his samādhi to conjure up visual apparitions of a leopard and a deer that other people could witness. Unlike the
illusions created by professional magicians, who rely on mechanical deception and sophisticated technologies, the illusions created by advanced yogins
are generated primarily by the power of their minds.

> Due to the assembly of a cause, consisting of radiant, clear
> space, and the contributing condition of warmth and mois-
> ture, a mirage appears, yet it is not established as real.

A desert oasis appears in the distance, but the thirsty traveler sees it recede
as fast as he approaches. In fact, it is only a mirage, appearing due to specific
atmospheric conditions and having no true existence whatsoever.

> Due to the interaction of a cause, consisting of the radiant,
> clear substrate consciousness and the contributing condition
> of grasping at identity, dream appearances arise that are non-
> existent; and people are deluded by grasping at them as real
> and clinging to them as truly existent as if they were appear-
> ances in the waking state.

In both waking and dream states, grasping to a supposed identity is the contributing condition that enables reified appearances of the substrate to arise
to the substrate consciousness: this is delusory. Becoming lucid within the
dream by realizing the empty nature of dream appearances is analogous to
realizing the empty nature of waking appearances.

> With the convergence of a cause, consisting of a lucid, clear
> mirror and the contributing condition of someone's face
> opposite, a reflection appears even though it is nonexistent.

You can take a picture of this reflection, but your camera will focus at the
distance of a spot behind the mirror, where no such image exists. The reflection you see is not only dependent on the mirror and its surroundings but
also on your location and gaze. The reflection has no existence independent
of these circumstances, even though it has the causal efficacy to appear in a
photograph as it is perceived by some conscious observer.

> In dependence upon a cause, the samādhi of meditation within *dhyāna*, in conjunction with the contributing condition of an environmental vessel and moisture, a city of gandharvas appears as an object.

A city of these celestial musicians appears like a mirage, as a result of one's samādhi and suitable conditions. Such displays must have been commonly known in ancient India to be included with these classic analogies.

> With the causes, consisting of a solid, high object, such as a boulder, and auditory consciousness, along with the contributing condition of making a noise such as shouting, an echo occurs from their dependent relation.

An echo of your shout coming from a great distance sounds like someone is answering you from atop the boulder, but of course no one is there. The echo arises only in dependence on an earlier sound, a reflective surface, and an observer positioned to hear both the original sound and the reflection at slightly different times.

> With the convergence of a cause, consisting of lucid, clear water and the contributing condition of planets and stars shining in the sky, reflections appear from their dependent relation.

Seeing reflections of stars in the water, they would seem to be millions of miles below the surface. Your camera will take a perfectly focused picture of them with the lens set to infinity. But there are no stars there.

> In dependence upon a cause, water, in conjunction with the contributing condition of stirring or agitation, bubbles emerge from their dependent relation.

Bubbles in water are not only fascinating to watch, but they are also effective in hydrotherapy for relieving sore muscles and in ultrasonic cleaners for cleaning jewelry. Nevertheless, they are only interdependent arisings with no independent existence.

> In dependence upon a cause, the eyes, in conjunction with the
> contributing condition of pressure applied to the optic nerve,
> a hallucination takes place from their dependent relation.

In this example of a very simple hallucination, the application of light pressure to the eyeballs produces a double image. But of course no such double object exists.

> With mastery of emanations as the cause, and entry into the
> samādhi of producing emanations as the contributing condition, emanations appear from their dependent relation, even
> though they do not exist.

The production of an emanation is like a 3D holographic projection that appears in space and can be photographed, even though it doesn't exist anywhere.

> Thus, for these ten analogies there are said to be (1) a *dependence* because of a reliance upon causes, (2) a *relationship*
> because the causes and the contributing conditions are nondual, and (3) *origination* because appearances emerge even
> though they do not exist.

Here our text is providing a contextual etymology for the term *dependent origination* (Skt. *pratītyasamutpāda*), which in Tibetan is rendered as *dependently*[188] *related*[189] *origination*.[190] The crucial point here is that because all phenomena are dependently related events, they must be empty of inherent existence.

> Likewise, in the displays of the unimpededly free, objectless
> expanse that is the all-encompassing absolute space of the
> ground—unceasing space, without basis and without root—
> the ground is divided by the consciousness that is continually
> holding the "I" to be a self.

The nature of primordial consciousness is indivisible from the dharmadhātu, the vast expanse of emptiness. Its nature is completely symmetrical and homogenous. But by grasping at identities as though they were real, consciousness creates a division between a reified self and everything else.

> Thus a self is maintained on this side and the ground that is the space of awareness is externalized; and from the radiant clarity of the mirror-like ground, where anything at all can arise, the appearances of the three realms proliferate.

By reifying the self, which is "in here," the external world appears to be "out there," but this expanse of emptiness—which appears to a mind of ignorance as the substrate—is not simply a vacuity. From the perspective of the wisdom that knows reality as it is, this objectless expanse is already nondual with the primordial consciousness that understands it to be emptiness, as well as with the all-pervasive energy of that consciousness.[191] Anything and everything can arise from this ground, yet when it is *not* understood, and when it is thus viewed from the perspective of ignorance, the energy of primordial consciousness manifests instead as the stirring of karmic energies, including the energy of the basic tendency to grasp at an identity. With these energies serving as contributing conditions, while the radiant clarity of the mirror-like ground itself now serves as a cause, the whole array of mundane appearances arise, which are classically analyzed into the three realms of desire, form, and formlessness.

> To give some examples of this: an ocean cannot be divided in two, but once foam has bubbled up, the ocean is set apart from it.

Here is an interesting example for anyone who has become absorbed in the sights and sounds of the surf. Even though foam is simply water with bubbles, it separates from the water, floating atop the waves and exhibiting its own dynamic identity.

> And in the sky, though there is nothing apart from space itself, when rainbows appear, they make it seem as though the sky were something else.

Similarly, a rainbow that appears before you in the sky can be seen by everyone viewing it from the right perspective and its location can be documented in a photograph; but if you rush to the spot where it touches the Earth, you will never find the rainbow there.

Every phenomenon in the universe is analogous to these ten classical examples of illusion because everything arises due to dependent origination. Here is a second contextual etymology for *dependent origination*:

> There are said to be (1) a *dependence* because of reliance upon the "I," (2) a *relationship* because self and other are nondual, and (3) *origination* because phenomena emerge even while lacking objective existence.

Each and every sentient being abides in the center of his or her unique world. This experience may be likened to what in Vajrayāna Buddhism is called a maṇḍala, or a sacred, secret world, where the principal divine figure emanates and withdraws magnificent worlds of pure beings and the distinct environments in which they dwell. Yet even as ordinary sentient beings, whose minds are not yet pure, it is still true that our minds emanate and withdraw the unique configurations of our experienced environments, as well as the particular characteristics we happen to observe in the other beings we encounter. Because all we can experience are the appearances unique to our own space of awareness, and because the way those appearances will arise depends intimately upon the karmic energies and mental formations coming to fruition within our substrate consciousness, at any given moment we paint the world with our own colors, so to speak. But this is not solipsism, because each one actually does engage and influence other sentient beings, who in turn dwell within their own maṇḍalas, viewing reality from their own unique perspectives. Multiple worlds are entangled and interact with one another, but they are alike in their common *dependence* upon grasping to the "I." The appearance of a self and all other phenomena arises from the very same fabric—the dharmadhātu—so their *relationship* is one of inseparability, like a body and its shadow. All phenomena in the universe *originate* like this and have no independent, objective existence apart from such a process. Within saṃsāra, at least, this is what it means to say that all phenomena are empty.

> So by investigating the nature of existence of the myriad appearances of all phenomena, the very way in which they

exist, recognize the crucial point that they are displays of the empty space of ultimate reality.

Ultimate reality (Skt. *dharmatā*) signifies the empty nature of all phenomena; all arise from the dharmadhātu and appear distinctly, while being ultimately inseparable.

Moreover, when you fall asleep, all objective appearances of waking reality—including the physical worlds, their sentient inhabitants, and all the objects that appear to the five senses—dissolve into the vacuity of the substrate, which is of the nature of space, and they infinitely pervade that vacuity.

Whether in deep, dreamless sleep, while resting in the substrate consciousness upon achieving śamatha, or at death, all objective appearances dissolve into the vacuity of the substrate, abiding as karmic seeds, or habitual propensities, where nothing is differentiated and everything is possible.

Then, once again, self-grasping consciousness is aroused by the conjured apparitions that come from the movements of karmic energies.

Transitioning from dreamless sleep into the microcosm of a dream, all appearances and the environment emerge from the substrate. Each individual's dream is uniquely dependent on the habitual propensities stored in his or her substrate. The movements of a person's karmic energies trigger the dream, and all appearances of other people and phenomena in the dream derive exclusively from that individual's substrate.

In addition to our individual karma we share collective karma. Many of our most significant activities are conducted with others, and this creates shared karmic propensities, which are experienced collectively. This is true for all sentient beings. For example, a devastating earthquake can be understood as the movement of tectonic plates, but this is not the whole explanation. The experience of an earthquake is also influenced by the collective karma of humans, animals, and other sentient beings.

> Consequently, from the appearance of a self, as before, all inner and outer phenomena—including the physical worlds, their sentient inhabitants, and sensory objects—proliferate as dream appearances within the ground space of awareness.

All appearances arise from the substrate, in both the dreaming and waking states. But the karmic seeds that give rise to specific appearances are your very own in the dream, whereas in the waking state they are collectively intertwined with those of many other beings.

> You firmly hold on to joy, sorrow, and indifference, and insistently believe them to exist truly. This is delusion, so recognize it!

Whether we are grasping at joy in fortunate situations, nursing sorrows in unfortunate situations, or simply indifferent to innocuous circumstances, we are grasping at reified, external objects as the sources of our joy, sorrow, or indifference. Reification must be recognized as the root of all delusion.

OBJECTIONS FROM A REALIST VIEWPOINT

At the beginning of the *Vajra Essence*, the retinue gathered around the Teacher in Düdjom Lingpa's pure vision is referred to as an illusory display of primordial consciousness. This is because each of the 84,000 disciples, including the bodhisattvas who are our interlocutors in this dialogue, is an archetypal personification of a faculty of Düdjom Lingpa's own mind. Bodhisattva Faculty Displaying All Appearances, who now rises to challenge the Teacher's preceding explanation, was introduced as Faculty Governing Outer Appearances, and below he is called simply Faculty of Appearances. His statements reflect our naïve belief that all the appearances we perceive really do exist in the outer world. Even though certain phenomena are obviously illusions, we cannot easily accept the Teacher's assertion that all phenomena are illusory, dependently related events.

> Then Bodhisattva Faculty Displaying All Appearances rose from his seat, bowed reverently, and said to the Bhagavān, "O Teacher, Bhagavān, I do not accept that all appearances dissolve like that. When I go to bed, wrap myself in warm

bedding, and fall asleep, this array of phenomena remains where it was."

It is hard to believe that the entire world of appearances arises from our substrate when we awaken and dissolves back into our substrate when we fall asleep. We intuitively feel these phenomena must exist independently from our perceptions of them: we believe they are real.

Although this text was revealed 150 years ago in Tibet, modern society now enjoys a much more sophisticated, scientific understanding of physical reality than was available in that place and time. What does modern physics tell us truly exists when we are not looking? Do the visual appearances of colors and shapes exist "out there" when nobody is looking? Are the walls white when we turn off the lights? Is the music playing when nobody is listening? Does food contain tastes and aromas when nobody is savoring them?

This crucial question was pondered by the founders of modern science, who sought to transcend fallible human perception by discovering objective truth: "What really exists—from God's perspective?" These early scientists, including Copernicus, Galileo, Kepler, Descartes, and Newton, were all devout Christians who believed that God created the universe in six days, with human beings and other land creatures appearing on the sixth and final day. They aspired to a God's-eye perspective that transcends the biases and limitations of human senses and language. They knew that subjective sense data, or qualia—our perceptions of colors, shapes, sounds, and tastes—all depend on human sensory faculties; everything we experience is anthropocentric. There are no qualia, colors, sounds, or tastes inherent in atoms themselves. But they assumed that even when nobody is looking, real atoms, molecules, and objects composed of them really exist. And likewise energy, which was eventually discovered to be interconvertible with mass, really exists. This view was the scientific consensus until the beginning of the twentieth century; and it's still a widespread assumption.

If the view of metaphysical realism is true, and configurations of mass-energy do exist absolutely and independently, then our text and all the other teachings on the Great Perfection are false. But the pioneers of quantum physics in the early twentieth century shattered the view of metaphysical realism by revealing some very counterintuitive properties of light. What is the intrinsic nature of light, from an absolute perspective? In some experiments, light was found to consist of tiny packets, or quanta, of energy called photons, which move through space as discrete particles. In other experiments, light was found to consist of electromagnetic waves, which interact by cancelling and reinforcing each other to form interference patterns. How can one thing be both a particle and a wave? These two are as mutually incompatible as a giraffe and a tomato. Yet light behaves like either one, depending upon how it is examined. So what is its true behavior, independent of any observer? This is unanswerable, because we can never observe light without relying upon some system of measurement, beginning with our own senses. One of the biggest surprises in the so-called delayed-choice experiments was that the act of measurement determined light's particle or wave behavior, and even its movements through space, *retroactively*, with the cause following the result in time, seeming to violate our notions of time and causality.

A quantum system exhibits properties quite different from those of the ordinary phenomena we encounter. Nothing truly exists in a definite location with definite momentum until a measurement is performed: prior to the act of measurement there is only a field of probabilities, and even that doesn't exist objectively. We cannot precisely measure both a particle's location and its momentum at the same time: our accuracy in measuring its location comes at the expense of uncertainty about its momentum, and vice versa. This Heisenberg uncertainty principle has been thoroughly proven by empirical evidence.

In another example, quantum objects such as photons, electrons, and even molecules can be "entangled," such that their states are interdependent, even when separated by an arbitrarily large distance. The measurement of one such object influences the state of its entangled twin immediately, seeming to violate our notion of causality. Einstein called it "spooky action at a distance," but this paradox has been repeatedly verified experimentally.[192] Most physicists believe that relativity theory, which prohibits faster-than-light travel, has survived every test, and so our ordinary notions of locality must be incorrect. Even more counterintuitively, in an experiment called "delayed-choice entanglement swapping," Zeilinger's and Brukner's team has demonstrated that the decision to make a measurement on entangled particles can affect their state in the past, again challenging our common beliefs about causality.[193]

The metaphysical realism that posits real atoms with definite locations and momentums has been demolished. A quantum system exists only in interdependence with its measurement system. The two are like a dream and the dreamer, in that the dreamscape does not exist independently of the dreamer, who in turn does not exist independently of the dream. This becomes most evident in a lucid dream, in which you recognize the nature of the experience you are having. By merely thinking you can walk on water, or pass through walls, you can learn to do such things and anything else you can imagine. Your reality is thoroughly participatory. It's also a very fragile reality that survives in a cocoon. When the dream collides with a real-world sound and you are stirred awake, the dreamscape vanishes instantly. Likewise, according to the most common interpretation of quantum physics, the spooky qualities of quantum systems in physicists' laboratories must be carefully protected from the random noise in the macroscopic world, or they will vanish, which is called decoherence.

There is also a strong parallel between a lucid dream compared with the waking state and a quantum system compared with the entire universe in its lifetime of 13.7 billion years. Objective, empirical evidence of lucid dreaming has been available to contemporary psychologists for about thirty years, due in part to the work of the pioneering Stanford PhD researcher Steven LaBerge.[194] There's no question that one can be awake and dreaming at the same time, because he has documented thousands of lucid dreams. In this perfect laboratory for studying the mind, absolutely everything is mind-made, including bizarre powers and miraculous feats that violate physical laws. It's a fascinating dimension of reality that can only be experientially explored by those who have found or developed the ability to dream lucidly. But the impact of research in lucid dreaming on modern psychology and our understanding of the mind has been almost nil. Research has not been funded by governments or the pharmaceutical industry, and Steven LaBerge has never been granted a tenure-track academic position. His work is considered by many an interesting oddity, but not of scholarly import in the "real world."

Similarly, even though quantum physics is a highly respected field, few cosmologists, geologists, chemists, biologists, and brain scientists have registered or even considered the profound implications of quantum mechanics for the phenomena they study. They simply ignore the quantum effects of elementary particles, explaining that in the macroscopic "real world," the coherence of such systems quickly decays and counterintuitive behaviors are lost in the noise. According to this view, both lucid dreams and quantum systems display extraordinary qualities that challenge our very sense of reality, but both vanish without isolation and protection from "real" macroscopic phenomena.

Yet instead of thinking of a dream world as a temporary experience isolated from the surrounding environment, consider the possibility that everything we experience *is* a dream.

Until quite recently, quantum phenomena were considered to be a category of "special effects," observable only under highly controlled conditions, just like lucid dreams. But when, as discussed earlier, John Wheeler proposed the whole of reality as a quantum system, he pointed out that decoherence does not feature in the equations for quantum mechanics: it is simply an ad hoc explanation for what happens in the lab.

Stephen Hawking, who held Isaac Newton's endowed chair at Cambridge University, is the most renowned theoretical physicist in the world today. He authored a paper with Thomas Hertog that further developed Wheeler's theory of quantum cosmology.[195] In quantum mechanics, prior to conducting a measurement, the system is said to be in a "superposition state," a field of possibilities or probabilities. Nothing is actually present until a measurement is taken. This is true not only for phenomena in the present but also for those in the past. Everything we know about the past is based on measurements made in the present, and our information always arises relative to systems of measurement and human interpretations of the data. Whether light appears to be a particle or a wave depends on the apparatus you choose and your conceptual interpretations. With a well-designed instrument and a coherent conceptual framework, your measurements are said to collapse the superposition state into actuality, and you can make true statements about the past. But such statements are always relative to your measurement systems and interpretations. They have no independent truth. Other measurement systems and conceptual frameworks may produce very different truths, even mutually incompatible ones, just like notions of light being waves or particles, which are contradictory characterizations.

Hawking and Hertog summarize their findings:

> The top down approach we have described leads to a profoundly different view of cosmology, and the relation between cause and effect. Top down cosmology is a framework in which one essentially traces the histories backwards, from a spacelike surface at the present time. The no boundary histories of the universe thus depend on what is being observed, contrary to the usual idea that the universe has a unique, observer independent history.

In some sense no boundary initial conditions represent a sum over all possible initial states. This is in sharp contrast with the bottom-up approach, where one assumes there is a single history with a well-defined starting point and evolution. Our comparison with eternal inflation provides a clear illustration of this. In a cosmology based on eternal inflation there is only one universe with a fractal structure at late times, whereas in top down cosmology one envisions a set of alternative universes, which are more likely to be homogeneous, but with different values for various effective coupling constants.[196]

In short, this quantum view suggests that everything we know about the past is entirely based on information we possess in the present. Any statements we make are dependent upon our measurement systems and interpretations. There is no single, true history of the universe. We have the freedom to choose the past of the entire universe by choosing the measurement system and conceptual framework we prefer. This is also true of the present and the future.

Now, when you close your eyes and fall asleep, what do you think is really out there when nobody's looking? Our thinking needs to evolve from the materialistic realism of the late nineteenth century to accord with the best understanding of today's first-rate physicists, such as John Wheeler, Stephen Hawking, and Anton Zeilinger.

If we wish to understand consciousness, we must directly challenge the materialist assumption that even immaterial consciousness must originate from the material brain. Instead of studying presumably correlated physical behaviors, we must honor the principle of empiricism by observing the widest possible range of states of consciousness itself, directly.

There's an old joke about the aspect of observational bias that causes people to look for things where it's easiest, which has been dubbed the "streetlight effect." The earliest version may appear in the kōan-like stories of the thirteenth-century Sufi wise man Mullah Nasruddin. A more recent and succinct rendition comes from the linguist Noam Chomsky: "Science is a bit like the joke about the drunk who is looking under a lamppost for a key that he has lost on the other side of the street, because that's where the light is. It has no other choice."[197]

Unfortunately, materialists are looking for consciousness where they can see most clearly, which is in the domain of matter and energy, where phenomena are physical, measurable, and quantifiable. But they need to investigate consciousness on its home turf instead, because it is nonphysical and unmeasurable by instruments of technology.

Nomadic Tibetans in Düdjom Lingpa's time would have had no need for the preceding arguments, because they had not been brainwashed by the doctrines of materialism and metaphysical realism that prevail in the modern world. They didn't need to unlearn such beliefs. Nevertheless, like our interlocutor, they would have believed instinctively that the entire world remained just as it was when they fell asleep, just as we do today.

> The Bhagavān countered, "O Faculty Displaying All Appearances, when you go to bed, wrap yourself in warm bedding, and fall asleep, if all waking appearances of the physical worlds, their sentient inhabitants, and all sensory objects stay where they are, where is the enormous physical world that objectively appears in the dream state? Where are the many beings who inhabit it? And where are those fine arrays of appearances to the five senses? Tell me, do those objects emerge outside or inside your body?"

If you reify all the appearances of your environment, convinced that they will continue unchanged when you fall asleep, then logically you should also be reifying the phenomena that you experience during dreams. In fact, an ordinary, nonlucid dream world—even one filled with bizarre and impossible contradictions—seems just as real as the world in the waking state: both are reified. But where are the phenomena of this dreamscape actually located?

> Faculty Displaying All Appearances replied, "I believe they emerge inside the body."

This is precisely what a neuroscientist would answer: dreams exist in your brain. It is well known that the brain is very active during dreaming, and there are strong correlations between mind and brain. But is there any empirical evidence that *the appearances in* dreams are actually located within the brain? Can any scientific instrument observe the phenomena of a dream in the brain or anywhere else?

> He replied, "O Vajra of Appearances, consider all the areas
> of the body from inside the head on down. Tell me, where
> do those vast and numerous phenomena, such as the many
> mountains and valleys, emerge?"

Pressing for evidence, today we would ask a neuroscientist for proof that
dream phenomena actually occur in the brain. But there is no evidence that
any subjective experience occurs inside the body. Demonstrated correlations between the mind and brain activity do not prove that the mind is
caused solely by brain activity or located therein. The common assertions
that dreams are literally located in the brain, emotions in the amygdala, discursive thoughts in the left frontal cortex, mental images in the right frontal
cortex, and visual appearances in the visual cortex are all based on the false
assumption that correlations between observed brain processes and experienced mental processes implies that they must be located in the same place.
But the fact that two processes are correlated doesn't logically imply that
they are located in the same place.

> Faculty of Appearances replied, "O Teacher, Bhagavān, if we
> examine and analyze in that way, the head is not large enough
> to hold such a proliferation of the phenomena of the physical
> worlds and their sentient inhabitants, nor are the limbs or the
> torso. Perhaps consciousness comes out of the body and per-
> ceives another realm."

On the other hand, perhaps consciousness does exit the body and travels
to another realm, such as a parallel universe, where all these dream phenomena exist. Is that even conceivable?

> He replied, "O Faculty of Appearances, if your awareness and
> material body separate like that and consciousness goes out-
> side, from what orifice does it emerge? And when it goes back
> into the body, by what orifice does it reenter? Identify this.
> Where is the location of objects in a dream: are they present in
> the cardinal directions, in the intermediate directions, above,
> or below? Tell me, do you think the objects that appear in
> a dream—including the physical worlds and their sentient

inhabitants—are the same as those in waking appearances, or are they different?"

If consciousness were to exit the body—perhaps with a sneeze, according to one explanation for the ancient custom of protecting the soul of the sneezer by saying, "God bless you!"—we should be able to determine its method of exit and reentry. But there is no evidence of an exit port or of some other location to which consciousness could travel.

> The bodhisattva replied, "I see no such orifice, nor can I identify the presence [of such dream appearances] in the east, south, west, or north. I think the objects that appear in a dream exist in some other dimension."

Where in the world might this dream dimension be found, and how could your consciousness travel there? This may sound silly, but if you insist on reifying all waking phenomena, then you should reify dream phenomena too, and they should exist in some physical location. Or are dream phenomena entirely different from waking phenomena?

> The Bhagavān continued, "Consider the possibility that consciousness passes through some aperture. In the waking state there are the appearances of doors that allow one to pass in and out of a house, and they can be identified. If you assert that consciousness goes somewhere in the cardinal or intermediate directions of this world of the waking state, then since all the elements and everything animate and inanimate in the dream world would be of the same taste as phenomena in the waking state, they would not really be dream phenomena at all. Moreover, if it were possible for awareness to reenter the material body after having been separated from it, there would be no reason why all the dead couldn't reenter their own bodies. If your body at night does not grow cold and lifeless due to the separation of awareness from matter, there would be no reason why it should grow cold at death, either. Therefore, if you believe that phenomena in the daytime and the nighttime are of the same type, are they differentiated by

sleep or not? If you believe they are different, then would they emerge together, as though one world is piled on top of the other, or one is outside and the other inside? Tell me what you think."

If dream phenomena were experienced when consciousness travels to some other location, then they would be no different from waking phenomena. Furthermore, the body should "die" when consciousness departs the body. And if it can reenter the body upon waking from a dream, why should it not be able to reenter a dead body?

In Vajrayāna Buddhism there is a method of practicing for the transference of consciousness at death called *phowa*,[198] wherein one visualizes one's consciousness shooting up from the heart and out through the crown cakra to a pure realm, such as Sukhāvatī. It's considered desirable for consciousness to exit from the top of the body rather than from the bottom.

There are many reported cases of Tibetan yogins who have died lucidly, in meditation. The mind dissolves into the substrate consciousness, which dissolves into pristine awareness, at which point a very subtle prāṇa remains inside the indestructible orb at the heart cakra. This state is called *tukdam*,[199] abiding in the clear light of death, which is beyond time. The breath and heart have stopped, and there are no detectable metabolic signs, but the yogin remains in meditation posture. It is extremely unlikely that brain activity continues for days on end without any circulation of the blood, but, inexplicably from the perspective of modern medicine, the body does not decompose. Because the very subtle energy of primordial consciousness abides in the heart center, which remains warm, the complexion remains fresh and the body does not decompose, even after many days at room temperature. When this final meditation is over, the very subtle energy leaves the body, which then begins to decompose.

He replied, "Teacher, Bhagavān, based on this kind of examination and analysis, if consciousness were to go elsewhere, the body would turn into a corpse, and all appearances of the physical worlds and their sentient inhabitants would have to be of the same type [during the waking and dream states]. So there would be no differentiation according to sleep, and at death there would have to be some way to reenter the body.

> If daytime and nighttime phenomena were different in type, then one set of appearances would have to emerge out from under the other, while the first was still there. If they were the same, there would be no distinction between phenomena in the states of waking and dreaming. So very well, I agree that dream phenomena emerge after waking phenomena have disappeared into the space of awareness."

If dream appearances were perceived because consciousness had traveled to some other location, and both waking and dream appearances were equally real, there would be no difference between them. If dream and waking phenomena were different, they would have to occupy different realms, one above and one below, or some such arrangement, so that they would not interfere with each other. This may seem absurd, as it should, but the problem comes from reifying them, which is what leads to these contradictions. The bodhisattva has seen the fallacy of what we would call naïve realism.

A naïve realist believes that our sensory faculties are fundamentally passive, and they detect colors, sounds, and forms that truly exist in the world outside us. Things are just as they appear to be. By this logic, dream appearances must exist in the same way. With the abandonment of metaphysical realism, the bodhisattva concludes that both dream and waking phenomena emerge in turn from the space of awareness and dissolve back into it. But he is acknowledging only that the appearances themselves emerge from the space of the mind, while still believing that the appearances that occur while one is awake do correspond to real phenomena that truly exist, independent of any observer.

> Again Faculty Displaying All Appearances addressed the Bhagavān, "O Teacher, Bhagavān, for this body to exist, it must depend upon the causes and contributing conditions of one's parents. But since the problem has come to light that appearances do not actually transform from one thing into another, why do these parents appear? And why does this body appear? Teacher, please explain."

We naïvely believe that even if our perceptions of our body are subjective and emerge from the space of the mind, the body itself is inherently real, and it was produced by our parents. But Padmasambhava maintains that nothing what-soever is truly existent. If there is no truly existent body, composed of truly existent atoms, and coming from truly existent parents, how could our per-ceptions of a body ever manifest? How do these appearances of a body arise?

> He replied, "O Faculty of Appearances, if you think both par-ents are necessary for the existence of a body, recall that a body in the intermediate period, a dream body, one that is born from heat and moisture, and one that is born spontaneously all arise without a mother or father."

Padmasambhava's counterexamples are bodies that arise without depen-dence on a mother or father, such as your body in a dream or in the bardo. In both cases your body appears as a form that moves from here to there and perceives various phenomena, but it is a mind-made body, not one born of parents. But the fact remains that human beings *are* born from their parents, so at first glance, the spontaneous birth of beings in the above cases don't seem pertinent. According to the Madhyamaka view, phenomena, including the human body, do conventionally arise in dependence upon prior causes and conditions, and this is not being refuted or challenged here. What is utterly crucial to recall as we read this passage is that a distinctive aspect of the Great Perfection is that it presents the ground of being, the path to enlightenment, and the fruit of perfect spiritual awakening from the per-spective of one who is already enlightened.

To understand the meaning of this perplexing passage, we may turn to Padmasambhava's parable of the prodigal prince: Long ago in the land of India there was a great king named Ākāśagarbha, whose son, the Crown Prince Kiraṇa, was immature and foolish. On one occasion the young prince attended a great festival near the palace in which a magician displayed such realistic illusions that the prince became utterly mesmerized by them. After the show, as the crowd dispersed, the prince became separated from his entourage and suffered from such a case of amnesia that he not only forgot the way back to the palace but even forgot who he was. Having nothing to eat and nowhere to stay, he took up with a band of vagrants, and wandering from one city to another, grew accustomed to eating beggars' food and wearing cast-off rags. Before long, he came to fully assume the identity of a homeless beggar and lived a destitute life of great misery.

Many months and years went by, and the kingdom, having lost its princely heir, was on the verge of collapse, and there was fear that the royal line of King Ākāśagarbha had come to an end. At that time, the young beggar-prince, while roving about the kingdom, happened to arrive at the home of the king's wise minister Sūryanaśim. The minister, immediately recognizing him as the prince, exclaimed, "Oh, our prince who was lost has returned! You need not beg. Come to the palace!" But the beggar-prince balked at this royal welcome, claiming that he was no prince but only a homeless beggar, and he refused to be taken in by the minister's advances.

The minister tried to persuade him that he had been so caught up in the magician's illusions that he had forgotten who he was and had mindlessly strayed into the lifestyle of a homeless vagrant and mistakenly taken on the identity of a beggar. But since the prince was still unpersuaded, the minister asked him details about his birthplace, his parents, childhood companions, and so on. When the prince found to his astonishment that he was unable to answer these simple questions, he asked Sūryanaśim to enlighten him as to his true background and identity. Upon receiving these "pointing-out instructions," the prince's awareness of own nature was restored, and he was immediately taken to the palace and crowned as the new king.[200]

To take another analogy, in the midst of a nonlucid dream, you have forgotten who you were in your waking state and have totally identified with your dreamed persona, who is deluded by all that is happening in the dream, taking it all to be real. Within the context of your dream, you may have a clear sense of who your parents are, and you may even have researched your genealogy for many generations back. You might even be able to recall who you were in your last dream—a previous incarnation, as it were—but without recognizing that you were dreaming then, too. But once you have awakened to the delusive nature of your dream and your mistaken identity within it, either by becoming lucid within the dream or by waking up completely, you recognize that the person with whom you identified in the dream never really existed and therefore had no parents. In the above passage, from the Teacher's perspective, Faculty of Appearances never existed as an unenlightened human being, so in reality he never had any parents.

If you believe this body exists in dependence upon one's parents, then before sentient beings became embodied, where did the very first father come from? Where did he live? Where

did he finally go? Examine the mother similarly—how she was born, lived, and passed away. Investigate thus step by step up to the parents of this present body. Understand this.

Whenever we investigate phenomena in our world, a universal human tendency is that an observation of the evidence is followed by a conclusion or discovery; and then we grasp to our discovery as being objectively true. We completely neglect the influences that our choices of both a conceptual framework and a method of observation bring to bear on the results we obtain. But it is delusional to think that these results were preexisting truths, independent of our methods of investigation. As Werner Heisenberg stated, "What we observe is not nature in itself but nature exposed to our method of questioning."[201] For the past four hundred years, scientists have been exploring reality with physical systems of measurement and posing questions about physical entities, all within the physical frameworks of physics, chemistry, and biology. *When you ask a physical question, you'll get a physical answer,* because this is ensured by your physical framework and methods.

But remember that as Stephen Hawking proposes, there is no single absolutely true history of the universe. Multiple histories exist, relative to the conceptual frameworks and measurement systems we choose. We can never witness something that is absolutely true, independent of any system of measurement. If you imagine that yours is the only framework and system of measurement, then you will believe that yours is the only truth: the absolute truth. Many types of religious fundamentalists have long fallen into this trap, as have scientific materialists—who assert that only physically measurable phenomena are real—thereby denying the truth of subjective experience as well as the validity of their own conceptually based theories. Oops!

The scientific story of evolution has great explanatory power regarding the evolution of species, but it is true only relative to the conceptual frameworks and measurements on which it is based. In Buddhism, which encompasses the Abhidharma, Mahayana, and Vajrayāna, there are multiple theories of the origin of the universe and human beings. According to the *Kālacakra Tantra*, no account of the history of the universe is absolutely true—but one or another account may or may not be true *relative to the cognitive framework* in which it has been formulated. These many stories may be mutually complementary, mutually incompatible, or some may be simply false, even in their own proper context. Critical research is needed in each case to determine which category applies.

The Buddhist theories of cosmogony do have some points that are in principle held in common with modern science: The universe is considered to be expanding, our particular cycle began billions of years ago, and it will end in a final cycle of destruction. According to the Kālacakra system, the universe emerged from "space particles," and from this formless realm emerged the form realm, from which emerged the desire realm. Each of these realms is populated by a wide variety of sentient beings, only some of whom possess physical bodies. The driving force behind the cycles of the universe is understood to be the karma of sentient beings. The collective karma of sentient beings gives rise to the formation of their shared environments. Our planet and its inhabitants are thoroughly entangled: this is the principle of interdependent arising.

According to Buddhist history, Buddha Śākyamuni was the fourth buddha of the present eon, in a series that would culminate in one thousand buddhas. During the time of his predecessor, Buddha Kāśyapa, a human lifespan was said to reach eighty thousand years, human bodies were more ethereal, and human minds were largely virtuous. Since those halcyon days— through the devolution of sentient beings—lifespans have shortened, bodies have coarsened, and minds have become plagued by mental afflictions. This history is clearly at odds with the history of biological evolution. But Buddhists employ radically different conceptual frameworks and methods of observation, so the mutual incompatibility of these respective histories does not necessarily invalidate either one.

The primary measurement technology in Buddhism, and in older Indian culture, is samādhi: "the mind's telescope." Using samādhi, one can escape the obscuring veils of the egocentric mind, with its gender, race, age, history, and personal attributes, just as the Hubble telescope escapes the distortions of Earth's atmosphere to see clearly galaxies that are billions of light-years away. As mentioned previously, achieving śamatha is an instrument for investigating the deep space of the mind, overcoming the distortions of your own personal narrative, and witnessing past-life memories extending far back in time. The Buddha explained that ancient contemplatives were able to recall a thousand lifetimes, including recollections of themselves and others as nonhuman beings that populated the world.

We have evidence that seafaring Indian traders traveled to Egypt and

Macedonia accompanied by yogins; one of them may have taught the technology of samādhi to the Buddha's contemporary Pythagoras (c. sixth century BCE). Pythagoras traveled to Egypt to study the ancient wisdom traditions, and may also have encountered Indian contemplative adepts. Pythagoras returned to form his eponymous community in Italy, where he taught not only philosophy, mathematics, and music but also advocated a diet and lifestyle that would support his followers in becoming true "lovers of wisdom," or "philosophers," a term that he coined. He may have taught contemplative practices as well, but since he insisted that his followers maintain a vow of secrecy, this remains a matter of speculation. He was renowned for claiming that he could recall his past lives, and for being a miracle-worker, or what in Indian terms would have been known as a siddha. Pythagoras didn't learn samādhi or the theory of transmigration from the Greeks or the Egyptians, for prior to that time it appears they did not have such contemplative training or theory. It seems most likely that he learned it from teachers in the well-developed Indian tradition and may even have traveled to India itself.

If your system of measurement is samādhi, and the questions you pose concern the nature of the mind, you will find answers that are quite different from those found using physical systems of measurement and materialist conceptual frameworks. The Madhyamaka view, and the view of our text, is that none of our accounts is absolutely true, neither the Buddhist descriptions of cyclical time nor the scientific explanations of a linear history to the universe. A description may be true relative to a particular cognitive frame of reference, and hidden from another perspective. The ancient Buddhist texts don't mention genetics or biological evolution, so they are incomplete in that respect. And evolutionary biology is excellent science, true in its frame of reference, but taking into account the long-standing discoveries of contemplative inquiry, we can recognize that such biology is also incomplete. Neither explanation portrays an absolutely objective reality, such as some grand, unified theory of everything would claim to do.

The Madhyamaka view asserts only one definitive truth, which is equally true in all times, places, and cognitive frames of reference: all phenomena are empty of inherent nature. This holds true for emptiness itself. Thus it is the only truth that is invariable across all cognitive frames of reference. All other truths are at most relatively true, but not inherently true. It is analogous to Einstein's assertion in relativity theory that the speed of light is invariant— whereas matter, energy, time, and space depend on a frame of reference. My body has no absolutely true mass, because the reading on my bathroom scale depends on the speed at which I am traveling relative to my inertial frame of reference. I can't currently travel close enough to the speed of light to be concerned about time-traveling weight gain, but many clever and sophisticated experimenters have tested and confirmed the theory of relativity and the invariance of the speed of light to a high degree of certainty.

Consider another analogy, one that will be much more complex to unfold: The nineteenth-century German philosopher Ludwig Feuerbach (1804–72) rejected the Christianity that dominated Europe in his time, advocated atheism, materialism, and communism, and explained God as a human projection of the ideal father figure. His best-known work, *The Essence of Christianity*,[202] was published in 1841. Feuerbach's book influenced an intellectual and revolutionary cohort that included Leon Trotsky, Karl Marx, Friedrich Engels, and Richard Wagner.

Feuerbach's anthropological explanation that man created God in his own image, rather than God creating man in his own image, was heretical in his time, but has become strangely commonplace today. Meanwhile, the dominant scientific view of planetary history is that consciousness emerged only after a very long evolutionary process, beginning with chemical reactions of inanimate matter and energy, which gradually led to organic compounds, which evolved into biological life forms, and some of these eventually developed brains and consciousness. The scientific method is credited for revolutionary discoveries in physics, chemistry, biology, and astronomy. With Charles Darwin's *Origin of Species* in 1859, it suddenly seemed the existence of life on Earth could be understood as a gradual process of physical evolution rather than the act of a creator God.

Over the past four hundred years, scientists have gradually come to the conclusion that the physical interactions of matter and energy explain the behavior of biological systems and that subjective psychological experiences can be reduced to biological processes in the brain. Neuroscientists enthusiastically present their field as the scientific discipline that will fully illuminate the nature of consciousness, free will, and religion, along with much else, by reducing psychology to biology. The marketing of this brand has been very effective in persuading the general population and research-funding agencies that they are the "go-to field" to solve the remaining mysteries of human identity, mind, and consciousness.

There is a telling parallel between the historical development of science and the current scientific story of our world. The first scientific revolution, attributed primarily to Galileo, was in the physical sciences; and the second, initiated by Darwin, was in the life sciences. The mind sciences emerged following the Darwinian revolution, at a time when scientific materialism was rapidly gaining dominion over all branches of natural science, exactly as Thomas Huxley orchestrated and anticipated. Following the same sequence of physical science to life science and mind science, science explains the history of the world as the evolution of matter and energy into living organisms, then on to conscious, intelligent beings. But there are skeptics regarding this belief even within mainstream science. The astrophysicist Paul C. W. Davies, for instance, comments that "a complete theory of the interactions of particles and forces would tell us little, for example, about the origin of life or the nature of consciousness."[203] So, as an analogous throwback to Feuerbach's claim that God is merely a projected super-dad, perhaps we might say that the scientific history of the world is merely a projection based on the particular historical evolution of Eurocentric science over the past four hundred years! This history wasn't inevitable; there could have been others, for the first scientific revolution could conceivably have been in biology or psychology.

In Galileo's time, before the mechanistic model of the universe came to dominate Western thought, there were rival attempts to explain the world, referred to as natural philosophies. In *organicism*, the universe and its parts are viewed as organic wholes, either analogous to living organisms or literally alive. Organicism goes back at least to Plato, who considered the universe to be an intelligent, living being; and it still informs the views of some modern biologists who stress the self-organizing nature of living systems over the properties of their parts. Perhaps the oldest explanations for life are expressions of *vitalism*, positing a living force, such as *vis viva*, *élan vital*, or a soul, that separates living things from nonliving matter. The term *vis viva* was first used by the German polymath Gottfried Leibniz (1646–1716) to describe the kinetic energy conserved in elastic collisions, such as in billiards. Generally speaking, the mechanistic model prevailed over such organic views of the universe, and it thoroughly pervades the modern scientific endeavor, with the goal of explaining all phenomena as purely mechanical interactions among component parts: the universe as machine.[204]

In an alternate reality, the trajectory of human scientific discoveries might have been entirely different. What if the first discoveries had been made in the realm of biology, with physics being understood only later? Our story of the history of the universe might now be that there was first a primeval universal life force, out of which the physical universe emerged to provide an environment that would be habitable to living organisms. A growing body of literature by physicists and biologists concerns what's called the *anthropic principle*, which observes that a large number of seemingly arbitrary but very specific constants in nature—such as the freezing point of water, or the slight density reduction when water freezes into ice, causing ice to float instead of sinking—had to be almost precisely what we observe in order for the life we know to exist. If these constants had been even slightly different, life as we know it would not be here. This view suggests that instead of the inanimate, physical universe being fundamental, and giving rise secondarily to life, it may be just the opposite. Perhaps a life principle, such as *prāṇa*, is fundamental, and it is responsible for giving rise to physical worlds in which living beings could manifest and evolve. We should recognize that there are still no proven scientific explanations for the origins of life. There are many different speculations, all untestable.

Now imagine that modern science had been pioneered by a psychologist who developed methods for achieving śamatha and utilizing vipaśyanā in the experiential exploration of the mind and its role in nature. The first scientific studies might have concerned the nature of consciousness itself, possibly even penetrating beyond the substrate consciousness to pristine awareness. Such a tradition might have considered consciousness to be the most fundamental aspect of the universe, with life a secondary derivation, and the inorganic physical universe a mere vessel to provide an environment for sentient beings.

But such wasn't the case for Western civilization. And our consensus history of scientific progress in physics, chemistry, biology, and psychology may be the reason we tell a similar story about the creation of the universe. Of course, the latter is a rich story with tremendous explanatory power regarding the objective, physical universe, and understanding it has radically improved human lives and potentials. But it's not the whole story, let alone the only plausible story, by any means. It's actually a very limited story, and it's only relatively true. Instead, highly replicable contemplative experience has revealed that the universe abides as a field of possibilities until self-grasping arises, appearances manifest, conceptualization differentiates object from subject, and the infinitely variegated stories of saṃsāra are spun, none of which are absolutely true.

Feuerbach's reduction of God to a creation of the mind of man and the above hypothesis—that the current scientific view of the evolution of the universe and life on our planet has developed as a direct reflection of our evolving methods of scientific inquiry—are equally anthropocentric. This is reminiscent of the famous declaration "Man is the measure of all things," by the Greek philosopher Protagoras (c. 490–c. 420 BCE). According to the Madhyamaka view, everything that is perceived and conceived by the human mind exists relative to the human mind; and the human mind, which is just as empty of inherent nature as everything else, exists only relative to the phenomena it apprehends. But the human urge toward transcendence is universal and timeless. Christian contemplatives sought such transcendence by looking inward, beyond the confines of the human soul—and its limited projections—to genuine mystical realization of the mind of God. Galileo, who was trained as a contemplative in his youth, later directed his yearning for transcendence outward, seeking to know the mind of the Creator indirectly, by way of His creation. Modern science, while setting aside Galileo's theistic framework, still seeks transcendence with the use of technological systems of measurement, which transcend the limitations of the human senses, and with the analytical use of mathematics, or the language of Nature, which transcends the limitations of human language and thought. In the practice of the Great Perfection, one first transcends the limitations of the human psyche by coming to rest in the substrate consciousness, which reveals a far broader range of phenomena than can be known with the physical senses. Then one cuts through the substrate consciousness to the timeless, nonlocal dimension of primordial consciousness, which reveals the whole range of possible worlds of saṃsāra and nirvāṇa. This, according to the Great Perfection, is the ultimate transcendence and the fulfillment of our innermost, eternal longing.

According to quantum cosmology, meaningful information lies at the foundation of the universe, and this necessarily implies the participation of an observer who acquires and records information. At a macrocosmic level, the universe is seen fundamentally as an information-processing system, relative to which matter and energy are derivative, emergent properties. At the microcosmic level, consider again the possibility that each sentient being may be regarded as a *conscious* information-processing system, and not simply a configuration of matter and energy relative to which consciousness is a derivative, emergent property. If this is correct, then the so-called placebo effect makes perfect sense for the first time: The power of expectation activates the information-processing system of a human body-mind, which then triggers the appropriate, complex, electrochemical processes in the body that bring about the expected change. While the materialist paradigm provides no explanation for the subject-expectancy effect, this explanation, based on the principles of quantum cosmology, presents a truly scientific explanation that lends itself to empirical research. Here is one more fertile area for contemplative-scientific inquiry.

THE VIEW FROM PRISTINE AWARENESS

We return to the preceding discussion on how to investigate the lineage of your parents leading up to your current body. Based on our shared cognitive frame of reference and modes of observation, our biological body, composed of atoms, was born from parents, each of whom had parents as well. The theory of evolution is not a fantasy; it's based on compelling evidence and rigorous logic. But it has no absolute truth that is independent of its methods of inquiry. Even according to the Madhyamaka view, your body is composed of atoms and molecules, whether you're looking or not. But in just the same way that the colors we perceive do not exist independently of our visual faculties, atoms and molecules as we understand them do not exist independently of the conceptual frameworks according to which they are discovered and measured. Both colors and our awareness of them are interdependent phenomena. None of them is inherently existent. Within the context of the nonlucid dream we call our life and family history, our biological parents gave birth to this body. But upon awakening, none of it is found to be true, just as when you awake from a dream, you know that the people in your dream had no existence apart from that imaginary reality.

The Bodhisattva Faculty of Appearances has expressed much skepticism concerning the Teacher's statements because he takes appearances seriously. If appearances truly represent reality, as we all instinctively assume, then the Teacher must be wrong.

> Faculty of Appearances responded, "All right, Teacher, Bhagavān—since it is I who established the appearances, I suspect it is solely my own appearances that don't exist but are merely appearances. Is that so or not? Teacher, please explain!"

In other words, the things that appear to me alone, as well as the "I" itself, may be mere appearances, but all the other phenomena in the world must be truly existent. Is this the answer? Many neuroscientists would be perfectly content with this answer, especially since very few of them are well versed in contemporary quantum physics. Your personhood, they may say, is an illusion, because there is no part of your brain that corresponds to your personal identity and controls the rest of the system. But your brain is real.

> He replied, "O great being, don't think like that! If you see everything to be empty only because you have established all appearances in that way, and that finally leads you to the conclusion that nothing is empty except what appears to you alone not to exist, then you are merely setting yourself up to stamp the seal of emptiness upon that which is not empty and to view that which exists as not existing."

Now you've fallen to both extremes simultaneously. You've fallen to the extreme of nihilism with respect to yourself and what appears to you— thinking that you and the qualia of your conscious experience don't exist. And you've fallen to the extreme of substantialism with respect to all other phenomena—thinking that they really exist out there, whether you perceive them or not.

> While regarding emptiness as deceptive and reifying existence as ultimately real, if you believe that you alone do not exist from your own side, then that understanding of the emptiness of yourself alone leaves you with the śrāvaka view of mere personal identitylessness.

The śrāvaka view recognizes the lack of a self that exists truly—your own personal identitylessness. But the five aggregates of form, feeling, recognition, compositional factors, and consciousness are considered real. The external universe is inherently real. Such metaphysical realism is common to the Theravāda view. But in the Mahāyāna teachings on the perfection of wisdom, even the five aggregates are asserted to be empty of inherent existence. For example, this is clearly stated in the *Heart Sutra*, where the dialogue is between Śāriputra, representing the śrāvaka view, and Avalokiteśvara, representing the Mahāyāna view. From the tiniest elementary particles all the way up to buddha nature, the sugatagarbha, all phenomena are said to be empty of inherent nature.

> By establishing the entire phenomenal world as being like the ten analogies of illusion, understand that they are not truly existent, just as there are no appearing objects that exist apart from an illusionist, and just as, from the very moment appearances appear, they vanish before the person to whom they appear. Regard this very lack of existing truly as ultimate emptiness.

If all appearances are like the creations of an illusionist, where is the illusionist who creates all the phenomena in the universe? From the perspective of the dharmakāya, all appearances are creative expressions of pristine awareness, rigpa. This is not someone else's pristine awareness but your very own.

> Faculty of Appearances replied, "Here is what I think: they are not the appearances of one sentient being. If all the three realms were merely my own appearances, when just my appearances changed, all the appearances of the three realms should change accordingly—they would certainly have to pass away, vanish, and be extinguished with me. Since that's not so, I don't think that due to my perception of external objects, the physical worlds and their sentient inhabitants in the three realms perish and vanish together with me. So, Teacher, please explain fully the meaning of this."

The Faculty of Appearances is rightly skeptical about the solipsism that thinks the whole world arises and passes because of himself alone. Here we must carefully examine the referent of the word "I" as the illusionist who creates all appearances in the universe. If the referent of this term is a particular individual with the characteristics of age, race, and gender, then it makes no sense, for it would falsely imply that everyone and everything apart from oneself is a figment of one's own imagination. Likewise, if the referent is a single continuum of substrate consciousness, manifesting the entire universe and then destroying it by reverting into the substrate, it makes no sense either. So what is the referent of the word "I" here?

Again, let's take an analogy: Great compassion is the driving engine of bodhicitta. The classic Tibetan liturgy for developing great compassion prays, "May all sentient beings be free of suffering and its causes!" With this aspiration one gives rise to immeasurable compassion, which is common to the Śrāvakayāna and the Mahāyāna. The next line asks, "Why *couldn't* we all be free?" After all, from the Mahāyāna perspective, everyone has a buddha nature, and all phenomena are empty, so why must we suffer? Next, the liturgy declares, "I shall free us all," as the resolve of great compassion (Skt. *mahākaruṇā*), which far exceeds the aspirations of the lower vehicles. This is a vast undertaking, and we're not relegating this responsibility to anyone else. Is this completely crazy?

If the referent of the word "I" in this liturgy is a particular individual with a limited number of years remaining and only two hands, it's certainly impossible. And it would take infinitely long for a single continuum of consciousness, reincarnating over and over, to liberate all beings, so this cannot be the referent of "I" either. From what perspective is it realistic to take this bodhisattva vow? From the perspective of pristine awareness, rigpa, you are Samantabhadra. You have no dependency on some other Samantabhadra for help. Your awareness pervades all space and all time. Your virtues are infinite, and you have all the time in the world. Here is the most profound referent of the word "I."

When the Teacher asks us to view everything as a dream, he's encouraging us to extend our awareness beyond identifying with the person in our dream life and personal history in the waking state. Furthermore, we must expand awareness beyond our personal substrate consciousness. We are encouraged to view life from the perspective of pristine awareness. From the Madhyamaka perspective, all phenomena are *like* a dream, but from the perspective of pristine awareness, all the phenomena in saṃsāra *are* a dream. We are seeking to propel our awareness out of the confines of delusional, dualistic grasping and release it into its ultimate ground state, pristine awareness. Therefore, in the presence of the buddhas, we vow to liberate all sentient beings from suffering and the causes of suffering, which only makes sense from the perspective of pristine awareness.

He responded, "O Faculty of Appearances, such thoughts of yours are familiar to all beings who are deluded by grasping at true existence. But knowing how to act like others is not

> the way to realize emptiness. For beginningless lifetimes, you have apprehended your own appearances as being other than yourself, and by closely identifying with them, you have become deluded."

We instinctively reify phenomena, just as the bodhisattva has done here, but conventional thinking will not lead us to the realization of emptiness or liberation. When we peer into the night sky, the vast universe of planets and stars does not consist of independently real entities: these are our own appearances. But we grasp at mere appearances as though they were planets and stars that are separate from ourselves and independent of all modes of observation. Likewise, we reify our identities as human individuals with particular ages, genders, races, and histories. In doing so, we demarcate all other species, ages, and genders as separate, external objects.

> The phenomenal world of a dream, with all its sensory objects, is not left behind and discarded when you wake up. Rather, they all vanish into the realm of the mind. Likewise, all appearances vanish into yourself. You must recognize that no autonomous physical worlds, sentient beings, or sense objects exist out there.

All appearances in dreams seem to exist from their own side. We grasp to appearances in a nonlucid dream, thereby experiencing hopes and fears that are wholly delusional. In exactly the same way, we grasp to appearances in the waking state as inherently real. This grasping, or reification, is the root of saṃsāra.

As discussed earlier, the view of metaphysical realism—the belief that there is an autonomous physical universe out there—has provided a philosophical foundation for virtually all of modern science since the time of Galileo. But again, the rise of quantum physics over the past century questions this fundamental belief. Niels Bohr, a founder of quantum physics, wrote, "In our description of nature the purpose is not to disclose the real essence of the phenomena but only to track down, as far as it is possible, relations between . . . aspects of our experience."[205] And Erwin Schrödinger, another of the great pioneers of this second revolution in physics, commented, "One can only help oneself through something like the following emergency decree: Quantum mechanics forbids statements about what really exists—statements about the object. Its statements deal only with the object-subject relation."[206]

One of the most provocative interpretations of quantum physics is called QBism, eloquently advocated by Christopher Fuchs. His fellow physicist Hans Christian von Baeyer addresses this view in his book *QBism: The Future of Quantum Physics*, in which he writes, "While the experimenter, the observer, and the theorist are investigating *something* external to themselves, what they are dealing with directly is not nature itself but nature reflected in human experiences."[207] QBism goes further than John Wheeler's theory of observer-participancy in the universe according to quantum cosmology. It makes the radical move of speaking not about human experiences in general but about the experience of each single agent, a particular human. This may be seen as implying that each and every sentient being, human and nonhuman, experiences its own universe, with all appearances of that universe being unique to each being. The science writer Amanda Gefter summarizes the gist of this new interpretation of quantum physics: "QBism would say, it's not that the world is built up from stuff on 'the outside' as the Greeks would have had it. Nor is it built up from stuff on 'the inside' as the idealists, like George Berkeley and Eddington, would have it. Rather, the stuff of the world is in the character of what each of us encounters every living moment—stuff that is neither inside nor outside, but prior to the very notion of a cut between the two at all."[208]

To relate this view of physical reality to classic accounts of the mundane siddhis that can be accomplished with advanced stages of samādhi, consider the siddhi of the ability to reach out and touch the moon and sun. The Buddha declared that when the mind has become concentrated, purified, cleansed, unblemished, and has gained imperturbability, a yogin applies and directs his mind to various supernormal powers.

> He then enjoys different powers: being one, he becomes many— being many, he becomes one; he appears and disappears; he passes through fences, walls and mountains unhindered as if through air; he sinks into the ground and emerges from it as if it were water; he walks on the water without breaking the surface as if on land; he flies cross-legged through the sky like a bird with wings; he even touches and strokes with his hand the sun and moon, mighty and powerful as they are; and he travels in the body as far as the Brahmā world.[209]

The Tibetan adept Karma Chagmé (1613–78) writes in a similar vein: "Moreover, those endowed with such great paranormal abilities, with such great might, and with such great power stroke the sun and moon with their hands."[210]

With our unquestioned assumption that that the moon and sun are objectively existent, these seem like utterly absurd claims. Tibetans tell a joke about a backward village in Ladakh that was secretly developing its own space program. When they were finally ready to launch, they held a press conference to announce their mission to land on the sun. "But you'll burn up!" objected a reporter. "No," replied the village astronaut with a knowing smile, "we're going to land at night!" Can we take such assertions by Buddhist adepts any more seriously than this comic story?

Everyone knows that we can't touch the sun, a ball of thermonuclear fire that could hold 1.3 million Earths. We are happily situated 93 million miles away, in the so-called Goldilocks zone: not too hot, not too cold, just right. Our instruments reveal astonishing pictures of the sun's dynamic beauty. Its energy powers photosynthesis, feeding the web of life on our planet. Its magnetic storms play havoc with telecommunications. Luckily, ours is a middle-aged star, with billions of years of life left; but it will eventually vaporize all life on Earth before swallowing our planet. Even though few people worship the sun as a deity anymore, it remains central to life on Earth. How could it not be truly existent, independent of anyone's conceptual designations of it? How could the teachings on emptiness be true?

Is the sun really there, independent of all observations, or not? Based on the methods of measurement we choose today, such as telescopes, along with our cognitive frame of reference, such as scientific materialism, the sun does exist. But, according to these teachings of the Great Perfection, which accord with the Madhyamaka view of Nāgārjuna, it has no absolute existence independent of measurements and conceptual frameworks.

What about the Earth? In 1966, we saw the first picture of it from the vicinity of the moon. Our tiny, strikingly colorful planet, floating in the blackness of space, is clearly different from the dead, gray surface of the moon in the foreground. Surely the earth exists, just as we photograph it. But the Buddhist scriptures describe our world as consisting of Mt. Meru and the four continents, with four subcontinents and a hierarchy of realms, including higher ones inhabited by devas. This description doesn't seem to match our maps and photographs of Earth. Is it mere superstition that's been debunked by modern technology and understanding?

In Indian Buddhist literature, the great siddhas, like Nāgārjuna, are said to have traveled to other continents by paranormal means. The Pāli canon describes a great famine during the Buddha's time. In response, his preeminent disciple Maudgalyāyana, whom the Buddha called foremost among the disciples in his accomplishment of siddhis, offered to transport the entire saṅgha to the northern continent of Uttara Kuru, where food was bountiful. But the Buddha rejected his offer (without questioning his ability to perform the service he offered), and the saṅgha survived the famine unharmed.

When I was studying in Dharamsala in the early 1970s, I learned something interesting about Uttara Kuru, one of the four continents, or world sectors, that surround Mt. Meru, according to Buddhist cosmology. My sister's husband was engaged in graduate studies in solar physics at UCLA, and the two of them traveled to Connecticut for the best view of a solar eclipse. At that time, my Tibetan language teacher, Tenzin Trinley, was a Tibetan astrologer who could make very accurate predictions of solar and lunar eclipses. With no access to Western sources, he mentioned to me that his calculations, based on the *Kālacakra Tantra*, indicated that there would be a full solar eclipse on the very same day predicted by modern astronomy. He added that this would be visible from the northern continent of Uttara Kuru, but not from the southern continent of Jambudvīpa, where India is located.

Consider the possibility that in the classical Buddhist explanation, the Earth's axis corresponds spatially to Mt. Meru. India and Central Asia would then correspond to the southern continent; North and South America, to the northern continent; Europe and Africa, to the western continent; and the Pacific and Australian region, to the eastern continent. But to my knowledge there is no mention in the ancient scriptures of people actually traveling on foot or by sea to the other continents surrounding Mt. Meru. Their technology centered on the dhyānas of the form realm, and they were traveling via samādhi. From those methods of investigation came the description of Mt. Meru and the four continents. Different perspectives may give rise to completely different truths, which are incompatible but complementary (like the wave-particle duality of light), while they are all equally empty of any independent, objective reality.

Here's another example. According to the *Kālacakra Tantra*, toward the end of the Buddha's life, the King of Shambhala and his entourage traveled to India to request the Buddha's teachings on this tantra. He gave them empowerment and teachings, and they returned to Shambhala, where these teachings were preserved; but they were unknown elsewhere until 1,500 years later, when they were first revealed in India. For hundreds of years, Tibetans and Mongolians have prayed to be reborn in Shambhala, which is so conducive to practicing the *Kālacakra Tantra* that, even though it is still a human realm, it is regarded as a pure land.[211] Here, enlightenment is said to be swiftly achieved. Nine hundred and sixty million households are reported to populate Shambhala, so it can't be located in Tibet. Where might Shambhala be found? Is it merely a myth?

In the Gobi desert of Mongolia there is a monastery called Khamaryn Khiid, founded in 1821 by the Mongolian yogin Danzan Ravjaa, who was an adept of both Kālacakra and Dzokchen. He called it a portal to Shambhala. Several years ago, I visited it with my wife, Prof. Vesna Wallace, who has translated major portions of the *Kālacakra Tantra* and its principal commentary, written, according to tradition, by one of the kings of Shambhala. A trail meanders off into the barren, red moonscape of the desert, but it is said that if one has purified one's mind and thereby one's vision of reality and follows this trail, one will arrive at Shambhala. If one's vision is not pure, one will be lost in the Gobi desert. With pure vision, you might encounter the vast population of Shambhala in the middle of the Gobi desert. But neither Shambhala nor the Gobi is inherently real.

> **Sentient beings become deluded by holding that solely from their own perspective there are no beings or appearances apart from themselves, and then mistakenly reifying appearances.**

It is solipsism to think that everything is merely your own subjective perceptions, or appearances, and equally delusional to think that appearances correspond to truly existent external objects.

> **So observe that tendency within your own mind! When the teachings of the Buddha degenerate, blind sentient beings establish emptiness merely by coming to the conclusion that although the physical worlds and their sentient inhabitants do not exist from one's own perspective, they do exist autonomously from their own side. From that conclusion, there are very few who identify the ultimate path of emptiness, so carefully examine the nature of this crucial point.**

It is incorrect to imagine that your own subjective perceptions are nonexistent, but that the sun is definitely located in the center of our solar system, the moon rotates about the earth, and the Gobi is a real desert. The delegitimization of subjective perceptions and the reification of material objects are the primary postulates of scientific materialism today: subjective perception is fantasy, but the objective physical world is real. Yet the Lake-Born Vajra is warning our own inner Faculty of Appearances not to fall into exactly this kind of thinking.

> Again Faculty of Appearances asked, "O Teacher, Bhagavān, if someone ascertains emptiness in terms of such nonexistence, doesn't that person have to ascertain that experiences of joy and sorrow and of moving from one place to another within the realms of the phenomenal world do not exist either? Teacher, please explain!"
>
> He replied, "O Faculty of Appearances, throughout beginningless lifetimes, such a great sentient being has never revolved within the three realms of saṃsāra. Although he may have traveled widely from one region to another, he does not exist. His eyes do not see the slightest trace of form. His ears have never heard even the sound of an echo, nor has his nose detected odors, his tongue experienced tastes, or his body felt tactile sensations. He has never taken even a single step in the three realms of saṃsāra. He has never exerted the slightest bit of effort toward making a living. He does not sit or rise, nor does he ever move any of his limbs. Know with certainty that he has never been subject to the experiences of birth, youth, adulthood, old age, illness, death, and so forth."

This is ontological shock therapy, like shaking awake someone who's suffering a nightmare: "What you're experiencing is not real. Wake up!"

From the Teacher's perspective of pristine awareness—like one who is awake within a dream—no truly existent person has ever transmigrated from one life to another. Dream forms and dream eyes are equally nonexistent, as are all other sense objects and faculties. From the perspective of one who has woken up, all the people, perceptions, actions, and experiences in the dream never occurred, just as from the perspective of Samantabhadra, sentient beings have never really existed.

> Again Faculty of Appearances asked, "O Teacher, Bhagavān, I can still certainly ascertain this beginningless and endless delusion, and there is surely much wandering about in saṃsāra."

The *Heart Sutra* says that from the perspective of realizing emptiness there is no form, no feeling, and no consciousness, but here the Faculty of Appearances reasserts his familiar perspective. All these phenomena certainly do exist, and we are obviously wandering in saṃsāra.

> "Moreover, countries are seen with the eyes, sounds and voices are heard with the ears, various odors are detected with the nose, and things that are experienced as the many kinds of tastes are also seen directly with the eyes. Ultimately, things are taken in hand, eaten, and tasted. All gentle and rough tactile sensations are experienced with the body. We do move around on the ground with our legs, and the phenomena of birth, aging, sickness, and death are incontrovertible. Moreover, people do try to make a living by moving about and exerting themselves. Why do you say that these don't exist? Teacher, please explain!"

Observe that anyone in a nonlucid dream would share these same observations about dream phenomena, equally certain that these phenomena are real.

> He replied, "O Faculty of Appearances, you do not travel from one region in a dream to somewhere else in the waking state. Rather, appearances simply shift, so to speak. Although you may have seen a country in a dream, upon looking for it today, not even a trace of it can be seen. While a variety of sounds, voices, smells, tastes, and different sorts of tactile sensations may have appeared in the dream, if you look for them today, you find the ears hear their own sounds and the nose detects

its own smells; and the tongue experiences its own tastes, other than which you have never tasted a single bite of food."

Whether in the dream state or in the waking state, all the sensations you perceive arise only from your own substrate. They don't arise from some separate, inherently existent reality. All apparent phenomena are your own perceptions.

> Although you may dream of traveling around a country on foot, you never take a single step.

Imagine undertaking a very long journey within a nonlucid dream, your feet dragging and body aching with exhaustion. From the perspective of one who is lucid, there is no journey taken, no exertion, and no traveler either. These are all empty appearances, like watching a 3D movie and imagining that you're traveling to another country.

> Although it may seem that you have exerted yourself in various ways to make a living in a dream, by observing your situation today you will see that not even an instant's worth of such work was done.

No matter how exhausting was your day chopping wood in a dream, when you awaken, you realize that everything you worked for was illusory. You accomplished nothing. Your own body was just another illusion. You were not really there.

> Likewise, all the appearances of birth, aging, sickness, death, walking, sitting, and movement are nonexistent. From the very moment that these delusive appearances arise, observe how they are nonobjective, nonabiding, baseless, never occurring, and unborn.

Here are the crucial vipaśyanā instructions. Why are appearances called *delusive*? They mislead us, like a con artist who tricks us into believing a lie. They are deceptive, not existing as they appear to be. Appearances seem to be equally tangible and real in both waking and dream states, but they are not. Examine them closely. Don't take them at face value. Appearances are not objectively real. They are not really located anywhere. They don't arise from some truly existent basis or foundation. They never occur and are never born.

A very effective training for vipaśyanā is to gain experience in lucid dreaming. Even though you know for sure that you're dreaming, appearances still seem to be there, truly existent, with their own inherent identities. How can you realize experientially that although phenomena appear, they don't exist as they appear? Not merely by practicing vipaśyanā in your dreams, any more than a one-year-old baby could learn about the world by pondering in its crib. Children learn by interactive exploration of the world. I witnessed my grandson's discovery of fire, in the form of a small candle on my altar, which he found to be hot!

Upon becoming lucid in a dream, you must actively explore these misleading, deceptive appearances instead of taking them for granted. If you wish to fly, you can do it. Your body is not physical, so you can simply imagine it as a flying body. With a little practice, you can walk through walls. Some people have to run through at first, or slip through backward, but once you get the hang of it, it's easy. You can transform your body from man to woman, adult to child, and human to animal, becoming anything you like.

With increasing experience, you find that there are no limits to what you can do in a lucid dream. You know with certainty that all appearances are malleable, insubstantial, and unreal. The dream is a microcosm, in which you have understood a limited aspect of emptiness. When you become adept at this, you are completely fearless in your dreams. Dream yoga will trigger your most dreaded nightmares. But when they come, you will know that you can transform them in any way you choose, or simply fly away. Ultimately, you will realize that there is no place to fly to, so when your worst nightmare arises, you simply relax into it: "Go ahead, give it your best shot, because nothing here can possibly harm me." Your invulnerability is not due to protective armor but because you have stopped reifying your body and mind and everything else in the dream. This matrix of empty appearances, with one imaginary appearance attacking another, can do no harm. This is vipaśyanā.

> Like these examples, all phenomena are mere appearances—
> they are empty and not established as real.

The Mahāyāna teachings state that an āryabodhisattva, with direct realization of emptiness, can give his own body parts to fulfill the needs of others, just as easily as we might give a vegetable. My own lama, the Ven. Gyatrul Rinpoché, told me that during the Cultural Revolution, one very accomplished Tibetan lama was captured by the communists. They wanted to break his will in order to make an example of him and prove their power over the Tibetans. He was tortured, nailed to a wall, and told to renounce the Buddha. He refused. The lama's disciples were grief-stricken to see his torture and humiliation, and they begged him to say the words that would free him. Nobody would believe it, anyway, they urged. He simply smiled at their request, saying, "How can I renounce the Buddha when I am a buddha?" For him, there was no suffering in an illusory body nailed to an illusory wall. This dream passed. He died in prison.

Another of my beloved lamas, an old friend of Gyatrul Rinpoché who has recently passed away, Ven. Yangthang Rinpoché, was held in a concentration camp for eighteen years, simply for being a great lama. Like the other monks and nuns, he was always on the verge of starvation. It was reported that he drew upon his power of samādhi to manifest food for his cellmates. He would appear outside the prison walls, making the guards scramble to capture and return him; and the next day he'd repeat the game. I heard him say that he experienced greater bliss in prison than most unconfined people ever know. Such accomplishments come about through the practices of śamatha, vipaśyanā, and Dzokchen.

> **Faculty of Appearances objected, "Dreams are not like phenomena in the waking state. Dreams seem to be delusive appearances, whereas phenomena in the waking state appear to be truly existent, stable, and incapable of being influenced by the mind. So how is that? Teacher, please explain!"**

As a faculty of Düdjom Lingpa's mind, Faculty of Appearances asserts what we instinctively assume to be true, which is that dreams are delusive, whereas in the waking state we witness a truly existent reality that is independent of our minds. Dreams are filled with logical inconsistencies, discontinuities, and sheer impossibilities; they are clearly delusive. The real, physical universe, in contrast, obeys the laws of nature.

In fact, such anomalies are keys to becoming lucid in a dream. A crucial aspect of lucid dreaming and dream yoga is developing a type of mindfulness called *prospective memory*. One trains to notice anything odd, under all circumstances. Adopting a critical-reflective attitude, whenever one encounters any kind of anomaly throughout the day and night, one asks, "*How* odd is this? Might I be dreaming right now?" Then one conducts what's known as a *reality check*. Here are three such checks: (1) Jump straight up in the air—if you float gently down, it's a dream. (2) Pinch your nose and close your mouth—if you can still breathe, it's a dream. (3) Read something, put it aside, then read it again—if the words have changed, it's a dream.

As with any skill, lucid dreaming abilities vary greatly. Some people are gifted, and this ability comes naturally to them, without training. But like most skills, anyone can have some experience of becoming lucid in a dream if they persist in effective practices to arouse such lucidity. If you generally can't remember your dreams, then even if you do have a lucid one, you probably won't remember it when you wake up. So develop dream recall, which also involves prospective memory. Fall asleep with this strong resolve: "Tonight I will certainly experience dreams, and I will recall them when I wake up." Here's a second key resolution: "When I first awake in the morning, I will remain absolutely still, not opening my eyes or moving at all." Then, when you first begin to awaken, try to recall exactly where you just were in the dream, and see if you can slip back into it. You may be able to reenter the dream while maintaining lucidity. But even if not, keep trying to retrace the sequence of your dreams. Keeping a dream journal is very helpful for developing the habit of dream recall. With a critical-reflective attitude, conduct reality checks throughout the day. Sooner or later, this habit will carry over into your dreams. Whenever you see something odd, conduct a reality check, and see whether you are dreaming.

> He responded, "O Faculty of Appearances, from the time this body of yours first appeared up until you recall them in your mind, there have been all kinds of waking appearances of working, finding employment, acquiring things, striving, and perceiving sensory objects. Where are they all now? What aims and tasks have been accomplished?"

How substantial are all the memories you hold of your experiences? Are memories of dreams and memories of waking experiences different or the same? The teachings concerning renunciation are a central finding of such investigations. At the end of your life, is there really any difference between your remembered life and a remembered dream?

> "Identify what is truly existent! Likewise, examine the ways in which they are and are not comparable to dream appearances. See whether or not there are differences between these two in terms of their duration and quantity."

If something were truly existent, it would be durable, unchanging over time. Both dream and waking appearances, on the other hand, are ephemeral and not as different as we habitually assume. Sometimes we have dreams in which it seems that a very long time has passed, or that there are innumerably many detailed experiences that follow one another in close succession. Is there anything about dream life that is necessarily shorter or less complex than waking life?

> There is no way to distinguish between saṃsāra and nirvāṇa apart from the presence and absence of delusion.

Bear in mind that nirvāṇa is equivalent to emptiness and the dharmadhātu. One who realizes nirvāṇa sees reality as it is. One who is caught up in saṃsāra is living in conditions much like a nonlucid dream; even while enjoying the best of life's circumstances, one is fundamentally deluded.

> If you take dreams to be delusive and unreal, and waking appearances to be nondelusive and real, do you think you are an undeluded buddha during the daytime and a deluded sentient being while dreaming?

This is a widespread assumption. Many people assume that in waking life, reality is perceived as it is. Dreams, on the other hand, are dismissed as the delusions of a confused mind. Many people believe that "normal" is as good as it gets. Until the recent emergence of positive psychology, possibilities for developing exceptional skills related to attention, compassion, empathy, mindfulness, and lucid dreaming were not a focus of scientific interest. As long as you're normal, it was assumed that our perceptions of the world are generally valid. Even when scientists study advanced meditators, there seems to be little appreciation for the extraordinary insights these adepts have gained through their contemplative training, many of which challenge the very foundations of modern psychology. Instead, their behavior, brain scans, and survey responses are analyzed and distilled into the "objective" data required of scientific studies. In the majority of meditation research conducted thus far, meditators are treated as subjects of experimentation rather than as experimental partners in a joint quest for knowledge. Until now scientists have displayed little interest in understanding the conceptual frameworks, observational methods, and results that have been developed and practiced by contemplatives over millennia. But change is in the air.

> **If so, saṃsāra and nirvāṇa would trade places in a single day, so there would certainly be no hope for either of them.**

If this were the case, you'd experience nirvāṇa during the daytime and saṃsāra at night, alternating uncontrollably, with no hope of escape from the cycle.

> **On the other hand, if you think they are both delusive but there is truth and falsity within each delusion, there is no reason to distinguish between delusive appearances.**

Perhaps you imagine that appearances in dreams are relatively more delusive, and daytime appearances less delusive; but if all appearances are mixtures of truth and falsity, they aren't really different at all.

> **Delusive appearances are so designated because something that is not so is taken to be so. In your dreams do you think, "This is a dream and this is delusive" without making any distinction between truth and falsehood?**

In the context of the dream, you may make correct or incorrect observations. Similarly, in the context of waking experience, you may make valid observations and form logical conclusions, or invalid and illogical ones. This is true even in science, which generally assumes that a real world exists out there and therefore that the scientist's task is to represent this preexisting truth with theories and data. But the measurement systems employed may be accurate or skewed, precise or unreproducible. The data collection and analysis may be rigorous or sloppy. Consequently, the results may be valid or not. How can we validate our observations?

According to the Madhyamaka view, if our perceptions cannot be validated with reference to an objective reality that exists in and of itself, how can we determine whether or not our observations are valid? The Tibetan master Tsongkhapa proposed three criteria for establishing the conventional existence of deceptive phenomena:

> How does one determine whether something exists conventionally? We hold that something exists conventionally (1) if it is known to a conventional consciousness; (2) if no other conventional valid cognition contradicts its being as it is thus known; and (3) if reason that accurately analyzes reality—that is, analyzes whether something intrinsically exists—does not contradict it. We hold that what fails to meet these three criteria does not exist.[212]

His Holiness the Dalai Lama has commented that these three criteria for existence can be understood as follows: (1) Something is known to worldly convention (i.e., commonly agreed upon as existing in the first place). (2) The known phenomenon should not be invalidated by any other valid cognition, which may include one's own subsequent cognitions. For example, you may perceive something and think it to be the case, but your subsequent perception of the phenomenon may ultimately invalidate it as a false perception. Similarly, it could be invalidated by valid cognitions of a third person. (3) The known phenomenon must not be invalidated by ultimate analysis.[213]

Regarding the second criterion for existence, since the dawn of the scientific revolution, as we have seen, Eurocentric civilization has focused primarily on improving third-person, scientific methods for enhancing valid cognition with progress in technology and scientific reasoning, and has paid almost no attention to improving first-person modes of perception, including introspection. As a result, virtually all progress in understanding the natural world has been confined to the third-person investigations of objective, physical, quantifiable phenomena, to the exclusion of all subjective, nonphysical, qualitative phenomena. This has produced a profoundly unbalanced understanding of reality as a whole, in which subjective experience has been marginalized or deleted from our understanding of the universe.

What is needed is a rigorous discipline for examining and exploring the nature, origins, and potentials of the mind through refined, sophisticated direct observation, which has been the hallmark of empiricism in all other branches of science. As noted previously, William James embraced this ideal when he declared that for the scientific study of the mind, introspective observation is what we have to rely on first and foremost and always. But the subjective nature of such first-person inquiry—in contrast to the third-person, objective perspective of all other branches of science—has been a stumbling block for the mind sciences over the past century. Tsongkhapa's three criteria for determining whether an observation of any kind is valid are extremely relevant here, along with James's statement that intersubjective consensus can be gained regarding introspective discoveries about the mind, with the final consensus being achieved through a process of "later views correcting earlier ones, until at last the harmony of a consistent system is reached."[214]

While the tremendous successes of the natural sciences have been based on objective, third-person observations, discoveries in mathematics, the logical foundation of science, are—like discoveries made through introspective, contemplative inquiry—based on subjective, first-person inquiry. Mathematicians evaluate, verify, and disprove each other's discoveries through intersubjective investigation: they don't attempt to validate them relative to some independent, objective reality.

A prime example of such consensual, intersubjective verification occurred with the recent discovery of a proof for Fermat's Last Theorem. Pierre de Fermat (1607–65), one of the world's greatest mathematicians, claimed to have proved that the equation $a^n + b^n = c^n$ has no whole number solutions when n is greater than 2, but his proof was never found. Later generations of mathematicians tried and failed to demonstrate a general proof, which is why it became known as Fermat's Last Theorem, namely, the last one to be proven. It was almost universally considered by contemporary mathematicians to be virtually impossible to prove.

Andrew Wiles first encountered the Last Theorem as a ten-year-old, and he spent the next thirty years working on the problem. When he eventually discovered a possible strategy for a proof, he worked in secrecy for seven years before revealing it. Wiles announced his proof on June 23, 1993, at a lecture in Cambridge entitled "Elliptic Curves and Galois Representations." In September 1993, the Princeton mathematician Nick Katz was appointed as one of the referees to review Wiles's manuscript. In the course of his review, he asked Wiles a series of clarifying questions that led Wiles to recognize that his proof contained a critical omission. One year later, on September 19, 1994, Wiles had a revelation that he would call "the most important moment of [his] working life, so indescribably beautiful . . . so simple and so elegant," and this insight allowed him to correct the proof to the satisfaction of the mathematical community.[215] The resulting proof, which is over 150 pages long, was published in May 1995. Wiles's success was such a major achievement that it resulted in awards, including the King Faisal International Prize (£140,000), the Wolf Prize (£70,000), a knighthood, and the Abel Prize for 2016 (£500,000).[216]

This historical example of intersubjective repudiation and verification illustrates William James's point that only a later consensus, based upon refinement of earlier views, can safeguard against the inherent difficulty and fallibility of introspective observation. When the scientific community fully recognizes the validity of this approach for the first-person contemplative investigation of the nature, origins, and potentials of the mind, contemplative science can be fully embraced within the context of the natural sciences as a whole. The implications of the inclusion of first-person empiricism in the natural sciences are bound to be far-reaching. As James declared, "Let empiricism once become associated with religion, as hitherto, through some strange misunderstanding, it has been associated with irreligion, and I believe that a new era of religion as well as philosophy will be ready to begin. . . . I fully believe that such an empiricism is a more natural ally than dialectics ever were, or can be, of the religious life."[217]

FATHOMING APPEARANCES

As difficult as it may seem to achieve verification and consensus concerning the nature of such subjective, nonphysical phenomena as the mind, awareness, and consciousness, it is not impossible. If we wish to make progress in this field comparable to the great advances achieved in the rest of the natural sciences, we should follow the lead of those other disciplines by directly observing the phenomena—in this case mental phenomena—that we seek to understand. We cannot succumb to materialist dogma that delegitimizes them—refusing even to look through the mind's telescope.

In determining the validity of dreaming and waking appearances, the Teacher asserts that we cannot simply dismiss dreams as delusional while reifying waking phenomena as truly existent—because actual observation reveals them to be equivalent as self-deceptions.

> "Is there no hatred toward your enemies, attachment to your friends, hope for good things, or fear of bad things? On the contrary, if you grasp and cling to the reality of good and bad, joy and sorrow, and all sensory objects during the waking state, and do the same for dream appearances as if they were waking appearances, then you are deceiving yourself. Presented with misleading appearances and mindsets, you cling to their reality and deceive yourself. Examine how this happens!"

The truth is that we almost always fail to question the reality of appearances in dream and waking states alike. In both cases, we deceive ourselves by reifying other people, joys, sorrows, and all phenomena, along with ourselves. Our friends, enemies, hopes, and fears in dreams are quite different from those in waking experience, but we fail to notice these inconsistencies. By clinging to the reality of ephemeral appearances, we delude ourselves and revolve endlessly in saṃsāra.

It should be clear by now that vipaśyanā is not a practice of simply observing with bare attention, but of probing deeply into the nature of appearances and their correspondence—or lack of correspondence—with reality.

> "O Faculty of Appearances, the appearance of going in all the different directions arises due to the power of conceptualization. From the mere appearance of taking one step after another, various indeterminate images of form and the like emerge from the space of awareness and at the same time [others] disappear back into the space of awareness."

In both dream and waking states, the power of conceptualization creates the framework for all experiences. In both cases, when you experience moving from one place to another, your perceptions include forms and other sensory objects that appear to awareness and then disappear, and this is interpreted as traveling. But from the perspective of the waking state, there is no real motion in the dream. And from the perspective of emptiness, there is no real motion in the waking state either.

"With regard to mountains and valleys, homes, possessions, and everything else—what appeared formerly vanishes as the later instances arise, but you do not arrive at the subsequent ones by leaving the former behind somewhere."

Those former appearances were never truly existent. They weren't there before you came along, and they won't remain after you pass by. But we grasp to them, imagining that all the changing appearances we perceive in passing are truly existent phenomena. In fact, all appearances freshly arise from and then dissolve back into the substrate, during both dream and waking states.

"Know that simply by opening and closing the eyes, all appearances dissolve into the space of awareness and subsequent ones emerge."

As mentioned earlier, each sentient being abides in the center of his or her unique world, or maṇḍala. If you were to follow the Buddhist path through all the stages of attainment, or grounds (Skt. *bhūmi*), you'd be very close to buddhahood as an āryabodhisattva on the tenth ground. No matter where others might locate you, from your own perspective, your location would be the highest pure land of Akaniṣṭha. This is the center of your maṇḍala.

In a dream, there is only one maṇḍala, with one center and one dreamer. There are no other observers. A lucid dreamer may close his eyes, whereupon the dream collapses and everyone in the dreamscape vanishes; still nobody is harmed, because everything is a creation of his substrate. In waking life, we share experiences and karma, closely similar sensory faculties, and common conceptual frameworks. We abide in the centers of our own maṇḍalas, which overlap and interact with others' maṇḍalas. When we close our eyes, other participants continue to see from their own perspectives. But no one looks out to perceive a truly existent world.

Faculty of Appearances responded, "I think these phenomena that appear right here are none other than all the people, places, and regions that were already present, and furthermore, they appear to the sense faculties. I don't think the later ones emerged after the earlier ones had disappeared into the space of awareness. The way that all appearing phenomena

> exist and the way they manifest invariably seems to be of one
> taste. But how do they exist? Teacher, please explain!"

Psychologists refer to *object permanence* as the understanding that objects continue to exist even when they cannot be observed. The Swiss developmental psychologist Jean Piaget (1896–1980) first studied the development of this understanding in human infants, whose behavior at an early age is consistent with "out of sight, out of mind." By about the age of two, they develop awareness that objects persist even when hidden. Piaget held that this ability is a key stage of human development. Subsequent studies have demonstrated the development of object permanence in many other animals. The belief that all the objects we perceive are truly existent, and independent of us, is very deeply ingrained. Faculty of Appearances has tenaciously expressed this belief that everything exists just as it appears.

> He replied, "O Faculty of Appearances, it's not like that. Do
> you believe the rainbow that appeared in the sky earlier and
> the one that appears today are identical? Do you think the
> clouds, mist, thunder, rain, and wind that occurred in the sky
> previously are the same as such events today? Do you believe
> that the appearances of your body and all sensory objects in
> a dream are identical to those in the waking state? If you do,
> examine where they all abide when they are not appearing.
> There would not be the slightest distinction in terms of how
> the form, shape, or color of any of them exists."

All phenomena, whether in the dream or waking state, have precisely the same ontological status: they are empty appearances to awareness. This nature is not easy to recognize because we are so accustomed to the idea of object permanence. If we didn't reify phenomena so instinctively, everyone would readily realize the truth of emptiness. In vipaśyanā, we are challenged to find the attributes of objects that exist when nobody is looking. But their shapes, colors, smells, sounds, and all other perceived characteristics arise only in dependence upon our sensory faculties. Such perceptions, or qualia, do not exist independently of a perceiver. Nevertheless, we instinctively assume that there must be a real attribute-bearer out there that corresponds to our perceptions in here. We must realize that nothing exists from its own side—while simultaneously avoiding the extreme of nihilism, the false conclusion that nothing exists at all.

> "Do you believe the people and animals that appear in the waking state are identical to, and thus in no way different from, those in a dream? If you think they are the same, you should recognize the obvious signs of their dissimilarity. For instance, in the waking state people may appear to be ill, be struck by weapons, and perish, but not in the dream state; and the various appearances of places and regions—land being destroyed, mountains crumbling—are also different."

Many years ago, Steven LaBerge and I led a lucid dreaming and dream yoga workshop in which this became very clear. One attendee, who was wheelchair-bound with continuous, debilitating pain, was able to have lucid dreams at will. She was so adept at shape-shifting that she could adopt virtually any form she liked. In one lucid dream that she shared with us, she transformed herself into a phonograph record. When circling endlessly became boring, she turned into a butterfly and flew away, a metamorphosis of suffering into liberation. Her waking appearances were of constant suffering, but in her dreams she saw this illusory reality as it is and was free.

> "You are deluded in regarding as permanent all the nonexistent, unestablished phenomena that appear."

To regard phenomena as permanent means to reify them. In a nonlucid dream we take appearances to be real, thereby subjecting ourselves to much unnecessary suffering. Likewise, we take waking appearances to be real phenomena. In both cases we are fundamentally deluded about the nature of appearances, and the result of suffering is the same.

> "In reality they are unestablished, impermanent, and mutable; and from the very moment they merely appear, they are empty and without objective existence. Knowledge of this state is the quintessence of all the tantras, oral transmissions, and pith instructions. So fathom this!"

The seeds of the teachings on emptiness are clearly found in the Pāli canon, although they had not yet blossomed into the elaborate gardens of the Mahāyāna. Within the Pāli canon, the Buddha simply refers to phenomena as "signless," which means that they have no intrinsic characteristics. Yet the emptiness of phenomena is a common thread running throughout all the Buddhist vehicles, including Dzokchen. If the emptiness of inherent nature is an invariant truth, then the more rigorously we investigate and penetrate phenomena, using finely honed attentional skills and sharp intelligence, the clearer this should become.

Among all the natural sciences, which are generally focused upon the external world, the one with the most advanced insights into the nature of matter and energy is physics. And within physics, the discipline that penetrates most deeply into the nature of the physical constituents of the world is quantum mechanics. It is here, on the cutting edge of science, that the Buddhist teachings on emptiness seem to resonate most profoundly with physical discoveries in the external world. If we probe deeply enough externally, we discover phenomena to be empty of any independent, objective reality. But scientists have not agreed upon any theory of consciousness.

Within Tibetan Buddhism, particularly in Mahāmudrā and Dzokchen, we find profoundly incisive probes into the nature of mind and consciousness. As a result of such persistent, phenomenological investigation, these too are found to be empty of inherent existence. But Buddhism has no theory of the outer world corresponding to that of modern physics. For the first time in history, we have the opportunity to see the world through both of these lenses on reality. Viewing scientific and Buddhist depictions of emptiness with binocular vision, perhaps we can fuse them into a three-dimensional theory of reality.

I do not believe that we need science in order to become enlightened, as the Buddhist teachings have done the job for millennia without science. It's also the case that the greatest discoveries made by Buddhist contemplatives cannot be proven with public, physical evidence. We can read about them and have faith, but there is nothing that compels the average person to accept them as true.

There is an extraordinary documentary video called *The Yogis of Tibet*, in which a very accomplished yogin, Drubwang Konchok Norbu Rinpoché (1921–2007), discusses his meditative practice with rare candor. He said, "When I meditate, I can see all my former lives," and "although I do appear like a human person outwardly, my mental state is so different."[218] Most lamas are not this frank; they're usually quite reluctant to speak publicly about any of their accomplishments. Did the confessions of this highly realized lama in a popular film precipitate a revolution in modern psychology? No, not a ripple.

In contrast, when physicists recently announced their discovery of the Higgs boson, there was a tsunami of media coverage and public interest. The difference is that the physicists' physical evidence was peer-reviewed and documented, yielding scientific, consensual knowledge, even though almost no nonscientist could actually understand it. The yogin's discoveries constitute private knowledge of nonphysical realities. But if something is true and has great implications for humanity, it should be known by as many people as possible. Understanding the nature of the substrate consciousness, primordial consciousness, and emptiness is far too important to keep private. The damage inflicted by materialist ideology is so serious that we need more than criticism—we need an antidote. The universal antidote to our fundamental misapprehension of reality is the realization of emptiness.

The Point of Realizing the Emptiness of Phenomena

Why must we strive so diligently to realize the emptiness of all phenomena, the truth that they lack inherent existence? We might be tempted to conclude that emptiness is an abstract concern of interest only to philosophers. Does our habit of reification really matter in daily life?

Here's a very practical tip. Whenever a mental affliction arises, whether it's directed toward another person or an inanimate object, the Buddhist assertion is that reification is at work. Without it, no mental affliction will manifest. When you reify an object, you grasp to it mentally by carving away everything that is not the object. Severing connections and ignoring dependencies, you elevate your object as a distinct, independent entity. This becomes most obvious when another person is involved, and the affliction is one of anger or desire. We may perceive a person as a wicked criminal or a loving friend, but what exactly constitutes this objectified person? A body or a mind? Permanent or impermanent? Arising in dependence on causes and conditions or independently? Likewise, if we occasionally feel high self-esteem, arrogance, and pride, while at other times we feel distinctly inferior, what exactly is this fickle self? If we examine closely, no independent self will be found. The way to demolish grasping to true existence is by investigating and precisely understanding dependent origination.

> Faculty of Appearances then commented, "In that case, all phenomena appear even though they are nonexistent. But even if one ascertains that all appearing phenomena have always been empty in this way, I don't see any point in determining it. After all, that fact is empty of itself, so I think that's enough. Is that so? Teacher, please explain!"
>
> He replied, "O Faculty of Appearances, all beings are identityless, without objective existence, and of the nature of emptiness. However, by failing to recognize this, beings wander endlessly in the three realms of saṃsāra, clinging to true existence. Establishing such nonexistence as the nature of emptiness, realizing it as it is, and causing this state to become manifest is the essential nature of meditation and the authentic path, the supreme quintessence of the teachings, oral transmissions, and pith instructions of the perfect Buddha. So know this!"

This is the central theme in Mahāyāna Buddhism. As Śāntideva says in *A Guide to the Bodhisattva Way of Life*, the perfections of generosity, ethics, patience, enthusiasm, and meditation are all to be accomplished for the sake of the perfection of wisdom.[219] There are many kinds of wisdom, but the perfection of wisdom is the realization of emptiness.

> If it is not realized, emptiness is reduced to an ethically neutral state that neither benefits nor harms. Knowledge of the nature of emptiness is the great wisdom of realizing identitylessness, which is the essential nature of all the grounds and paths.

If emptiness is treated as an intellectual abstraction, without ethical consequences, there will be no benefit and no enlightenment. The grounds and paths are described differently in various Buddhist vehicles. In the Mahāyāna, there are five bodhisattva paths: (1) the path of the accumulation of merit, which entails the achievement of śamatha, bodhicitta, and the initial conceptual realization of identitylessness; (2) the path of preparation, which entails a deepening realization of emptiness and bodhicitta; (3) the path of seeing, which occurs when a bodhisattva first has a direct, nonconceptual realization of emptiness, corresponding to the first āryabodhisattva ground, the Very Joyous; (4) the path of meditation, during which afflictive and cognitive obscurations are purified, corresponding to the second through tenth grounds; and (5) the path of no more training, where vajra-like samādhi leads to the full enlightenment of a buddha on the eleventh ground, Universal Radiance. The central themes common to all these grounds and paths are the realization of emptiness and bodhicitta.

> Faculty of Appearances then asked, "Even though all phenomena of the appearing worlds are perfectly empty, the mere realization of this doesn't cause them to become nonexistent. So couldn't it be that physical or verbal virtues surpass this realization? Teacher, please explain the meaning here."

Even if it's true that all phenomena are empty, perhaps realizing this is not so important; it won't change the world. It might be better to engage in physical and verbal virtues, such as prostrations and recitations, or throwing ourselves into humanitarian work and philanthropy. This attitude is like accepting the findings of quantum mechanics as true, while thinking that this truth has no impact on one's daily life. In fact, the discoveries of quantum mechanics have enabled many of today's ubiquitous technologies, including transistors, lasers, LEDs, atomic clocks for GPS navigation, and MRI scanners for medical imaging. New developments in quantum computing and cryptography promise dramatic performance gains over classical methods. In parallel fashion, directly realizing emptiness and the *ultimate* nature of reality will transform one's life so profoundly as to be inexpressible.

> The Bhagavān replied, "Don't think like that. Even if you spent your entire life practicing virtues that exist deceptively, such as prostrations and circumambulations with your body and mere oral recitations with your mouth, how could liberation ever be achieved? Since you won't become liberated even by such mental virtues as meditating on a deity, cultivating the dhyānas, or merely recognizing your thoughts, what's the

point of frustrating yourself by thinking that liberation won't be attained simply by knowing emptiness? If you think that, you are obscured by a great darkness of stupidity and foolishness, and your eye of wisdom with which to investigate the nature of existence of all phenomena is blinded."

Physical and verbal practices alone are inadequate, and you won't become liberated even by practicing mental virtues like Vajrayāna deity meditation, śamatha, or settling the mind in its natural state. However, if these practices are fused with the realization of emptiness, then you are definitely on the path to liberation. Merely recognizing thoughts with bare awareness means nothing—unless you realize the empty nature of those thoughts.

Faculty of Appearances is seeking the benefits of realizing emptiness in the wrong place. One's realization of emptiness doesn't magically change the outer world. For example, the Buddha's disciple Maudgalyāyana was beaten to death despite his exceptional supernormal abilities. Having committed in a previous life the deed of killing his parents, known as one of the five deeds of immediate retribution, he knew he could not avoid the weighty consequences. His realization of identitylessness didn't negate his karma.

> Faculty of Appearances asked, "Nowadays some people venture into meditation and strive in practice, and some masters acquire knowledge through the teachings, tantras, oral transmissions, and pith instructions of the Buddha and through their own training, yet they do not succeed in meditation or realization. Each must judge this for himself. After passing through many pleasant and difficult stages, there are people who finally identify some degree of knowledge and claim it to be authentic. Are such claims true or not? Teacher, please explain!"

Padmasambhava states explicitly that these Great Perfection teachings are taught to benefit future disciples, who will fathom the essential points and vanquish all doubts.[220] And Düdjom Lingpa's commentary to *The Sharp Vajra of Conscious Awareness Tantra* describes these teachings as an inheritance granted so that many people in the future will achieve liberation by depending upon this path.[221] These concerns voiced by Faculty of

Appearances are shared by many contemporary practitioners. Do people today practice these teachings successfully and attain authentic knowledge and realization, as described in the ancient scriptures and commentaries? There are many who practice recitations and visualizations, but far fewer earnestly devote themselves to rigorous, sustained training in śamatha and vipaśyanā. Some practice Vajrayāna meditations intensively in retreats for three years and longer. But have their practices degenerated into shallow and ineffective rituals, or do people still succeed in meditation and attain the same realization as all the bodhisattvas and buddhas of the past?

> He replied, "O Faculty of Appearances, the buddhas have taught that all phenomena, ranging from form up to the omniscient mind, are of the nature of emptiness. They have taught the characteristics of all phenomena because yogins must know and realize them. The path of their followers accords with this, so it is crucial for that path to conform to all the tantras, oral transmissions, and pith instructions as well. For beginningless eons, beings have failed to discover the path by themselves, and they have been deluded by clinging to the experiences of a constant stream of joyful and painful appearances. If they still fail to conform to the teachings, tantras, oral transmissions, and pith instructions of the buddhas, they will not discover the grounds and paths to liberation on their own. And the appearances of pleasant and painful sensations make their claim to having attained the state of omniscience like that of asserting the horns of a hare. Know that their speech is very stupid and foolish, and their words indicate a lack of investigation, analysis, and realization."

The point of these teachings is not merely to believe, study, analyze, or even teach them—but to realize them. To follow any path that comports with the teachings of the Buddha, it's essential to realize the meaning of emptiness.

I have found writings by Western philosophers such as Hilary Putnam that resonate quite strongly with the Buddhist teachings on emptiness, and quantum cosmology seems remarkably congruent with Buddhist explanations of the ultimate nature of reality. Yet we have seen that most of the sophisticated theories about physical phenomena developed by our leading scientists and philosophers are framed as intricate interactions of matter and energy. They typically ignore the importance of mind and awareness, or dismiss them as emergent phenomena, mere artifacts of physical processes in the brain. No development of morality, emotional balance, mental stability, or attentional refinement is considered necessary for a career in science or philosophy. The trend of modernity offers no path to liberation from inner human suffering, dismissing such notions in favor of economic growth and better consumer goods.

Sentient beings have a hard time finding the path to enlightenment on our own. We spend our lives chasing after desirables and trying to avoid undesirables. Someone who has ingested poison is not in a good position to discover the antidote. This is why the Buddha revealed not only the teachings on emptiness but also the path that leads to realization and liberation.

Just as Einstein and his fellow scientists called for a new type of thinking to defuse the threat of nuclear annihilation, the Buddha called for a realization of emptiness to liberate the mind and extinguish the suffering of saṃsāra. The path he described leads to the realization of emptiness and direct, nonconceptual knowledge of the ultimate nature of reality. Hence the importance of taking refuge in the Buddha, Dharma, and Saṅgha, as well as refuge in one's Guru, without whom we will continue to wander in the vast, endless reaches of saṃsāra. Enlightenment is not something we can get from a book, seminar, or retreat. We will not realize emptiness by casually sampling the Dharma, indulging our likes and dislikes as if choosing flavors of ice cream.

> **Faculty of Appearances then asked, "Even though I know that phenomena are empty due to their nonexistence, anxiety and fear still arise when things happen such as being attacked by others, falling over a cliff, or being assaulted with water, fire, or weapons; and experiences such as pain, illness, loss, and regret do occur. So it seems to me they must exist. Please explain how this happens."**

A merely intellectual grasp of emptiness is no match for our deeply ingrained habits of reification. The phenomena we encounter in our daily lives continue to appear as tangible, independent, and real, and they have real consequences. Even if we experience profound insights in our formal meditation practice, these are all too easily lost in the thick of worldly engagements. If all phenomena are empty, why do they still seem to exist and bear the same consequences?

> He replied, "O Faculty of Appearances, when appearances arise such as an attacker beating you with a weapon or a stick, or frightening situations occur involving water, fire, or a cliff, sensations of suffering and pain certainly arise due to dualistic grasping."

We habitually blame all our suffering on such things as bad people, weapons, fires, floods, earthquakes, microbes, accidents, genetic mutations, prejudice, and luck. But in all cases, one primary cause is responsible: grasping to subjects and objects as inherently different. Virtually anything can make us suffer, but we are vulnerable only because of grasping. Even the buddhas cannot eradicate the power of sentient beings' karma. But liberating the mind from grasping extinguishes all suffering. Stop reifying the subject internally. Stop reifying the object externally. Stop reifying the duality of subject and object. All appearances arise due to dualistic grasping—which is delusional.

> "But in reality there is no injury or entity that inflicts harm. The fires of hell do not burn, pretas are not tormented by hunger or thirst, and *asura*s are not hacked up with weapons of war. Likewise, in terms of phenomena, all misery and pain merely appear; but in terms of emptiness, they are not established as being anything real at all."

From the perspective of emptiness, nothing whatsoever has true, inherent existence, even though everything seems to appear, abide, and disappear, and all the realms of the hells, pretas, and asuras, as well as our own human realm, are equally creations of our own minds.

> "O son of the family, the primordial ground, appearing as space, is apprehended as something other. Once space appears as earth, earth is apprehended as being a real substance. Similarly, space appears as sensory objects such as water, fire, air, and sentient beings, and these appearances are taken to be real things. For example, various reflections of the sun, moon,

planets, stars, and so on appear in the ocean, but they have no existence apart from the ocean. In this way, recognize that everything is subsumed in space itself."

The dharmadhātu, the primordial ground, which we misconstrue as "empty" space, gives rise to all material substances, here collectively called *earth*. Although material objects consist of nothing but space—which is consistent with the quantum mechanical view of matter as a specific configuration of space—we reify material things as having inherent solidity. The same is true for the other classical elements of water, fire, and air, constituting the whole of the external phenomenal world. And it's equally true for sentient beings and our inner phenomenal worlds. All outer and inner phenomena arise from the dharmadhātu, due solely to our dualistic grasping and reification.

The theory that all physical phenomena emerge from space figures prominently in quantum field theory. The physicist Henning Genz states it clearly:

> Real systems are, in this sense, "excitations of the vacuum"— much as surface waves in a pond are excitations of the pond's water . . . the properties of the physical vacuum define the possible excitations—the possible systems that can emerge from the physical vacuum . . . The vacuum in itself is shapeless, but it may assume specific shapes: In so doing, it becomes a physical reality, a "real world."[222]

The science writer K. C. Cole adds, "The closest we can probably come to imagining perfect symmetry is a smooth, timeless, featureless empty space— the proverbial blank slate, the utter silence. It can't be perceived because nothing can change. Everything would be one and the same; everything would be the same, as far as we could tell, as nothing."[223] Using an analogy that is remarkably similar to one found in Dzokchen literature, she writes, "Like water freezing into ice and releasing its energy into its surroundings, the 'freezing' of the vacuum liberates enormous amounts of energy . . . As simply as water freezing into ice, the inflated vacuum froze into the structure that gave rise to quarks, electrons, and eventually us."[224] And the physicist John March-Russell declares, "The current belief is that you have to understand all the properties of the vacuum before you can understand anything else."[225] Finally, on a note that is strikingly reminiscent of the relation between relative space and the dharmadhātu that it conceals, the physicist Steven Weinberg suggests that our vision of the world we see around us is "only an imperfect reflection of a deeper and more beautiful reality."[226]

The Buddhist theory that all the material elements of the universe emerge from space is certainly not unique to Dzokchen. In his book *The Universe in a Single Atom*, His Holiness the Dalai Lama comments that according to the *Kālacakra Tantra*, space is quantized into particles from which all other configurations of matter and energy emerge:

> According to Buddhist cosmology, the world is constructed of the five elements: the supportive element of space, and the four basic elements of earth, water, fire, and air. Space enables the existence and functioning of all the other elements. The Kālachakra system presents space not as a total nothingness, but as a medium of "empty particles" or "space particles," which are thought of as extremely subtle "material" particles. This space element is the basis for the evolution and dissolution of the four elements, which are generated from it and absorbed back into it. The process of dissolution occurs in this order: earth, water, fire, and air. The process of generation occurs in this order: air, fire, water, and earth . . . If we go back to the ultimate cause of the material objects of the world, we arrive finally at the space particles. They precede the big bang (which is to say any new beginning) and are indeed the residue of the preceding universe that has disintegrated. I am told that some cosmologists favor the idea that our universe arose as a fluctuation from what is termed the quantum vacuum. To me, this idea echoes the Kālachakra theory of space particles.[227]

Our final analogy is one of Düdjom Lingpa's favorites, appearing dozens of times in the *Vajra Essence*. To landlocked Tibetans, the ocean is a vast and mysterious expanse that can hold many meanings. In this case, imagine a very calm ocean on a clear night, far from city lights. A seaside cliff is your retreat cave, from where you gaze down upon the reflections in the ocean. The ocean represents the dharmadhātu, in which appear vivid reflections representing objects that seem to be real but have no true existence apart from the ocean. All appearances, internally and externally, manifest like reflections in the ocean of the dharmadhātu. All phenomena emerge from the dharmadhātu, consist of it, and dissolve back into it. They are never anything other than the space of emptiness.

Recounting his pure vision in the opening scene of the *Vajra Essence*, Düdjom Lingpa first uses this same analogy to describe the appearance of the Teacher, Samantabhadra, the Lake-Born Vajra, Guru Padmasambhava, who appears as an eight-year-old youth: "Within the realm of his oceanic, radiant, transparent body, all the peaceful and wrathful buddhas and myriads of buddha fields and emanations naturally appeared, like planets and stars reflected brightly in a lake."

Surrounding the Teacher is an illusorily displayed buddha field and a retinue of 84,000 disciples and bodhisattvas who bow in reverence before the Teacher, when a song of realization spontaneously emerges from pristine space. Here is its final stanza:

> All displays of the buddha field, Teacher, and retinue
> exist not, yet from nonexistence they appear—to exist.
> We sing its praises in awestruck exaltation!

Try to imagine how recognizing the ubiquitous truth of emptiness could lead directly into an experience of transcendent wonder at the mystery of existence itself. How similar or different might this be to the theological idea of "creation out of nothing"? We must leave such vast questions for another exploration, but for now we have been given a completely balanced vision of appearances and emptiness, which in Düdjom Lingpa's revelation will take the disciple straight into a realization of the creative source of all appearances, pristine awareness itself. May you study the whole of this pure vision—granted directly from the enlightened mind of Padmasambhava himself—and then go on to meditate sincerely upon it. Finally, may you arrive at the same realization of emptiness and pristine awareness that all the buddhas have realized, for the infinite benefit of all who still think they are no more than sentient beings.

Epilogue

All of us sentient beings in saṃsāra suffer and wish to be free. But we human beings have exceptional mental abilities of intelligence, memory, language skills, and imagination to enable us to explore the scope of suffering to which we are vulnerable, the true sources of our suffering, the possibility of genuine, lasting freedom, and the way to realize such freedom. But so many of us squander our extraordinary mental gifts by focusing primarily on the pursuit of hedonic satisfaction through the acquisition of material goods, influence, and prestige. In this way, our precious human lives pass by in vain. For many people in our modern world, the meaninglessness of the natural world in general and of human existence in particular is regarded as self-evident. The universe is a mindless machine, and we are biological robots programmed to survive and procreate. This view is said to be supported by scientific evidence. Likewise, the belief that human existence ends in oblivion—the total annihilation of our awareness and personal existence—is accepted by many as an incontrovertible, scientific fact, which only "religious believers" fail to accept. So the cessation of all experience at death is something that we both fear and, at times, quietly, long for. But simply believing something doesn't make it true.

Over the past 150 years, with the domination of science and the media by the unquestioned beliefs of materialism, and the domination of human civilization by materialistic values and consumerism, due to overpopulation and rampant overconsumption (especially by the very wealthy), we are fouling and depleting the entire ecosystem to such an extent that we are rapidly driving other species into extinction and imperiling the survival of our own species. It is well documented that humanity has killed off 50 percent of the wildlife on our planet within just the past forty years, and the trend continues.[228] While human history is filled with the tragic consequences of people justifying the most vicious behavior in the name of religion, materialism threatens to bring human history itself to an untimely and violent end.

We suffer because of the ignorance of not knowing the nature of reality and the delusion of misapprehending the nature of our own existence and of the world around us. Some such delusion we acquire through our social upbringing. Materialism is a primary example. But the deeper delusion, one that we are all born with, is the tendency to reify ourselves as subjects and all other phenomena as objects. All other innate and acquired delusions and their derivative mental afflictions, such as greed and hatred, are based on it.

By using our exceptional capacity of intelligence in the most meaningful ways, we can explore the reality of suffering and the nature of our ordinary consciousness to discover that, as much as we may resist the idea, our own personal suffering does not cease at death. There is no such easy escape from reality. With the penetrating use of our intelligence we may inquire and gain insight into the true sources of our suffering. In so doing, we may discover that the origins of suffering are not inherent to our existence as sentient beings either. True freedom is a possibility. Guided by those who have come before us and found such freedom for themselves, we may then discover the path to liberation and spiritual awakening. This is the meaning of existence.

The Buddha has shown us the way to fulfill our innermost potential, to realize our heart's desire for freedom by coming to know reality as it is. The remedy for ignorance is knowledge, and the methods of inquiry known as vipaśyanā provide the means to gain such insight through deep, experiential realization. It is not enough to listen to lectures on emptiness and dependent origination or to read profound treatises on the nature of existence. We must meditate in order to internalize these truths. But if vipaśyanā is not supported by and integrated with śamatha, the insights it yields will not penetrate to the core of our being and cut the roots of ignorance and delusion from their source. Furthermore, many great yogins of the past have attested that it is difficult or impossible to make progress in the "swift" practices of the stage of generation and completion without already being grounded in the firm stability of mind that is śamatha. As the great Shabkar Tsokdruk Rangdröl (1781–1851) wrote:

The distance covered by a great ship
pulled on land by a hundred men for a hundred days
can be covered in a day when it is put to sea.
In the same way, a single day of meditation
performed with real stability of mind
brings more progress than a hundred days
practicing generation and completion stages
before stability of mind has been attained.[229]

Given the indispensable role that the full achievement of śamatha plays in reaching the path to enlightenment, thus bringing about irreversible purification and transformation of the mind, we may well ask: How long does it take to achieve such sustainable mental balance and what are the necessary conditions for doing so? Buddhist contemplatives have found that śamatha is most effectively attained if one devotes oneself to this practice full-time and continuously until it is fully achieved. In addition, one must see that all the inner and outer prerequisites for such an attainment have been acquired.

While the inner prerequisites are of primary importance, particularly for the cultivation of śamatha, one must also practice in a conducive, supportive environment. This is one that satisfies the following conditions:

+ Your basic necessities, such as food and clothing, are easily obtained.
+ There is no danger from predators, enemies, and so on.
+ Your retreat setting is pleasant and healthy.
+ You share the companionship of other ethical, like-minded people.
+ Your environment is well-situated, such that there are few people about during the daytime and little noise at night.

As for the all-important inner prerequisites, the following qualities have been found to be indispensable:

+ Having few desires for things you don't have.
+ Contentment with what you do have.
+ Having few concerns and activities that may distract you from your śamatha practice.
+ Maintaining pure ethical discipline.

❖ Utterly dispensing with rumination involving desire and so on, not only while in formal meditation but also between sessions.

Particularly within the context of Mahāyana practice, the cultivation of bodhicitta and the first four perfections of generosity, ethics, patience, and enthusiasm are necessary preconditions for achieving the perfection of meditative stabilization, the fifth perfection, which is the final preparation for cultivating the perfection of wisdom through the practice of vipaśyanā.[230] If one has fulfilled all the outer and inner prerequisites for achieving śamatha, Buddhist contemplatives have found that it may be achieved within one year of full-time practice in a suitable environment. But if such prerequisites have not been met, śamatha may never be achieved, no matter how long or how hard you try, as Atīśa warns in his *Lamp for the Path to Enlightenment*: "As long as the conditions for śamatha are incomplete, samādhi will not be accomplished even if you meditate diligently for a thousand years."[231] Finally, since many inner and outer challenges, or "upheavals," are bound to arise in the course of intensive śamatha practice, it is imperative to know how to transform adversity so that it enriches your practice rather than obstructs it. For this, the Tibetan Buddhist practices of "mind training,"[232] such as Atīśa's *Seven-Point Mind Training*, can be wonderfully helpful.[233]

While there is good reason to believe that śamatha has been achieved in one year by traditional Asian Buddhists, is it still feasible for people in today's world—with its materialism, hedonism, and consumerism—to do so? This is a question that can be answered only through experience and only by people who are deeply dedicated to achieving śamatha and proceeding along the path to enlightenment. While we may have faith in the great contemplatives of the past, to know for ourselves whether this path is viable for us in the present, we must also have faith in ourselves. As William James comments, "In what manner do we espouse and hold fast to visions? By thinking a conception *might* be true somewhere, it *may* be true even here and now; it is *fit* to be true and it *ought* to be true; it *must* be true; it *shall* be true for *me*."[234]

In my experience over the past forty-five years, it is very difficult to find a genuinely conducive environment in which one can continue practicing for as long as it takes to achieve śamatha. So I have concluded that it is necessary to create facilities that are specifically designed for such long-term practice. Since very few people with intense dedication to practice are financially independent, it is also necessary to provide financial support for them and, if they are in retreat outside their own homeland, they must be able to acquire long-term, renewable visas. The creation of a worldwide network of such "contemplative observatories" has therefore become one of my highest priorities.

Just as astronomers need observatories and neuroscientists need laboratories to conduct their research, so do contemplatives need supportive environments, companions, and mentors to optimally develop the contemplative technology of śamatha and the contemplative science of vipaśyanā. For their discoveries to gain scientific recognition and public acceptance, these observatories should provide facilities where professionally trained contemplatives fully collaborate with scientists to explore the nature, origins, and potentials of the human mind. In this way, the first-person methods of contemplatives can be thoroughly integrated with the third-person methods of modern science, thus enriching humanity's understanding of our inner potentials. As William James wrote in reference to a future science of religions as he envisioned it, such collaboration between contemplatives and science "can offer mediation between different believers, and help to bring about consensus of opinion."[235] Such an integral contemplative science could earn public acknowledgment comparable to that presently granted to the physical sciences, such that "even the personally nonreligious might accept its conclusions on trust, much as blind persons now accept the facts of optics—it might appear as foolish to refuse them."[236]

I consider this interdisciplinary, cross-cultural research to be even more significant for the world than the international Human Genome Project, Europe's Human Brain Project, and the American Brain Initiative. Such research could be a major step toward discovering the common ground among the world's great contemplative traditions, for bridging spiritual and scientific views of human nature and the universe at large, and for tapping into the inner resources of the human spirit that are the source of sustainable well-being for all.

Afterword

New Frontiers in the Collaboration of Buddhism and Science

Over the past thirty years, I have participated in and listened to many conferences and dialogues about the nature of the mind and consciousness held between scientists and Buddhist scholars, primarily from the Tibetan Buddhist tradition. Time and again, experts from diverse fields, including psychology, neuroscience, and philosophy, have presented their cutting-edge research to Buddhists and then invited their response to these advances in modern science. In virtually all such meetings, it is the Western scientists who dominate, speaking for over 90 percent of the time, while His Holiness the Dalai Lama and other Buddhists in attendance have brief opportunities to respond and ask questions of the Western experts. Overall, I have found much greater openness on the part of Buddhists to learn about scientific discoveries in the mind sciences than I have found open-mindedness on the part of scientists eager to learn about Buddhist discoveries. For example, His Holiness has often commented that if scientists present evidence that clearly refutes any Buddhist belief, he would abandon that Buddhist belief. But it is rare to find any scientist who would likewise agree that if Buddhist contemplatives make replicable, intersubjectively validated discoveries that clearly refute certain materialist beliefs, they would abandon those beliefs. When scientists meet eminent Buddhist scholars and contemplatives, they might open such a conversation in a spirit of humility, acknowledging the following points:

✢ Although the scientific study of the mind has been pursued for more than 135 years, there has been no progress in solving the "hard problem," or the question of *how* brain activity and conscious experiences are correlated.

✢ While hundreds of scientific and philosophical books and articles have been published about the nature of consciousness, there is currently no scientific definition of consciousness, no objective means of detecting mental phenomena, the neural correlates of consciousness itself have yet to be discovered, and it is unknown whether organic processes are universally necessary for the generation of all possible states of consciousness.

✢ Since 1950 tremendous advances have been made in understanding the neural conditions that contribute to mental diseases, a great number and variety of psychopharmaceutical drugs have been developed and have been widely prescribed by medical professionals, especially in wealthy countries, and over two hundred schools of psychotherapy have been devised to help people with psychological problems. Yet, despite all these advances, during this same period there has been a tenfold increase in depression, which is now the number-one cause of disability worldwide, with the risk of depression 32 percent higher in wealthy countries.

✢ Since 1950 in the United States, the gross domestic product has increased fiftyfold, but the reported change in well-being has remained unchanged. So, despite the recent advances in positive psychology, there appears to be little or no improvement in humanity's overall mental health and well-being.

So, they might say, in light of the evident limitations of materialist approaches to understanding the mind, consciousness, and mental health and well-being, we scientists are keen to learn about Buddhist theories, methods, and discoveries in these fields. Buddhists might respond in a similar spirit of humility by acknowledging that over the past 2,500 years, Buddhism has not developed any quantitative, scientific study of behavior or the brain, and there is no branch of Buddhist psychology specifically devoted to diagnosing and treating mental illness. However, the Buddhist tradition has developed highly sophisticated means of developing and utilizing attention and introspection in the direct study of consciousness and a broad range of mental states and processes.

I would love to participate in conferences with dialogues between Buddhists and scientists in which they are both given the same time to present their views, and with mutual open-mindedness, which has been exceedingly rare thus far. For example, in numerous such meetings with scientists, when His Holiness has spoken of empirical evidence concerning both children and contemplatives who have expressed clear past-life recollections, the scientists have quickly shifted the topic without giving such evidence any credence or inquiring about Buddhists theories to explain such memories. Such closed-mindedness is frustrating, and it generally pertains to any evidence or reasoning that challenges the unquestioned assumptions of scientific materialism.

While the theories and methods of science in general are largely compatible with, or complementary to, those of Buddhism, the beliefs and methodological constraints of scientific *materialism* are fundamentally incompatible with all schools of Buddhism throughout history. The relationships between proponents of scientific materialism and those of Buddhism are complex, but might nonetheless be characterized by way of the following metaphors, shocking though they may be:

1. Communist regimes, such as the former Soviet Union and the People's Republic of China, which embrace scientific materialism as their state religion, are like wolves in wolves' clothing, for they have consistently committed genocide against Buddhism, often bent on its total destruction and delegitimization as well as the mass murder and incarceration of its proponents.

2. Scientists who embrace materialism as their unquestioned ideology are like wolves disguised as sheepdogs, who have taken on the apparently benign role of leading the Buddhist flock to the slaughterhouse, where Buddhism is butchered and a "filet of Buddhism" is sold to the public, from which all the bones of contention where Buddhism is incompatible with materialism have been carefully removed.

3. Many people posing as "secular Buddhists," but who in fact unquestioningly adopt the beliefs of scientific materialism, are like wolves in sheep's clothing, for they try to blend in with the flock of Buddhists, urging everyone around them that their Buddhism is the new, improved version, freed from all the superstitions of religion, including the Buddha's own account of his enlightenment and the myriad accounts of later Buddhist adepts who have fathomed the nature of the mind and from that perspective reveal materialism to be intellectually and morally bankrupt.

4. Buddhists who fail to challenge these assaults on Buddhism are like neutered sheep who keep their heads down and their eyes closed as they passively witness the integrity of their own tradition being sacrificed on the altar of materialism, nihilism, consumerism, and hedonism.

As the Harvard psychologist Jerome Kagan remarked during the Mind and Life conference at MIT in 2003, "Humans do not like being wolves," and I might add, we don't like being led to the slaughter by them, either. At the conclusion of this meeting, the MIT geneticist Eric Lander commented:

> What are the foundations for any kind of dialogue between different traditions? The first foundation is a commitment to openness, to debate, to evidence, to a nondogmatic approach, and to respect. What does it really mean to be open? It means to be willing to change your mind and say you might be wrong. . . . It's not enough for the Buddhists to be open to rethinking. Science also must be open to rethinking. At its best, science is about constantly being in doubt and maintaining a constant humility about how little we know. In practice, day to day, that humility doesn't always emerge. . . .
>
> [Buddhists] bring traditional practices that have been worked out through experimentation and careful thought over some 2,500 years. How should we regard such traditional practices? One way is to regard them as something like folk wisdom, the way that pharmaceutical companies might regard a folk remedy: They're on to something and now we'll work out what the real basis of it is. I don't think that's the right way to regard it. I am persuaded that we have every reason to regard it as a refined technology that could play a critical role in science. . . .
>
> Lastly, what can the world gain? Several things: specific knowledge about the mind and the brain. The questions are very challenging and we need all the help we can get. But there are some other things the world can gain. I'll speak now as a scientist concerned about our society. We live in a world where science is a very powerful and effective paradigm, and yet we know it does not contain all the answers to all human needs. Like any one-dimensional diet, consuming only science leads to malnutrition. The fact that science does not contain the answer to all human

needs has produced in many people, in our country at least, what some have called a flight from reason: a rejection of science and the appeal of fantastical things. . . . This debate is remarkably different from this. It is not about any flight from reason, or flight from science. It is possible for science and Buddhism to recognize happily that science is only one way of understanding the world. It can be incorporated; it can be worked with; it need not be rejected. I think that is really important. Our world would be much better with debates that are based on respect and an attempt to understand. Science very much needs to be willing to participate in those debates because it has much, but not everything, to offer the world.[237]

Jerome Kagan then offered his own reflections, including the following:

The primary purpose of this meeting was to consider whether individuals trained in the Buddhist form of introspection could discover significant facts about the human mind that no other method could reveal; and secondly, whether those facts had a special or privileged access to what was true. . . . Although the Buddhists contend that specially trained introspection can reveal deep truths about the human mind that Richard Davidson's EEG or fMRI scanner could never discover, I remind you that Niels Bohr, the great Danish physicist who's a hero for me, suggested that no method has a uniquely privileged power to reveal the true nature of the human mind or the true nature of anything. It does not matter whether we record neuronal activity, behavior, latencies in a priming experiment, or the products of trained introspection. Each method reveals something different about the whole, and we need a variety of procedures to come closer to answers that, of course, we will never possess. . . .

I do believe, however, that trained introspection can reveal subtleties of perception and feeling that no other current scientific method can discover. That's why I came to this meeting, and therefore this information is useful. And I agree with Eric Lander and the consensus in this meeting that that evidence should be incorporated into our studies of human psychology.

I welcome the contribution of Buddhist scholars to this mission. They have something important to tell us about mind and perhaps brain. Although their insights are not more valid, or, if you prefer, more true than any other corpus, trained introspection is a valuable source of evidence, another instrument to be added to those of the geneticist, the cell biologist, the neuroscientist, the historian, the psychologist, the sociologist, the anthropologist, the novelist, the poet, and all others who wish to be wiser observers of the phenomena that we can never know completely.[238]

Finally, Eric Lander offered this wonderful challenge to Buddhists:

I'd like to emphasize the importance of the point that the Buddhists may be better able to tell us what kinds of psychological and psychophysical tests one would apply to capture whether someone has or hasn't attained an ability to attend or to control emotion. I would like to push the point because some of those tests can be done without the MRIs in Wisconsin. They could be done by Buddhists in Dharamsala. For a meaningful research collaboration to go on, it must go on in India and Tibet as well. It's just good science. We must both actually be engaged in designing experiments to have the best conversation. A great outcome would be Tibetan Buddhists doing and publishing experiments there with colleagues in the next few years. That's something demonstrable one could try to accomplish. I think they would be different experiments and very interesting. The experiments would get picked up and then tried in the West.[239]

His Holiness the Dalai Lama's response to the above comments was clear and succinct:

As I listened to the presentations of Eric Lander and Jerome Kagan, who made a beautiful summation of some of the salient points that were raised in the conversations, I felt deeply impressed and the only thing I could say is, yes, I agree with you.... We human beings have a physical body, but we also have this mind. To have a happy, meaningful life, we have to take care of our body as well as our mind. So I think spiritual traditions and material progress should go together in combination.[240]

Unfortunately, since that historic meeting, very little has been done by either the scientific or Buddhist communities to implement these provocative, groundbreaking suggestions from Lander and Kagan, enthusiastically endorsed by His Holiness the Dalai Lama. It is high time to start organizing conferences on Buddhism and science to which are invited truly openminded scientists, philosophers, and Buddhists who are willing to question their beliefs and the limitations of their respective modes of inquiry. These would be true dialogues, where both sides are given equal time to share the discoveries and insights of their traditions, in contrast to the current approach in which scientists provide tutorials for Buddhists and invite them to respond. Genuine cross-cultural, interdisciplinary collaboration must be based on mutual respect, in which all participants are not only willing but eager to question even their most cherished assumptions, which are to be examined and appraised in the light of compelling evidence and sound reasoning. This is the common ideal of both Buddhism and science.

It is also high time for Buddhists to establish our own centers for contemplative research, based primarily on the contemplative technology of "higher training in samādhi"[241] and the contemplative science of "higher training in wisdom,"[242] with both of these rooted in "higher training in ethics."[243] Since śamatha and vipaśyanā are widely regarded as the essential practices of Buddhist meditation, their cultivation and achievement should be central to all Buddhist contemplative training and inquiry. While virtually all scientific research on meditation thus far has entailed scientists studying the brains and behavior of meditators as subjects of scientific inquiry, true collaborative research must entail the *integration* of the third-person methods of science and the first-person methods of contemplation.

In short, what is needed in these modern times, in which humanity and the ecosphere at large are beset with so many human-made crises, is a true revolution in the mind sciences and a true renaissance in contemplative inquiry. If these two great transitions are achieved, we may be able to restore balance and harmony where it has been lost in the lives of individuals and our global community as a whole. These ideals may be achieved through close collaboration between scientific and contemplative researchers, which has the potential to open vast new horizons of knowledge that will transcend the current boundaries between science and religion.

As a step toward realizing these ideals and carrying through with the suggestions of Kagan and Lander, the Center for Contemplative Research (CCR) is, at the time of writing, currently under construction on the outskirts of the village of Castellina Marittima in the region of Tuscany, Italy. It will provide an environment for exploring the inner potentials of the human mind and the nature and origins of consciousness, integrating the first-person methodologies of contemplative inquiry with the third-person methodologies of scientific inquiry. It is a branch of the Santa Barbara Institute for Consciousness Studies, which I founded in Santa Barbara, California, in 2003 as a nonprofit organization dedicated to research and education in the field of cross-cultural and interdisciplinary studies on the nature and potential of the mind.

Over the past few decades, world-class scientists have begun to explore the benefits of meditation and are eager to work with contemplative traditions. This center will be the first facility in the world that is dedicated to research into the nature of the mind and consciousness by contemplatives and scientists working hand-in-hand in a spirit of open-minded mutual respect and appreciation. There is already enthusiastic interest on the part of international experts in these fields of study, and the only missing link so far has been the creation of such a center designed to provide the optimal environment for such long-term, in-depth research.

The center, located on six hectares of land overlooking the Mediterranean Sea, includes a three-story building that will be its research headquarters and up to thirty-five individual retreat cabins for contemplatives to receive long-term, professional training in meditation in collaboration with scientists working closely with them. In accordance with the wishes of His Holiness the Dalai Lama, the nearby Lama Tsong Khapa Institute (LTKI) is developing a Mindscience Academy in which scientists and religious leaders from different traditions join together to study the mind, emotions, and secular ethics. The CCR and the LTKI have formed a close association to see that the experiential research and academic study of the mind conducted in these two organizations will mutually support and enrich each other.

While great progress in the mind sciences has been made over the past century, the nature and origins of consciousness remain as much a mystery now as ever, and no significant breakthroughs have been made regarding the so-called mind-body problem, or the way in which the mind interacts with the body. Likewise, in quantum physics, the "measurement problem," which pertains to the role of the observer in making quantum measurements, remains unsolved. A working hypothesis for research in the CCR is that the lack of progress on these two fronts is because the radical empiricism that has been the hallmark of the great scientific revolutions of the past has been neglected when it comes to the scientific study of the mind. Galileo applied such a radically empirical approach to the study of astronomy and physics, Lavoisier adopted this approach for chemistry, and Darwin applied it to the study of biological organisms. In short, it entails the rigorous, open-minded, direct observation of the natural phenomena one seeks to understand. While the mind sciences have developed a sophisticated array of methods for studying the mind indirectly through the investigation of the neural correlates of mental activity and its behavioral expressions, they have failed to develop any rigorous methods for observing and investigating the mind firsthand. This can be done only through introspection, which has been largely neglected in the mind sciences for over a century.

Such radically empirical methods of observing and exploring the nature and origins of the mind have been developed over many centuries in the East and West, mostly notably by Buddhist, Hindu, Jain, Taoist, Jewish, Christian, and Sufi contemplatives. But these methods have never been integrated with those of modern science, and in today's world they have commonly been marginalized by the traditions in which they were originally developed. The core mission of the CCR is to help catalyze the first, true revolution in the mind sciences and a renaissance in contemplative inquiry.

The CCR will provide facilities for qualified individuals to engage in extensive, professional training in meditative practices, beginning with the cultivation and achievement of śamatha and vipaśyanā, and then moving on to more advanced contemplative practices, especially those taught in the Dzokchen tradition. By dedicating oneself to these practices over years of full-time training, levels of expertise can be achieved that are virtually unknown in the modern world. With the close collaboration between such highly trained contemplatives and psychologists, neuroscientists, physicists, and philosophers, our core mission is to unveil the deepest mysteries of consciousness and the role of the mind in nature for the benefit of humanity.

In the spring of 2017 the CCR and the LTKI began a long-term collaboration in hosting an annual series of intensive, eight-week contemplative training programs focusing on the five visionary Dzokchen treatises revealed by Düdjom Lingpa. During this first retreat, I gave the oral transmission and commentary to Düdjom Lingpa's *Foolish Dharma of an Idiot Clothed in Mud and Feathers* and *Buddhahood Without Meditation*. In 2018 we turned to the *Sharp Vajra of Conscious Awareness Tantra* and Düdjom Lingpa's commentary, entitled the *Essence of Clear Meaning*. Over the coming years, we intend to complete this series of retreats by focusing on the *Enlightened View of Samantabhadra* and the *Vajra Essence*. These retreats are personally attended by scores of people, with hundreds more participating from around the world by listening to podcasts of the oral transmissions and commentaries. In 2017 participants in the eight-week retreat collaborated with an international team of scientists to explore the effects of such training from first-person and third-person perspectives. We anticipate further studies of this kind throughout the entire series of these retreats.

The scientific study of the effects of meditation is still in an early phase of development, and until now it has been limited to scientists conducting their studies on meditators, who are simply subjects—not true collaborators—in such research. The CCR will explore unprecedented ways of supporting mutually respectful, truly collaborative research between contemplatives and scientists, each drawing on the unique strengths of their respective traditions. Graduates from these eight-week programs will be prepared to bring the benefits from such contemplative training into all aspects of modern society, including education, business, healthcare, government, the arts, and athletics.

The CCR will explore methods to improve attention, memory skills, mindfulness, and emotional balance. Such research will explore the potential benefits of meditation as an alternative to drugs for the prevention and treatment of mental disorders, including depression, attention deficit/hyperactivity disorder (ADHD), general anxiety disorder (GAD), and post-traumatic stress disorder (PTSD). An additional field will be the study of the value of different types of meditation to develop high levels of mental health and well-being. These studies will focus on the cultivation of genuine well-being that arises from the realization of inner peace and mental balance, without dependence on external conditions. To achieve this, we hypothesize that it is necessary to develop and sustain four kinds of mental balance: (1) conative, entailing the cultivation of intelligent desires and intentions, (2) attentional, entailing the ability to focus one's attention with stability and clarity, (3) cognitive, entailing discerning mindfulness, and (4) emotional, entailing the development of emotional intelligence. In my forty-two years of experience as a teacher of meditation, I have found that exceptional mental health and well-being is the natural result of such training in these four aspects of mental balance. Now we will have the opportunity to put such hypotheses to the test of rigorous scientific study.

The contemplatives and scientists dedicated to the creation of CCR envision this center becoming the hub of an international network of such centers belonging to the Association for Research in Contemplative Science (ARCS). Great interest in such an interdisciplinary, cross-cultural network has already been expressed by individuals and institutions in countries throughout the world, including India, Singapore, Mongolia, Brazil, Mexico, the United States, Australia, the United Kingdom, Spain, Italy, Austria, and Russia. The vision is to model this association after the Human Genome Project, with multiple research centers collaborating to make fundamental discoveries about the mind and its role in nature.

The idea of creating this research facility has aroused a high level of international enthusiasm, in part because it has been inspired and fully supported by His Holiness the Dalai Lama. The Santa Barbara Institute for Consciousness Studies has already conducted such research at multiple campuses of the University of California, at Emory University, the University of Arizona, and at the University of Vienna, and it has collaborated with many scientists around the world. As mentioned above, such a mutual relationship has already been formed with the Lama Tsong Khapa Institute, and in the future we anticipate working with other contemplative centers and scientific institutions worldwide, thus beginning the formation of a network of international, spiritual, cultural, and scientific collaboration known as the Association for Research in Contemplative Science.

Glossary

absolute space of phenomena (Tib. *chos kyi dbyings*, Skt. *dharmadhātu*). The expanse of all phenomena in saṃsāra and nirvāṇa. This does not refer to space in the reified, Newtonian sense, but rather to an ultimate dimension of space out of which all manifestations of relative space-time and mass-energy emerge, in which they are present, and into which they eventually dissolve. Likewise, all manifestations of relative states of consciousness and mental processes emerge as displays of primordial consciousness, which according to the Great Perfection tradition has always been indivisible from the absolute space of phenomena.

Akaniṣṭha (Skt., Tib. *'og min*). Lit. "unsurpassed," the buddha field of Samantabhadra, in which every being finally achieves supreme enlightenment.

arhat (Skt., Tib. *dgra bcom pa*). One who has achieved nirvāṇa, the complete cessation of the causes of suffering and their effects.

āryabodhisattva (Skt., Tib. *'phags pa'i byang chub sems dpa'*). A bodhisattva who has gained a direct, nonconceptual, unmediated realization of emptiness on the path of seeing.

asura (Skt., Tib. *lha ma yin*). A titan, or demigod, whose existence is characterized by aggression and conflict with the devas.

awareness (Tib. *rig pa*, Skt. *vidyā*). The basic act of cognizing. See also *pristine awareness.*

bardo (Tib. *bar do*, Skt. *antarabhāva*). See *transitional phase* and *intermediate period* for both a broader and more specialized meaning.

Bhagavān (Skt., Tib. *bcom ldan 'das*). Lit. "Blessed One," an epithet of the Buddha. The Tibetan term has the connotation of one who has overcome all obscurations, is imbued with all excellent qualities, and who has transcended saṃsāra.

bindu (Skt., Tib. *thig le*). An orb of light or fluid. In the present book, this refers to the vital essences, or the red and white essential drops of vital fluids within the subtle body, included within the triad of channels, orbs, and vital energies.

bodhicitta (Skt., Tib. *byang chub kyi sems*). Lit. "awakening mind," it is described as having two *relative* aspects, called aspirational and engaged, along with its absolute, *ultimate* aspect. The nominal cultivation of aspirational bodhicitta means wishing to achieve enlightenment in order to liberate all sentient beings in saṃsāra. Bodhicitta is called engaged when one actually practices with this motivation to achieve buddhahood. In the Great Perfection, bodhicitta is the primordial, originally pure ground, which pervades the whole of saṃsāra and nirvāṇa. In that context, then, the realization of ultimate bodhicitta is the actualization of identitylessness as the play of the consummation of saṃsāra and nirvāṇa, free of activity and conceptual elaboration. Precious bodhicitta subsumes all authentic realities and is the ultimate source of all phenomena; it manifests the wisdom of realizing identitylessness, liberating the three realms of saṃsāra as the play of the three kāyas.

bodhisattva (Skt., Tib. *byang chub sems dpa'*). A being in whom bodhicitta arises effortlessly and who devotes himself or herself to the cultivation of the six perfections in order to achieve enlightenment for the benefit of all beings.

Bodhisattvayāna (Skt., Tib. *byang chub sems dpa'i theg pa*). The spiritual vehicle of the bodhisattvas, in which one seals saṃsāra and nirvāṇa with bodhicitta.

brāhmin (Skt., Tib. *bram ze*). In the caste system of India, a member of the priestly class who engages in pure conduct, partakes of pure food, and is seen to have virtuous attitudes.

buddha (Skt., Tib. *sangs rgyas*). Lit. "awakened one," an enlightened being in whom all mental afflictions and obscurations are dispelled and all excellent qualities brought to perfection.

buddha field (Tib. *sangs rgyas kyi zhing khams*, Skt. *buddhakṣetradhātu*). Lit. "buddhafield realm," a "pure realm" that is brought forth spontaneously from a buddha's enlightened mind.

buddha nature (Tib. *sangs rgyas kyis rigs*, Skt. *buddhadhātu*). The primordially pure, essential nature of the mind, equivalent to pristine awareness, which is none other than the dharmakāya, but may be regarded provisionally as one's capacity for achieving spiritual awakening.

cakra (Skt., Tib. *rtsa 'khor*). A "wheel" of channels through which vital energies course. The fivefold classification of the cakras includes the cakra of great bliss at the crown of the head, the cakra of enjoyment at the throat, the dharma cakra at the heart, the cakra of emanation at the navel, and the cakra of sustained bliss at the genital region.

clear light (Tib. *'od gsal*, Skt. *prabhāsvara*). The illuminating nature of pristine awareness.

close applications of mindfulness, four (Tib. *dran pa nyer bzhag bzhi*, Skt. *catursmṛtyupasthāna*). The foundational practices of vipaśyanā in which mindfulness is closely, discerningly applied to the body, feelings, mind, and phenomena.

completion stage (Tib. *rdzogs rim*, Skt. *utpanna-* or *niṣpannakrama*). See *stage of completion*.

conceptual elaboration (Tib. *spros pa*, Skt. *prapañca*). Conceptual constructs such as those regarding existence, nonexistence, birth, and cessation. This term can also refer, without negative connotation, to the use of the imagination in a ritual of empowerment or advanced practice of tantra.

connate (Tib. *lhan skyes*, Skt. *sahaja*). Lit. "born together at the same time," this term is used in various contexts for that which is natural or spontaneous, whether referring to a process as it occurs within cyclic existence or to exalted spiritual qualities that emerge as part of the path beyond cyclic existence (as in "connate primordial consciousness").

consciousness (Tib. *shes pa*, Skt. *jñāna*). The basic experience of knowing, cognizing, or being aware.

consciousness, conditioned (Tib. *rnam par shes pa*, Skt. *vijñāna*). The clear and knowing qualities of the mind that emerge in the aspect of the object and are bound by reification. See by comparison *primordial consciousness*.

cooperative condition (Tib. *lhan cig byed rkyen*, Skt. *sahakārikāraṇa*). An auxiliary factor in bringing about an effect, which occurs at the same time as the substantial cause yet is not of the same substance as its effect. For example, it is like the field workers who plant the seeds for a resultant harvest, the efforts of the person making a pot, or the sensory faculty that governs a moment of awareness.

creative displays, creative expressions (Tib. *rtsal*). Effulgences or manifestations, such as the creative displays of primordial consciousness.

cutting through (Tib. *khregs chod*). The first of the two major phases in the practice of the Great Perfection, aimed at gaining direct, sustained realization of the original purity of pristine awareness.

ḍākinī (Skt., Tib. *mkha' 'gro ma*). A highly realized female bodhisattva, who manifests in the world in order to serve sentient beings. The Tibetan term means a female "sky-goer," referring to the fact that such beings course in the expanse of absolute space.

deeds of immediate retribution, five (Tib. *mtshams med pa lnga*, Skt. *pañcā-nantarya*). Actions with such negative karmic force that upon death the perpetrator is reborn immediately in hell, bypassing the intermediate period: patricide, matricide, killing an arhat, maliciously drawing the blood of a buddha, and causing a schism in the Saṅgha.

deity (Tib. *lha*, Skt. *deva*). Within the context of Buddhist Vajrayāna, this refers to an enlightened being who is manifest within a maṇḍala, or secret, pure abode.

deity, personal (Tib. *yi dam*, Skt. *iṣṭadevatā*). The enlightened manifestation, or embodiment, chosen as one's primary object of refuge and meditative practice.

delusion (Tib. *'khrul pa, gti mug*, Skt. *bhrānti, moha*). Principally the delusion of reifying oneself and other phenomena, which acts as the root of all other mental afflictions.

delusive appearances (Tib. *'khrul snang*). The reified appearances of phenomena that arise on account of delusion.

desire realm (Tib. *'dod khams*, Skt. *kāmadhātu*). The level of existence that includes hell beings, pretas, animals, humans, demigods (or asuras), and the gods (or devas) belonging to the realm of cyclic existence.

deva (Skt., Tib. *lha*). Within the present book, this term generally refers to a "god" within saṃsāra, who experiences great joy, extrasensory perception, and paranormal abilities, but who suffers greatly when faced with death. For an alternate meaning, see *deity*.

Dharma (Skt., Tib. *chos*). Spiritual teachings and practices that lead one irreversibly away from suffering and the source of suffering and toward the attainment of liberation and enlightenment.

dharmadhātu (Skt.). See *absolute space of phenomena*.

dharmakāya (Skt., Tib. *chos kyi sku*). The "enlightened embodiment of truth," which is the mind of the buddhas.

dharmatā (Skt., Tib. *chos nyid*). See *ultimate reality*.

dhyāna (Skt., Pāli *jhāna*). Advanced states of meditative concentration, generally presented in four progressively deeper levels.

direct crossing over (Tib. *thod rgal*, Skt. *vyutkrāntaka*). The second of the two phases of the practice of the Great Perfection, which is aimed at realizing the spontaneous manifestations of the dharmakāya.

display (Tib. *rol pa*, Skt. *lalita*). The manifestation of reality unfolding as a "dance" or "sport."

Dzokchen (Tib. *rdzogs chen*). See *Great Perfection*.

emptiness (Tib. *stong pa nyid*, Skt. *śūnyatā*). The absence of true, inherent existence with respect to all phenomena. Emptiness itself is not to be reified.

energy-mind (Tib. *rlung sems*). A term based upon the idea common to many presentations of Vajrayāna and the Great Perfection, namely, that the subtle and very subtle vital energies run in tandem with consciousness (*rlung sems 'jug pa gcig pa*), or that both are of the same essential nature, understood from different points of view (*ngo bo gcig ldog pa tha dad*). The pair of energies and mind are frequently referred to by a single compound term. In general this refers to the karmic energies and conditioned mind, but since there is sometimes reference in Great Perfection texts to a purified energy-mind, or in unsurpassed yoga tantra texts to the indwelling, very subtle energy-mind associated with the clear light, it seems the same term can also refer to the energies of primordial consciousness.

enlightenment (Tib. *byang chub*, Skt. *bodhi*). Spiritual awakening.

ethically neutral (Tib. *lung ma bstan*, Skt. *avyākṛta*). A characteristic of all those phenomena that are not by nature either virtuous or nonvirtuous.

excitation (Tib. *rgod pa*, Skt. *auddhatya*). Mental agitation aroused by the mental affliction of attachment. One of the two attentional imbalances to which the mind is habitually prone and that is overcome through the cultivation of stability in the practice of śamatha. For the other, see *laxity*.

extremes of conceptual elaboration, eight (Tib. *spros pa'i mtha' brgyad*, Skt. *aṣṭānta*). The eight philosophical assertions of origination, cessation, existence, nonexistence, coming, going, diversity, and unity.

form realm (Tib. *gzugs khams*, Skt. *rūpadhātu*). A dimension of saṃsāra in which beings imbued with luminous bodies dwell in any of the four dhyānas, free of the attachments of the desire realm but still prone to attachment to the form realm.

formless realm (Tib. *gzugs med khams*, Skt. *arūpyadhātu*). A dimension of saṃsāra in which beings dwell in any of the formless absorptions (Skt. *samāpatti*) up to the pinnacle of mundane existence. Imbued with transparent mental bodies, devoid of coarse form, they are free of attachments to the desire and form realms but still cling to the formless realm.

gandharva (Skt., Tib. *dri za*). (1) An ethereal being who is said to subsist on fragrances. (2) A "celestial musician." (3) A being in the intermediate period.

generation stage (Tib. *bskyed rim*, Skt. *utpattikrama*). See *stage of generation*.

glow, inner (Tib. *mdangs*). The natural glow (*rang mdangs*) of pristine awareness, which is transcendently present in the ground and expresses itself as self-emergent, indwelling primordial consciousness.

Great Perfection (Tib. *rdzogs pa chen po*, Skt. *mahāsandhi*). Dzokchen, or *atiyoga*, the pinnacle of the nine vehicles transmitted by the Nyingma school. The clear light absolute space of phenomena, having no center or periphery, from which all phenomena of saṃsāra and nirvāṇa spontaneously arise as creative displays.

ground of being (Tib. *gzhi*, Skt. *āśraya*). The ground of the whole of saṃsāra and nirvāṇa, which is the dharmakāya. This Tibetan term is sometimes translated as "the condition of the ground" when referring to that which exists in the natural state even without relying upon practice of the path.

grounds and paths (Tib. *sa lam*, Skt. *bhūmimārga*). The stages of attainment and the paths that lead to them. There are five sequential paths culminating in the liberation of a śrāvaka, five culminating in the liberation of a pratyekabuddha, and five bodhisattva paths culminating in the perfect enlightenment of a buddha. According to the sūtra tradition, there are ten āryabodhisattva grounds. According to the Great Perfection tradition, there are twenty āryabodhisattva grounds, followed by the culmination of the twenty-first ground.

guru (Skt., Tib. *bla ma*). A spiritual teacher or mentor who leads one to the state of liberation and spiritual awakening.

identitylessness (Tib. *bdag med*, Skt. *nairātmya*). Selflessness or a lack of inherent identity. There are two types: (1) the identitylessness of persons, and (2) the identitylessness of phenomena.

indwelling (Tib. *gnyug ma*, Skt. *nija*). That which has remained naturally within oneself from the very beginning (without beginning) and abides continuously. It can also be translated as "fundamental" or "innate."

inherent existence (Tib. *rang bzhin gyis grub pa*, Skt. *svabhāvasiddhi*). The quality of existence in and of itself that is mistakenly projected onto phenomena. While phenomena appear as if they exist in this way, independently of the mind that apprehends them, if anything existed in this way, it would be immutable and unknowable.

insight (Tib. *lhag mthong*, Skt. *vipaśyanā*). See *vipaśyanā*.

instruction, pith (Tib. *man ngag*, Skt. *upadeśa*). A succinct and powerful practical instruction, coming from the experience of the guru and the lineage.

instruction, pointing-out (Tib. *mdzub khrid, ngo sprod pa*). An introduction to the nature of the mind.

intermediate period (Tib. *bar do*, Skt. *antarabhāva*). The interval between death and one's next rebirth, which includes two of the six transitional phases, namely, the transitional phase of the actual nature of reality and the transitional phase of becoming.

introspection (Tib. *shes bzhin*, Skt. *samprajanya*). The mental faculty by which one monitors how one's own body, speech, and mind are functioning. This is crucial to all forms of spiritual practice, including meditation, and in the practice of śamatha in particular this pertains to monitoring the flow of attention, being on guard for the occurrence of laxity and excitation.

karma (Skt., Tib. *las*). Actions defiled by mental afflictions, especially the delusion of self-grasping.

karmic energy (Tib. *las rlung*). A vital energy that courses through the body and is propelled by one's previous karma. See also *prāṇa*.

karmic imprint (Tib. *bag chags*, Skt. *vāsanā*). The potentiality stored in the substrate consciousness by one's past actions and intentions that will ripen as an experience upon meeting suitable conditions. See also *propensities, habitual*.

kāya (Skt., Tib. *sku*). An aggregate of spontaneously actualized facets of primordial consciousness and qualities of enlightenment, designated as a composite body.

laxity (Tib. *bying ba*, Skt. *laya*). The loss of clarity of attention, which is counteracted through the cultivation of vividness in the practice of śamatha. See also *excitation*.

luminosity (Tib. *gsal ba*, Skt. *prabhāsvara*). The natural clarity of awareness that makes manifest all appearances.

Madhyamaka (Skt., Tib. *dbu ma*). The Middle Way, the higher of the two Mahāyāna philosophical schools in the sūtra system, especially associated with the writings of the second-century Indian master Nāgārjuna. Within Tibetan Buddhism, the Middle Way view is in turn understood according to two traditions of interpretation: the Svātantrikas (Tib. *rang rgyud pa*), who espouse the efficacy of an autonomous line of reasoning for demonstrating that phenomena are not truly existent, and the Prāsaṅgikas (Tib. *thal 'gyur ba*), who claim that the only type of argument that can instill authentic understanding of emptiness is one that leads to an absurd consequence, or a kind of *reductio ad absurdum*.

Mahāmudrā (Skt., Tib. *phyag rgya chen po*). The "Great Seal," which is a synonym for emptiness, the absolute space of phenomena. Also refers to a system of practice designed to lead to the realization of emptiness with the very subtle mind of clear light.

Mahāyāna (Skt., Tib. *theg pa chen po*). The "Great Vehicle," by which one proceeds to the state of the perfect enlightenment of a buddha in order to liberate all sentient beings.

maṇḍala (Skt., Tib. *dkyil 'khor*). (1) A symbolic representation of the world, which is ritually offered. (2) A sacred, secret world, where the principal divine figure emanates and withdraws perfect worlds consisting of pure beings and the distinct environments in which they dwell. (3) A representation of such a pure abode of an enlightened deity.

mantra (Skt., Tib. *sngags*). Sanskrit syllables, words, or a series of words imbued with special symbolic significance or spiritual blessings.

meditative equipoise (Tib. *mnyam bzhag*, Skt. *samāhita*). Undistracted, even placement of the mind upon its object for as long as one wishes, first achieved with the attainment of śamatha.

mental afflictions (Tib. *nyon mongs*, Skt. *kleśa*). Craving, hostility, delusion, and so forth; mental disturbances that propel us to perform negative actions and perpetuate saṃsāra.

mental process (Tib. *sems byung*, Skt. *caitta*). A mental event that arises in conjunction with consciousness, by means of which one engages in various ways with the objects of apprehension.

mentation (Tib. *yid*, Skt. *manas*). The activity of the mind that is the basis for the emergence of all manner of appearances, thereby revealing the luminous aspect of consciousness. From this "refraction" of the light of consciousness into the five modes of sensory appearances, reification of those appearances tends to follow, resulting in close identification and delusion.

mentation, afflictive (Tib. *nyon yid*, Skt. *kliṣṭamanas*). A primitive, preconceptual, subjective sense of personal identity, over here, that is separate from the objective space of awareness, which is perceived as being something other, over there. It is the most primal expression of grasping to the idea of "I" (Tib. *ngar 'dzin pa*), which in Sanskrit is literally known as the "I-maker" (Skt. *ahaṃkāra*).

merit (Tib. *bsod nams*, Skt. *puṇya*). Karmic potential generated through performing positive actions with a virtuous motivation.

mind (Tib. *sems*, Skt. *citta*). Within the texts discussed here, this usually refers to the dualistic awareness that clings to appearances, conceptually observes its own processes, and arouses pleasure and pain through intellectual fabrications and the acceptance and rejection of virtue and vice.

mind, ultimate nature of the (Tib. *sems nyid*, Skt. *cittatā*). Pristine awareness, the *sugatagarbha*. Also, the empty nature of the mind, or its lack of inherent identity.

mindfulness (Tib. *dran pa*, Skt. *smṛti*). The mental faculty of attending continuously, without forgetfulness, to an object with which one is already familiar.

mode of existence (Tib. *gnas tshul*). How things actually are, in contrast to their mode of appearance (Tib. *snang tshul*).

mundane existence (Tib. *srid pa*, Skt. *bhava*). The cycle of existence in which one is propelled from life to life by the force of mental afflictions and karma. Equivalent to *saṃsāra*.

natural liberation (Tib. *rang grol*). Lit. "self-liberation" or "self-release," this may also be translated as "releases itself" or "natural release." When there is no grasping, thoughts and afflictions are naturally liberated without any need for antidotes, interventions, or outside forces.

nature (Tib. *rang bzhin*, Skt. *prakṛti*). The quality or feature of some phenomenon, such as the mind, whose nature is luminosity.

nature, essential (Tib. *ngo bo*, Skt. *svabhāva*). The fundamental nature of a phenomenon, as in the case of awareness being the essential nature of the mind. This can also refer to emptiness, as the ultimate essential nature of any phenomenon, such as the mind.

nature of existence (Tib. *gnas lugs*, Skt. *tathātva*). The fundamental mode of existence of all phenomena, which is emptiness. This is often contrasted with the way things appear (Tib. *snang lugs*).

nihilism (Tib. *med par lta ba*). A doctrine that denies the possibility of objective knowledge, meaning, values, or morality.

nirmāṇakāya (Skt., Tib. *sprul pa'i sku*). An "emanation embodiment" of the sugatagarbha that may appear anywhere in the universe in order to benefit sentient beings, with four types: living-being, teacher, created, and material nirmāṇakāyas.

nirvāṇa (Skt., Tib. *mya ngan las 'das pa*). Spiritual liberation, in which one is forever freed from delusion and all the other mental afflictions, which are what give rise to suffering.

obscuration, afflictive (Tib. *nyon mongs pa'i sgrib pa*, Skt. *kleśāvaraṇa*). The coarse obscurations that consist of manifest mental afflictions and their seeds, which are abandoned on the path of meditation, after the path of seeing the nature of reality directly.

obscuration, cognitive (Tib. *shes bya'i sgrib pa*, Skt. *jñeyāvaraṇa*). The subtle mental obscurations that impede the achievement of omniscience, including the habitual propensities for phenomena to appear as though they had inherent existence.

one taste (Tib. *ro gcig*, Skt. *ekarasa*). (1) The third of the four stages of Mahāmudrā meditation. (2) The empty nature of all phenomena of samsāra and nirvāṇa: equally nonexistent, equally pure, naturally arising from the expanse of the ground, and not established as anything else.

perception, extrasensory (Tib. *mngon par shes pa*, Skt. *abhijñā*). Heightened modes of perception that are developed through the practices of śamatha and vipaśyanā. Five kinds of such perception are commonly listed in Buddhist texts: (1) extrasensory perception by which paranormal abilities are enacted, (2) clairvoyance (remote viewing), (3) clairaudience, (4) recollection of past lives, and (5) awareness of others' minds.

perfections, six (Tib. *pha rol tu phyin pa drug*, Skt. *satpāramitā*). The principal practices of a bodhisattva, as imbued with bodhicitta: generosity, ethical discipline, patience, enthusiasm, meditation, and wisdom.

phowa (Tib. *'pho ba*, Skt. *samkrānti*). See *transference*.

pliancy (Tib. *shin sbyang*, Skt. *praśrabdhi*). The suppleness and buoyancy of the body and mind that is cultivated through the practice of śamatha. The achievement of this quality makes the mind optimally efficient for engaging in the cultivation of relative and ultimate bodhicitta.

poisons, five (Tib. *dug lnga*). Delusion, hostility, pride, craving, and envy.

prāṇa (Skt., Tib. *rlung*). Vital energy, known as "winds" or energy currents in the body. See also *karmic energy* (Tib. *las rlung*) and *vāyu*.

pratyekabuddha (Skt., Tib. *rang sangs rgyas*). Lit. "solitary buddha," a person who is committed to his or her own individual liberation by solitary practice.

preta (Skt., Tib. *yi dvags*). A spirit whose existence is dominated by insatiable hunger, thirst, and craving.

primordial consciousness (Tib. *ye shes*, Skt. *jñāna*). The manifest state of the ground, which is self-arisen, naturally luminous, and free of outer and inner obscuration; this is indivisible from the all-pervasive, lucid, clear expanse of the absolute space of phenomena, free of contamination. The word is used in many contexts within Buddhist literature, where it can also simply refer to a timeless kind of knowing, free of conceptual elaboration, which realizes emptiness.

primordial consciousness, discerning (Tib. *so sor rtog pa'i ye shes*, Skt. *pratyavekṣaṇajñāna*). Primordial consciousness that unimpededly discerns the displays of pristine awareness, which knows reality as it is and perceives the full range of all phenomena.

primordial consciousness, five facets of (Tib. *ye shes lnga*, Skt. *pañcajñānāni*). Mirror-like primordial consciousness, discerning primordial consciousness, primordial consciousness of equality, primordial consciousness of accomplishment, and primordial consciousness of the absolute space of phenomena.

primordial consciousness, mirror-like (Tib. *me long lta bu'i ye shes*, Skt. *ādarśajñāna*). Self-illuminating primordial consciousness, which is of a lucid, clear nature, free of contamination, and allows for the unceasing appearances of all manner of objects.

primordial consciousness, three facets of (Tib. *ye shes gsum*). This refers to the empty essential nature, the luminous manifest nature, and all-pervasive compassion as the threefold division of primordial consciousness, or pristine awareness, as it resides in the ground, and can thus be actualized, through practice, into the three kāyas of a buddha.

primordial consciousness of the absolute space of phenomena (Tib. *chos kyi dbyings kyi ye shes*, Skt. *dharmadhātujñāna*). The self-emergent essential nature of the pure ground, which is primordial great emptiness, and which subsumes all phenomena of saṃsāra and nirvāṇa.

primordial consciousness of accomplishment (Tib. *bya ba sgrub pa'i ye shes*, Skt. *kṛtyānuṣṭhānajñāna*). Primordial consciousness by which all pure, free, simultaneously perfected deeds and activities are accomplished naturally, of their own accord.

primordial consciousness of equality (Tib. *mnyam pa nyid kyi ye shes*, Skt. *samatājñāna*). Primordial consciousness of the equal purity of saṃsāra and nirvāṇa in great emptiness.

pristine awareness (Tib. *rig pa*, Skt. *vidyā*). In the context of the Great Perfection, this refers to the ultimate dimension of consciousness, which is primordially pure, beyond time and space, and transcends all conceptual constructs, including the eight extremes of conceptual elaboration.

pristine awareness that is present in the ground (Tib. *gzhir gnas kyi rig pa*). The all-pervasive, fundamental nature of awareness, which is equivalent to the dharmakāya.

propensities, habitual (Tib. *bag chags*, Skt. *vāsanā*). Mental imprints accumulated as a result of previous experiences or actions, which influence later events and conduct.

radiance (Tib. *gdangs*). The natural luminosity of pristine awareness.

rainbow body, great transference (Tib. *'ja' lus 'pho ba chen po*). The highest form into which the aggregates of a practitioner of the Great Perfection path can be liberated upon reaching perfect enlightenment. See *vajrakāya* (Tib. *rdo rje sku*).

realization (Tib. *rtogs pa*). Direct insight into some fundamental aspect of reality. In the context of the Great Perfection, this refers to the subtle, exact knowledge of how all appearing phenomena are nonobjective and empty from their own side, culminating in the decisive knowledge of the one taste of great emptiness—the fact that the whole of saṃsāra and nirvāṇa naturally arises from the expanse of the ground and is not established as anything else.

realms, sentient beings of the six (Tib. *'gro drug*). This usually refers to beings born into one of the six domains of the desire realm, whether those of the gods, asuras, humans, animals, pretas, or hell beings.

realms, three (Tib. *khams gsum*, Skt. *tridhātu*). The desire, form, and formless realms.

reification (Tib. *bden 'dzin*, Skt. *satyagrāha*). Grasping to the idea of inherent existence; falsely apprehending any phenomenon as existing by its own nature, from its own side, independent of conceptual imputation.

rigpa (Tib. *rig pa*, Skt. *vidyā*). See *pristine awareness*.

rūpakāya (Skt., Tib. *gzugs kyi sku*). A form embodiment of an enlightened being, including nirmāṇakāyas and sambhogakāyas.

samādhi (Skt., Tib. *ting nge 'dzin*). Meditative concentration. In the narrow sense of the term, this means focused concentration (achieved specifically through the practice of śamatha), but in the broader sense it is one of the three "higher trainings," together with ethics and wisdom. In that context it refers to exceptional states of mental balance and well-being.

Samantabhadra (Skt., Tib. *kun tu bzang po*). Lit. "all good," with many meanings, depending upon the context: (1) the name of a particular bodhisattva who is one of the eight principal bodhisattva disciples of the Buddha Śākyamuni, (2) a synonym for buddha nature in general, and (3) a synonym for the dharmakāya, in the form of the primordial Buddha Samantabhadra, from whom, according to the Nyingma tantras, the diverse buddha bodies emanate and from whom the higher tantric lineages arise. As such, Samantabhadra is also the result attained through the Great Perfection practice of cutting through.

śamatha (Tib. *zhi gnas*). An advanced degree of meditative concentration in which attentional stability and vividness have been developed to the point that one can fully engage in the cultivation of insight, or vipaśyanā.

sambhogakāya (Skt., Tib. *longs spyod rdzogs pa'i sku*). The "full enjoyment embodiment" of an enlightened being, which is perceptible only to ārya-bodhisattvas and buddhas. It is complete with the *signs and symbols of enlightenment* (see entry below), and is usually adorned with elaborate jewels and elegant apparel.

saṃsāra (Skt., Tib. *'khor ba*). The cycle of existence, perpetuated by compulsively taking rebirth due to the power of one's mental afflictions and karma.

Saṅgha (Tib. *dge 'dun*). Technically, the assembly of āryas (i.e., those who have realized emptiness directly), but more generally the congregation of Buddhist practitioners.

self-appearing (Tib. *rang snang*). Manifesting from itself, a characteristic of primordial consciousness. Also translated as "your own appearances."

self-emergent (Tib. *rang byung*). Emerging from itself, a characteristic of primordial consciousness.

self-grasping (Tib. *bdag tu 'dzin pa*, Skt. *ātmagrāha*). Grasping to a supposed inherently existent identity of persons or things.

settling the mind in its natural state (Tib. *sems rnal du babs pa*). The dissolution of the coarse mind into its underlying subtle continuum of mental consciousness (*substrate consciousness*), which is accomplished through the full accomplishment of śamatha.

siddha (Skt., Tib. *sgrub thob*). One who has accomplished one or more *siddhi*s (see entry below). A great siddha (or *mahāsiddha*) is one who has accomplished both the common and supreme abilities and realizations.

siddhi (Skt., Tib. *dngos grub*). A supernormal ability or achievement. The supreme siddhi is the perfect enlightenment of a buddha, while the eight common siddhis include: (1) the siddhi of celestial realms, the ability to dwell in celestial realms while still alive, (2) the siddhi of the sword, the ability to overcome any hostile army, (3) the siddhi of medicinal pills, the ability to become invisible by holding blessing pills in your hand, (4) the siddhi of fleet-footedness, by which you can walk around a lake in an instant by wearing boots you have blessed, (5) the vase siddhi, by which you can create a vessel that renders inexhaustible anything you put inside it, food or money, for example, (6) the siddhi of yakṣas, the power to make yakṣas your servants, (7) the siddhi of ambrosia (Skt. *amṛta*), which gives you a lifespan as long as the sun and the moon, the strength of an elephant, and the beauty of a lotus, and makes you feel as light as cotton wool whenever you arise from your seat, and (8) the siddhi of the balm of clairvoyance, which, when applied to your eyes, allows you to see things beneath the earth, such as treasures and so on.

sign (Tib. *mtshan ma*, Skt. *nimitta*). An object grasped by the conceptual mind.

signs and symbols of enlightenment (Tib. *mtshan dang dpe byad*). The thirty-two excellent signs and eighty symbols of a supreme nirmāṇakāya buddha.

space (Tib. *dbyings*, Skt. *dhātu*). On the relative level this refers to the *space of awareness* (Tib. *chos kyi khams*, Skt. *dharmadhātu*), which in its primal manifestation is the *substrate* (Tib. *kun gzhi*, Skt. *ālaya*). On the ultimate level it refers to the *absolute space of phenomena* (Tib. *chos kyi dbyings*, Skt. *dharmadhātu*), which is synonymous with emptiness.

space of awareness (Tib. *dbyings*, Skt. *dhātu*). The Tibetan term *dbyings* can mean the relative "space of awareness," when it is not an abbreviation of *chos kyi dbyings*, or the "absolute space of phenomena." The term *space of awareness* may be regarded as identical to the term *element of phenomena* (Tib. *chos kyi khams*, Skt. *dharmadhātu*), which denotes the range of phenomena that can be perceived by the mind and is one of the eighteen elements (Tib. *khams*, Skt. *dhātu*) commonly cited in Buddhist phenomenology.

spontaneous actualization (Tib. *lhun grub*, Skt. *anābhoga*). The spontaneous emergence of qualities and activities from the dharmakāya, the realization of which is the central aspect of the practice of direct crossing over.

śrāvaka (Skt., Tib. *nyan thos*). Lit. "hearer," a disciple of the Buddha who is committed to his or her own individual liberation by following the path set forth by the Buddha.

Śrāvakayāna (Skt., Tib. *nyan thos kyi theg pa*). The spiritual vehicle of the śrāvakas, which is perfected by realizing personal identitylessness.

stage of completion (Tib. *rdzogs rim*, Skt. *utpanna-* or *niṣpannakrama*). A Vajrayāna system of practice, corresponding to anuyoga, which is based on the practice of the stage of generation, and which utilizes that which is already "complete" within the human body—namely, the channels, orbs, and vital energies—in order to bring about realizations of indivisible great bliss and emptiness and to manifest the indwelling mind of clear light joined with the illusory body.

stage of generation (Tib. *bskyed rim*, Skt. *utpattikrama*). A Vajrayāna system of practice, corresponding to mahāyoga, in which one's own body, speech, and mind are regarded as displays of the vajra body, speech, and mind of one's personal deity. As a result of such practice, (1) one achieves stability in one's own awareness, (2) ordinary appearances, along with the clinging that believes them to be real, are transferred to the nature of buddha fields, and (3) one's body, speech, and mind are transformed into the three vajras.

substantial cause (Tib. *nyer len gyi rgyu*, Skt. *upādānakāraṇa*). A prior cause of something that actually transforms into its effect, as a seed transforms into a sprout, or matter transforms into energy.

substantialism (Tib. *dngos por lta ba*). The view that phenomena exist by their own inherent natures, prior to and independent of conceptual designation.

substrate (Tib. *kun gzhi*, Skt. *ālaya*). A vacuous, immaterial, nonconceptual state experienced in deep, dreamless sleep, when one faints, when one dies, and when the mind has settled in its natural state through the achievement of śamatha, in which appearances to the mind have vanished. It is the primal manifestation of the *space of awareness*.

substrate consciousness (Tib. *kun gzhi rnam shes*, Skt. *ālayavijñāna*). An ethically neutral, inwardly directed state of consciousness, free of conceptualization, in which appearances of self, others, and objects are absent. It is into this dimension of consciousness that the coarse mind dissolves upon achieving śamatha.

suchness (Tib. *de bzhin nyid*, Skt. *tathatā*). The ineffable reality of emptiness; the ultimate nature of all phenomena.

suffering (Tib. *sdug bsngal*, Skt. *duḥkha*). The unsatisfying nature of saṃsāra, the reality of suffering, consisting of blatant suffering, the suffering of change, and existential suffering.

sugata (Skt., Tib. *bde bar gshegs pa*). Lit. "well-gone one," an epithet of a buddha, meaning one who has gone to the far shore of liberation, fulfilling one's own and others' needs by achieving perfect enlightenment.

sugatagarbha (Skt., Tib. *bde gshegs snying po*). The essence, or womb, of the sugatas; synonymous with "buddha nature."

Sukhāvatī (Skt., Tib. *bde ba can*). Lit. "land of bliss," this is the buddha field of Amitābha in the western direction.

sūtra (Skt., Tib. *mdo*). Discourses attributed to the Buddha but not included among the tantras.

svabhāvikakāya (Skt., Tib. *ngo bo nyid kyi sku*). The "natural embodiment" of the buddhas, which is the one nature of the dharmakāya, sambhogakāya, and nirmāṇakāya.

tantra (Skt., Tib. *rgyud*). A thread or continuum. A scripture belonging to the class of Vajrayāna Buddhism, as opposed to the exoteric teachings of the sūtras. Many of these scriptures are also attributed to the historical Buddha (as in the case of the *Guhyasamāja* and *Kālacakra Tantras*) or to later emanations of the buddhas, such as those revealed to Düdjom Lingpa.

tathāgata (Skt., Tib. *de bzhin gshegs pa*). Lit. "one who has gone to (or arrived at) suchness," an epithet for a buddha.

terma (Tib. *gter ma*). A "treasure," or hidden text or object, which may be hidden in the ground, water, space, or even mindstream of an adept, waiting to be discovered by a "treasure-revealer" when the time is most propitious. See *tertön*.

tertön (Tib. *gter ston*). A revealer of treasures hidden by great masters of the Great Perfection tradition for the benefit of future generations.

thoughts (Tib. *rnam rtog*, Skt. *vikalpa*). In most contexts, this refers to ordinary, dualistic thoughts concerning the objects of saṃsāra.

transference (Tib. *'pho ba*; Skt. *saṃkrānti*). Transference of consciousness from one type of existence to the next. According to the Great Perfection, the unsurpassed transference is the realization of the pristine domain of the absolute space of phenomena, the sugatagarbha.

transitional phase (Tib. *bar do*, Skt. *antarabhāva*). Any one of the six transitional phases of living, meditation, dreaming, dying, the actual nature of reality, and becoming. See also *intermediate period*.

transitional phase of becoming (Tib. *srid pa bar do*). The dream-like intermediate period immediately following the transitional phase of the actual nature of reality, in which one is on the way to one's next rebirth.

treasure-revealer (Tib. *gter ston*). A highly realized being who reveals Dharma teachings concealed in the physical world or in the nature of mind. See *tertön*.

tulku (Tib. *sprul sku*, Skt. *nirmāṇakāya*). A realized being who is either firmly on the path to enlightenment or who has already achieved enlightenment and becomes incarnate for the sake of the world.

ultimate reality (Tib. *chos nyid*, Skt. *dharmatā*). The ultimate, essential nature of all phenomena, which is emptiness.

vajra (Skt., Tib. *rdo rje*). A symbol of ultimate reality, with the seven attributes of invulnerability, indestructibility, reality, incorruptibility, stability, unobstructability, and invincibility. Also, in Vajrayāna, the "three vajras" can refer to the body, speech, and mind of an enlightened being, or to the subtle vibrations of mantra that are their source.

vajrakāya (Tib. *rdo rje sku*). Lit. "vajra embodiment," a term with which *great transference rainbow body* is often combined. It emphasizes the indestructibility and incorruptibility of such an embodiment—the fact it will never again undergo a transference of consciousness—whereas *rainbow body* emphasizes its illusory appearance as light of five colors. See *rainbow body, great transference*.

Vajrayāna (Skt., Tib. *rdo rje'i theg pa*). The vehicle of esoteric Buddhist teachings and practices aimed at bringing one swiftly to the state of enlightenment.

vāyu (Skt., Tib. *rlung*). Usually refers to one or all of the five primary and five secondary subtle energies that course within the body of a human being in the original condition. The term *prāṇa-vāyu* sometimes refers specifically to just one of the five primary energies, the "vital energy of the life force" (Tib. *srog 'dzin gyi rlung*), though the word *prāṇa* alone can also be used more generally.

vipaśyanā (Skt., Tib. *lhag mthong*). Lit. "superior vision," contemplative insight into fundamental aspects of reality, such as impermanence, suffering, identitylessness, and emptiness.

vīra (Skt., Tib. *dpa' bo*). Lit. "heroic being," one who shows great courage in not succumbing to mental afflictions and in striving diligently in spiritual practice. A highly realized male bodhisattva who manifests in the world in order to serve sentient beings.

vital energy. See *prāṇa* and *vāyu*.

wisdom (Tib. *shes rab*, Skt. *prajñā*). In general this refers to the faculty of discerning intelligence. More specifically in these contexts, it refers to the knowledge that determines everything included in the phenomenal world of saṃsāra and nirvāṇa as being empty, identityless, and nonobjective, such that all appearances and mindsets are gradually extinguished in the space of awareness.

yakṣa (Skt., Tib. *gnod sbyin*). One of the eight classes of haughty, nonhuman beings who cause harm to human beings.

yāna (Skt., Tib. *theg pa*). A vehicle for spiritual practice leading to varying degrees of spiritual liberation and enlightenment.

yidam (Tib. *yi dam*, Skt. *iṣṭadevatā*). See *deity, personal.*

yoga (Skt., Tib. *rnal 'byor*). Lit. "yoke," a meditative practice involving the mind and body.

yogin (Skt., Tib. *rnal 'byor pa*). A man who is adept in the practice of yoga.

yoginī (Skt., Tib. *rnal 'byor ma*). A woman who is adept in the practice of yoga.

Notes

1 Majjhima Nikāya, *Ariyapariyesana Sutta*, No. 26.

2 Aṅguttara Nikāya 3.65, *Kalama Sutta*.

3 Tib. *gter ston*.

4 Traktung Dudjom Lingpa, *A Clear Mirror: The Visionary Autobiography of a Tibetan Master*, trans. Chönyi Drolma (Hong Kong: Rangjung Yeshe Publications, 2011).

5 B. Alan Wallace, *Stilling the Mind: Shamatha Teachings from Düdjom Lingpa's Vajra Essence* (Boston: Wisdom Publications, 2011).

6 Tib. *khregs chod*.

7 Tib. *thod rgal*.

8 Düdjom Lingpa, *The Vajra Essence*, vol. 3 of *Düdjom Lingpa's Visions of the Great Perfection*, trans. B. Alan Wallace (Boston: Wisdom Publications, 2015), 102.

9 Düdjom Lingpa, *Heart of the Great Perfection*, vol. 1 of *Düdjom Lingpa's Visions of the Great Perfection*, trans. B. Alan Wallace (Boston: Wisdom Publications, 2015), 27–38, 163–212.

10 See B. Alan Wallace, *Minding Closely: The Four Applications of Mindfulness* (Ithaca, NY: Snow Lion Publications, 2011).

11 See Gen Lamrimpa, *Realizing Emptiness: Madhyamaka Insight Meditation*, trans. B. Alan Wallace (Ithaca, NY: Snow Lion Publications, 2002).

12 See for example B. Alan Wallace, *The Attention Revolution: Unlocking the Power of the Focused Mind* (Boston: Wisdom Publications, 2006); and Wallace, *Minding Closely*.

13 Düdjom Lingpa, *Heart of the Great Perfection*, 145.

14 Tib. *lus dben*. This stage of practice is typically explained to mean that one is isolated, or separated from, the tendency to think of one's body as something

ordinary, and to experience it rather as being inseparable from the body of an enlightened being.

15   Tib. *ngag dben*. During this completion-stage practice, one is separated from the tendency to think of one's speech as ordinary and learns to experience the subtlest manifestation of inner speech, or the movements of *prāṇa* in one's heart cakra, as being inseparable from the mantra of a buddha.

16   See Padmasambhava, *Natural Liberation: Padmasambhava's Teachings on the Six Bardos*, commentary by Gyatrul Rinpoche, trans. B. Alan Wallace (Boston: Wisdom Publications, 2015), 105. These teachings by Padmasambhava were discovered as an "earth terma" by the fourteenth-century treasure-revealer Karma Lingpa (1326–1386).

17   Tib. *sems dben*. At this advanced level of the completion stage, one realizes an approximation of the indwelling mind of clear light and is thus separated from the tendency to regard one's own mind as something ordinary.

18   Tib. *shin sbyang*, Skt. *praśrabdhi*.

19   Dīgha Nikāya 1.74–75.

20   As quoted by Jé Tsongkhapa in his *Small Exposition of the Stages of the Path to Enlightenment*. See B. Alan Wallace, *Balancing the Mind: A Tibetan Buddhist Approach to Refining Attention* (Ithaca, NY: Snow Lion Publications 2005), 198.

21   Saṃyutta Nikāya 54.9.

22   Ānāpānasati Sutta, Majjhima Nikāya, 118. Bhikkhu Ñāṇamoli and Bhikkhu Bodhi, trans., *The Middle Length Discourses of the Buddha: A Translation of the Majjhima Nikāya* (Boston: Wisdom Publications, 1995), 943, with modification of the original translation.

23   Düdjom Lingpa, *Vajra Essence*, 15–16.

24   *Dhammapada* 1.1. The *Dhammapada* is the second book of the Khuddaka Nikāya.

25   From the *Ratnamegha Sūtra* (*Cloud of Jewels Sūtra*), quoted in Nyanaponika Thera, *The Heart of Buddhist Meditation: Satipaṭṭhāna* (San Francisco: Red Wheel/Weiser, 1996), 198, with modification of the original translation.

26   John R. Searle, *The Rediscovery of the Mind* (Cambridge, MA: MIT Press, 1994), 1.

27   Ibid., 23, 92.

28   John R. Searle, *Mind: A Brief Introduction* (New York: Oxford University Press, 2004), 115.

29   Searle, *Rediscovery of the Mind*, 91, 76–77.

30   Ibid., 100. I have provided an extensive analysis of the ideological and methodological inconsistencies in Searle's writings in my book *The Taboo of Subjectivity: Toward a New Science of Consciousness* (Oxford: Oxford University Press, 2000).

31   Thomas H. Huxley, "Materialism and Idealism," in *Collected Essays*, vol. 1, *Methods and Results* (New York: Cambridge University Press, 2011), http://www.bartleby.com/library/prose/2766.html.

32   Thomas H. Huxley, "On the Physical Basis of Life," *Fortnightly Review* 5 (1868).

33   Thomas H. Huxley, "Science and 'Church Policy,'" *The Reader*, December 1864.

34   William James, *The Principles of Psychology*, 2 vols. (New York: Dover Publications, 1950), 1: 1.

35   Ibid., 1: 185.

36   John B. Watson, *Psychology from the Standpoint of a Behaviorist* (London: Frances Pinter, 1983), 3.

37   John B. Watson, "Psychology as the Behaviorist Views It," *Psych. Rev.* 20 (1913): 166.

38   R. P. Feynman, R. B. Leighton, and M. Sands, *The Feynman Lectures on Physics* (Reading, MA: Addison-Wesley, 1963), 1: 1–4.

39   Sean Carroll, *The Big Picture: On the Origins of Life, Meaning, and the Universe Itself* (New York: Dutton, 2016), 3.

40   Stephen Jay Gould, *Rocks of Ages: Science and Religion in the Fullness of Life* (New York: Ballantine, 1999).

41   Steering Committee on Science and Creationism, "Science and Creationism: A View from the National Academy of Sciences" (Washington, DC: NAS Press, 1999).

42   *The Big Picture*, 384.

43   Martina Amanzio and Fabrizio Benedetti, "Neuropharmacological Dissection of Placebo Analgesia: Expectation-Activated Opioid Systems versus Conditioning-Activated Specific Subsystems," *Journal of Neuroscience* 19, no. 1 (1999): 484–94.

44   Raúl de la Fuente-Fernández, et al., "Expectation and Dopamine Release: Mechanism of the Placebo Effect in Parkinson's Disease," *Science* 293, no. 5532 (2001): 1164–66.

45   Anne Harrington, ed., *The Placebo Effect: An Interdisciplinary Exploration* (Cambridge: Harvard University Press, 1997), 5.

46   Irving Kirsch, "Conditioning, Expectancy, and the Placebo Effect: Comment on Stewart-Williams and Podd (2004)," *Psychological Bulletin* 130, no. 2 (2004): 341–43.

47   Patrick David Wall, "Pain and the Placebo Response," in *Experimental and Theoretical Studies of Consciousness*, ed. G. R. Bock and J. Marsh (Chichester, UK: John Wiley & Sons, 1993), 214.

48   Sharon Begley, *Train Your Mind, Change Your Brain: How a New Science Reveals Our Extraordinary Potential to Transform Ourselves* (New York: Ballantine Books, 2007), viii–ix.

49   See Daniel 12: 3-4: "Those who are wise shall shine like the brightness of the firmament, and those who turn many to righteousness like the stars forever and ever. But you, Daniel, shut up the words, and seal the book until the time of the end; many shall run to and fro, and knowledge shall increase."

50   Francis Bacon, "Idols Which Beset Man's Mind," http://www.sirbacon.org /baconidols.htm.

51   See David Ritz Finkelstein, "Emptiness and Relativity," in *Buddhism and Science: Breaking New Ground*, ed. B. Alan Wallace (New York: Columbia University Press 2003), 365–84.

52   Carroll, *Big Picture*, 295.

53   James, *Principles of Psychology*, 2: 290–91.

54   Ibid., 2: 322n.

55   B. F. Skinner, *Science and Human Behavior* (New York: Macmillan, 1953).

56   B. F. Skinner, *About Behaviorism* (New York: Alfred A. Knopf, 1974), 216.

57   For a compelling explanation of the complex reasons for the demise of introspection in modern psychology, see Kurt Danziger, "The History of Introspection Reconsidered," *Journal of the History of the Behavioral Sciences* 16 (1980): 241–62.

58   Donald Hoffman, "Do We See Reality as It Is?" June 11, 2015, https://www .ted.com/talks/donald_hoffman_do_we_see_reality_as_it_is/transcript? language=en.

59   Alex Rosenberg, "Why You Don't Know Your Own Mind," *New York Times*, July 18, 2016, http://www.nytimes.com/2016/07/18/opinion/why-you-dont -know-your-own-mind.html. For scientific proofs to the contrary, see C. Petitmengin, A. Remillieux, B. Cahour, and S. Carter-Thomas, "A Gap in Nisbett and Wilson's Findings? A First-Person Access to Our Cognitive Processes," *Consciousness and Cognition* 22, no. 2 (2013): 654–69. For a broader philosophical argument, see M. Bitbol and C. Petitmengin, "On the Possibility and Reality of Introspection," *Mind and Matter* 14, no. 1 (2016): 51–75.

60   For an illuminating account of how this occurred, see Joëlle M. Abi-Rached and Nikolas Rose, "The Birth of the Neuromolecular Gaze," *History of the Human Sciences* 23, no. 1 (2010): 11–36.

61   Eric R. Kandel, "The Origins of Modern Neuroscience," *Annual Review of Neuroscience* 5 (1982): 299–303.

62   Eric R. Kandel, "The New Science of Mind," *New York Times*, September 6, 2013, http://www.nytimes.com/2013/09/08/opinion/sunday/the-new-science-of -mind.html.

63   Daniel M. Wegner, *The Illusion of Conscious Will* (Cambridge: MIT Press, 2003), 341–42.

64   Stephen Hawking, "10 Questions for Stephen Hawking," *Time*, November 15, 2010, http://content.time.com/time/magazine/article/0,9171,2029483,00.html.

65   Stephen Hawking, interviewed by Ken Campbell, *Reality on the Rocks: Beyond Our Ken*, aired February 26,1995.

66   Stephen Jay Gould, *Ever Since Darwin: Reflections in Natural History* (New York: W. W. Norton, 1992), 14.

67   Steven Weinberg, *The First Three Minutes: A Modern View of the Origin of the Universe* (New York: Basic Books, 1993), 154.

68   Michael S. A. Graziano, "Are We Really Conscious?" *New York Times*, October 10, 2014, https://www.nytimes.com/2014/10/12/opinion/sunday/are-we-really-conscious.html.

69   Michio Kaku, "Consciousness Can Be Quantified," https://www.youtube.com /watch?v=0GS2rxROcPo&feature=youtu.be.

70   Searle, *Rediscovery of the Mind*, 48–49.

71   Ibid., 95.

72   Ibid., 227.

73   William James, "A Plea for Psychology as a 'Natural Science,'" *The Philosophical Review* 1, no. 2 (1892): 146.

74   Sigmund Freud, "The Future of an Illusion," in *Mass Psychology and Other Writings*, trans. J. A. Underwood (London: Penguin Books, 2004), cited in N. David Mermin, "Physics: QBism Puts the Scientist Back into Science," *Nature* 507, no. 7493 (2004): 423.

75   Thomas H. Huxley, "Science and Religion," *The Builder* 17 (January 1859).

76   "Atomic Education Urged by Einstein," *New York Times*, May 25, 1946, 13.

77   James, *Principles of Psychology*, 1: 191–92.

78   Edward B. Titchener, *A Primer of Psychology*, rev. ed. (New York: Macmillan, 1899), 24–25. See also Edward B. Titchener, *Experimental Psychology: A Manual of Laboratory Practice* (New York: Macmillan, 1901–5). For modern advances in this field see Claire Petitmengin, "Describing One's Subjective Experience in the Second Person: An Interview Method for the Science of Consciousness," *Phenom. Cogn. Sci.* 5 (2006): 229–69.

79   Tib. *gsal ba*.

80   Tib. *rig pa*.

81   Thomas H. Huxley, *The Elements of Physiology and Hygiene: A Text-Book for Educational Institutions* (New York: D. Appleton & Co., 1868), 178.

82   See William James, *A Pluralistic Universe* (Cambridge: Harvard University Press, 1977).

83   John R. Searle, *Consciousness and Language* (Cambridge: Cambridge University Press, 2002), 34.

84 George F. R. Ellis, "True Complexity and Its Associated Ontology," in *Science and Ultimate Reality: Quantum Theory, Cosmology, and Complexity*, ed. John D. Barrow, Paul C. W. Davies, and Charles L. Harper, Jr. (Cambridge: Cambridge University Press, 2004), 621.

85 For a clarification of this distinction see Marcia Bates, "Fundamental Forms of Information," *Journal of the American Society for Information and Technology* 57, no. 8 (2006): 1033–45.

86 Norbert Wiener, *Cybernetics: Or Control and Communication in the Animal and the Machine* (Cambridge: MIT Press, 1961), 132.

87 Časlav Brukner and Anton Zeilinger, "Information and Fundamental Elements of the Structure of Quantum Theory," in *Time, Quantum and Information*, ed. Lutz Castell and Otfried Ischebeck (Berlin: Springer-Verlag, 2003), 352.

88 Andrei Linde, "Inflation, Quantum Cosmology and the Anthropic Principle," in Barrow, Davies, and Harper, *Science and Ultimate Reality*, 449; Paul Davies, "That Mysterious Flow," *Scientific American* 16, no. 1 (2006): 6–11.

89 Paul C. W. Davies, "An Overview of the Contributions of John Archibald Wheeler," in Barrow, Davies, and Harper, *Science and Ultimate Reality*, 10.

90 John Archibald Wheeler, "Law without Law," in *Quantum Theory and Measurement*, ed. John Archibald Wheeler and Wojciech Hubert Zurek (Princeton, NJ: Princeton University Press, 1983), 194.

91 Brukner and Zeilinger, "Information and Fundamental Elements of the Structure of Quantum Theory," 352.

92 James, *A Pluralistic Universe*, 89.

93 Edward Caird, *Hegel* (Edinburgh: W. Blackwood, 1883), 162; cited in James, *A Pluralistic Universe*, 47.

94 Saṃyutta Nikāya 2.36.

95 Ven. Weragoda Sarada Maha Thero, *Treasury of Truth: Illustrated Dhammapada* (Taipei, Taiwan: The Corporate Body of the Buddha Education Foundation, 1993), 61.

96 Tib. *ngo bo*.

97 Tib. *rang bzhin*.

98 See Wallace, *Minding Closely*, 175–204.

99 Düdjom Lingpa, *Vajra Essence*, 20.

100 Ibid., 28.

101 Tib. *nyer len gyi rgyu*.

102 Tib. *lhan cig byed rkyen*.

103 Tib. *rten*.

104 Tib. *brten pa*.

105 *Bodhicittavivāraṇa*, v. 34. The interpolation is based upon the explanation of Jé

Tsongkhapa Lozang Drakpa in his *Illumination of the True Thought: An Extensive Explanation of "Entering the Middle Way"* (Tib. *Dbu ma la 'jug pa'i rgya cher bshad pa dgongs pa rab gsal*), in vol. *ma* of the Tashi Lhunpo block-print edition of the *Collected Works of the Lord* (*Rje'i gsung 'bum*) (Dharamsala, India: Sherig Parkhang, 1997), 149b2–150a3 (300–301).

106 *Kathāvatthu* 615.

107 Aṅguttara Nikāya 1.8–10, cited in Peter Harvey, *The Selfless Mind: Personality, Consciousness and Nirvana in Early Buddhism* (Surrey, England: Curzon Press, 1995), 166, with modification of the original translation.

108 Aṅguttara Nikāya 1.10–11, cited in Harvey, *Selfless Mind*, 167.

109 Pāli, *pabhassara*, Skt. *prabhāsvara*, Tib. *'od gsal*.

110 Pāli, *cittassa nimittaṁ*.

111 Saṃyutta Nikāya 5.150–52.

112 Karma Chagmé, *A Spacious Path to Freedom*, commentary by Gyatrul Rinpoche, trans. B. Alan Wallace (Ithaca, NY: Snow Lion Publications, 2009), 100–101.

113 Lerab Lingpa, "Vital Essence of Primordial Consciousness," in Wallace, *Open Mind*, 63.

114 Jé Tsultrim Zangpo, "An Ornament of the Enlightened View of Samantabhadra," in Wallace, *Open Mind*, 164–65.

115 Lozang Do-ngak Chökyi Gyatso Chok, "Oral Instructions of the Wise," in Wallace, *Open Mind*, 214.

116 Pāli, *attakāra*.

117 Pāli, *attasaraṇa*.

118 Saṃyutta Nikāya 5.10.

119 *Milindapañhā*, 25.

120 Düdjom Lingpa, *Vajra Essence*, 178.

121 Düdjom Lingpa, *Buddhahood Without Meditation*, 39 (translation slightly modified). According to Sera Khandro's commentary, *Garland for the Delight of the Fortunate* (Ibid., 253) the nine kinds of activity (Tib. *bya ba dgu phrugs*) include the body's (1) outer activities, such as walking, sitting, and moving about, (2) inner activities of prostrations and circumambulations, and (3) secret activities of ritual dancing, performing mudrās, and so on; the speech's (4) outer activities, such as all kinds of delusional chatter, (5) inner activities, such as reciting liturgies, and (6) secret activities, such as counting propitiatory mantras of your personal deity; and the mind's (7) outer activities, such as thoughts aroused by the five poisons and the three poisons, (8) inner activities of mind training and cultivating positive thoughts, and (9) the secret activity of dwelling in mundane states of *dhyāna*.

122 See Sarah H. Jacoby, *Love and Liberation: Autobiographical Writings of the*

Tibetan Buddhist Visionary Sera Khandro (New York: Columbia University Press, 2014).

123 Sera Khandro, *Garland for the Delight of the Fortunate*, in Düdjom Lingpa, *Buddhahood Without Meditation*, 251 (translation slightly modified).

124 This verse, often quoted in Tibetan Buddhist literature, is cited from Puṇḍarīka's *Vimalaprabhā* commentary on the *Kālacakra*, although it appears in the Pāli canon as well. The Sanskrit occurs as a quotation in Śāntarakṣita's *Tattvasaṃgraha*, ed. D. Shastri (Varanasi, India: Bauddhabharati, 1968), k. 3587.

125 Dīgha Nikāya 1.223.

126 Huxley, "Science and Religion," 35.

127 Ibid.

128 Dudjom Lingpa, *A Clear Mirror*, 57–59.

129 Sogyal Rinpoche, preface to *Düdjom Lingpa's Visions of the Great Perfection*, vols. 1–3, xvii.

130 Düdjom Lingpa, *Vajra Essence*, 274–75.

131 Düdjom Lingpa, *Heart of the Great Perfection*, 59.

132 Düdjom Lingpa, *Vajra Essence*, 20–21. See also Wallace, *Stilling the Mind*, 120.

133 Aṅguttara Nikāya 1.10-11.

134 Udāna §73. Unpublished translation by Bhikkhu Bodhi.

135 Padmasambhava, *Natural Liberation*, 106.

136 Düdjom Lingpa, *Heart of the Great Perfection*, 166–67.

137 Padmasambhava, *Natural Liberation*, 115.

138 Lozang Chökyi Gyaltsen, *Collected Works (Gsung 'bum) of Blo bzang chos kyi rgyal mtshan, the 1st Paṇchen Lama, Reproduced from Tracings from Prints of the Bkar shis lhun po Blocks* (New Delhi: Mongolian Lama Gurudeva, 1973), 4: 84. This passage translated by B. Alan Wallace.

139 Zara Houshmand, Robert B. Livingston, and B. Alan Wallace, eds., *Consciousness at the Crossroads: Conversations with the Dalai Lama on Brain Science and Buddhism* (Ithaca, NY: Snow Lion Publications, 1999), 72.

140 Cristof Koch, *The Quest for Consciousness: A Neurobiological Approach* (Englewood, CO: Roberts and Company Publishers, 2004), 19.

141 Catherine de Lange, "The Fragility of You and What It Says about Consciousness," in *Untold Story*, July 26, 2017, https://www.newscientist.com/article/mg23531360-600-the-fragility-of-you-and-what-it-says-about-consciousness/.

142 Padmasambhava, *Natural Liberation*, 106.

143 LiveScience Staff, "Girl Sees Fine with Half a Brain," July 27, 2009, http://www.livescience.com/health/090727-one-eye-vision.html; see also Lars Muckli, et al., "Bilateral Visual Field Maps in a Patient with Only One Hemisphere," *PNAS* 106, no. 31 (2009): 13034–39, doi:10.1073/pnas.0809688106.

144 Roger Lewin, "Is Your Brain Really Necessary?" *Science* 210 (December 12, 1980): 1232–34.

145 Ibid., 1233.

146 Ian Stewart, *Concepts of Modern Mathematics* (New York: Dover Publications, 1995), 286.

147 Pim van Lommel, *Consciousness Beyond Life: The Science of Near-Death Experience* (New York: HarperOne, 2010); Edward F. Kelly, Emily Williams Kelly, Adam Crabtree, Alan Gauld, Michael Grosso, and Bruce Greyson, *Irreducible Mind: Toward a Psychology for the 21st Century* (Lanham, MD: Rowman & Littlefield, 2007), chap. 6, "Unusual Experiences Near Death and Related Phenomena."

148 Richard P. Feynman, *The Character of Physical Law* (Cambridge: MIT Press, 1967), 127, 148, 158.

149 Atīśa, *Lamp for the Path to Enlightenment* (Tib. *Byang chub lam gyi sgron ma,* Skt. *Bodhipathapradīpa*), vv. 35, 36, 38.

150 For a very cogent Western philosophical critique of metaphysical realism, see Hilary Putnam, *Realism with a Human Face*, ed. James Conant (Cambridge: Harvard University Press, 1990).

151 Düdjom Lingpa, *Vajra Essence*, 262.

152 Padmasambhava, *Natural Liberation*, 235–56.

153 Ibid., 141–68; B. Alan Wallace, *Dreaming Yourself Awake: Lucid Dreaming and Tibetan Dream Yoga for Insight and Transformation* (Boston: Shambhala Publications, 2012).

154 Tib. *mir chags pa.*

155 For an overview, see Christopher C. French, "Near-Death Experiences in Cardiac Arrest Survivors," *Progress in Brain Research* 150, ed. Steven Laureys (Amsterdam: Elsevier Science, 2005), 351–67.

156 Bruce Greyson, "The Near-Death Experience Scale: Construction, Reliability, and Validity," *Journal of Nervous and Mental Disease* 171, no. 6 (1983): 369–75.

157 Padma Sambhava and Karma Lingpa, *The Tibetan Book of the Dead: Liberation through Understanding in the Between*, trans. Robert A. F. Thurman (New York: Bantam Books, 1994), 11.

158 Lee W. Bailey, "A 'Little Death': The Near-Death Experience and Tibetan Delogs," *Journal of Near-Death Studies* 19, no. 3 (2001): 139–59.

159 Tib. *'das log.*

160 Delog Dawa Drolma, *Delog: Journey to Realms Beyond Death*, trans. Richard Barron (Chökyi Nyima) with His Eminence Chagdud Tulku Rinpoche (Junction City, CA: Padma Publishing, 1995), vii.

161 *Rājaparikathā ratnamālī*, Tib. *Rgyal po la gtam bya ba rin po che'i phreng ba*, as

quoted by Tsongkhapa in his *Illumination of the True Thought [of the Middle Way]*, vol. *ma*, 87b3 (176), in the Tashi Lhunpo block-print edition of the *Collected Works of the Lord*. (There is a textual variant of the last word in Tibetan editions of this verse from the Tengyur, as *yin* rather than *med*, but I follow the latter, as it is the reading most frequently glossed by contemporary teachers, such as His Holiness the Dalai Lama.)

162 Tsongkhapa, *Illumination of the True Thought*, vol. *ma*, 87b4–5 (176).

163 An edited transcript of this meeting appears in Arthur Zajonc, ed., *The New Physics and Cosmology: Dialogues with the Dalai Lama* (New York: Oxford University Press, 2004).

164 Tib. *srid pa*.

165 B. Alan Wallace, "A General Theory of Ontological Relativity," in *Hidden Dimensions: The Unification of Physics and Consciousness* (New York: Columbia University Press, 2007), 70–84.

166 Hugh Everett, "Short Article," *Reviews of Modern Physics* 29 (1957): 454.

167 Thomas Nagel, *The View from Nowhere* (New York: Oxford University Press, 1986).

168 Richard Conn Henry, "The Mental Universe," *Nature* 436 (July 7, 2005): 29.

169 Leonard Susskind, "The World as a Hologram," SU-ITP-94-33, September 1994, arXiv:hep-th/9409089.

170 Philip Ball, "We Might Live in a Computer Program, but It May Not Matter," BBC Earth, September 5, 2016.

171 See also Düdjom Lingpa, *Vajra Essence*, 40–41, and Sera Khandro, *Garland for the Delight of the Fortunate*, in *Buddhahood Without Meditation*, 91–101.

172 Quoted by Aage Petersen, in "The Philosophy of Niels Bohr," *Bulletin of the Atomic Scientists* 19, no. 7 (1963): 8-14.

173 *Probability and Uncertainty: The Quantum Mechanical View of Nature*, dir. Richard P. Feynman, British Broadcasting Corp. Television, London, November 18, 1964, http://www.richard-feynman.net/videos.htm.

174 Carroll, *Big Picture*, chap. 17.

175 Hilary Putnam, *Realism with a Human Face*, 28.

176 Lerab Lingpa, "How to Settle the Mind in Its Natural State, Since This Method Is So Crucially Important," from "The Vital Essence of Primordial Consciousness," in Wallace, *Open Mind*, 32.

177 Aṅguttara Nikāya 4.36, trans. Thanissaro Bhikkhu, with abridgements, http://www.accesstoinsight.org/tipitaka/an/an04/an04.036.than.html.

178 Tib. *kun rdzob*, Skt. *saṃvṛti*. This adjective usually occurs as a modifier of one of the two kinds of reality. The Tibetan and Sanskrit adjective means "totally obscuring," for this reality totally obscures the deeper dimension of ultimate real-

ity (Tib. *don dam bden pa*, Skt. *paramārthasatya*). "Totally obscuring reality" seems too awkward in English and also does not quite get at the meaning, since, according to Candrakīrti, it is *ignorance* that obscures the nature of the reality, not the appearances themselves. Hence the appearances are "deceptive," but for those who are deceived by the obscuring veil of ignorance, they appear to be "real." Thus they are "deceptively real" and constitute what is known as "deceptive reality."

179 See B. Alan Wallace, *Choosing Reality: A Buddhist View of Physics and the Mind* (Ithaca, NY: Snow Lion Publications, 1996), chap. 2, "Exploring the Nature of Empty Space."

180 B. Alan Wallace, "Vacuum States of Consciousness: A Tibetan Buddhist View," in *Buddhist Thought and Applied Psychological Research: Transcending the Boundaries*, ed. D. K. Nauriyal (London: Routledge, 2006), 112–21; Henning Genz, *Nothingness: The Science of Empty Space*, trans. Karin Heusch (Cambridge, MA: Perseus Books, 1999); K. C. Cole, *The Hole in the Universe: How Scientists Peered Over the Edge of Emptiness and Found Everything* (New York: Harcourt, 2001). On the other hand, in his first of five Messenger lectures at Cornell University on "The Future of Fundamental Physics," October 4, 2010, the theoretical physicist Nima Arkani-Hamed stated: ". . . many, many separate arguments, all very strong individually, suggest that the very notion of space-time is not a fundamental one. Space-time is doomed. There is no such thing as space-time, fundamentally in the actual, underlying description of the laws of physics. That's very startling, because what physics is supposed to be about is describing things as they happen in space and time. So if there is no space-time, it's not clear what physics is about. That's why this is a hard problem. That's a serious comment . . ." http://www.cornell.edu/video/nima-arkani-hamed-quantum-mechanics-and-spacetime.

181 Tib. *rgyu*.

182 Tib. *rkyen*.

183 Searle, *Rediscovery of the Mind*, 112.

184 Alex Rosenberg, *The Atheist's Guide to Reality: Enjoying Life without Illusions* (New York: W. W. Norton, 2011), 6.

185 Rosenberg, "Why You Don't Know Your Own Mind."

186 *Opere*, II, 564, which is a letter from Paolo Gualdo to Galileo. Galileo Galilei, *Le opere di Galileo Galilei*, ed. Antonio Favaro, 20 vols. (Florence: Barbera, 1890–1909), vol. 2, no. 564, p. 165.

187 For a flagrant example of this ethnocentric bias, see Daniel J. Boorstin, *The Discoverers: A History of Man's Search to Know His World and Himself* (New York: Vintage Books, 1985). In this entire historical overview of humanity's discoveries, the author cites only two outstanding figures in human history for their

discoveries regarding the mind: Freud and Jung. Five thousand years of civilization in Asia is utterly ignored.

188 Tib. *rten cing.*

189 Tib. *'brel bar.*

190 Tib. *'byung ba.*

191 Tib. *ye shes kyi rlung.*

192 Juan Yin, et al., "Bounding the Speed of 'Spooky Action at a Distance,'" *Phys. Rev. Lett.* 110, no. 26 (2013): http://arxiv.org/abs/1303.0614.

193 Xiao-song Ma, et al., "Experimental Delayed-Choice Entanglement Swapping," *Nature Physics* 8, no. 6 (2012): 479–84.

194 Stephen LaBerge and Howard Rheingold, *Exploring the World of Lucid Dreaming* (New York: Ballantine Books, 1990).

195 S. W. Hawking and Thomas Hertog, "Populating the Landscape: A Top Down Approach," *Physical Review D* 73, no. 12 (2006): 123527-1–9.

196 Hawking and Hertog, "Populating the Landscape," 123527; Martin Bojowald, "Cosmology: Unique or Not Unique?" *Nature* 442 (August 31, 2006): 988–90.

197 Quoted in Robert F. Barsky, *Noam Chomsky: A Life of Dissent* (Cambridge: MIT Press, 1998), 95.

198 Tib. *'pho ba.*

199 Tib. *thugs dam.*

200 Karma Chagmé, *Naked Awareness: Practical Instructions on the Union of Mahāmudrā and Dzogchen*, commentary by Gyatrul Rinpoche, trans. B. Alan Wallace (Ithaca, NY: Snow Lion Publications, 2000), 81–87.

201 Werner Heisenberg, *Physics and Philosophy: The Revolution in Modern Science* (New York: Harper & Row, 1962), 58.

202 Ludwig Feuerbach, *The Essence of Christianity*, trans. Marian Evans (New York: Calvin Blanchard, 1855).

203 Davies, "An Overview of the Contributions of John Archibald Wheeler," 20.

204 See also Wallace, *Taboo of Subjectivity*, 43–47.

205 Christopher A. Fuchs, N. David Mermin, and Rüdiger Schack, "An Introduction to QBism with an Application to the Locality of Quantum Mechanics," *American Journal of Physics* 82, no. 8 (2014): 749.

206 Ibid., 757.

207 Hans Christian von Baeyer, *QBism: The Future of Quantum Physics* (Cambridge: Harvard University Press, 2016), 188.

208 Amanda Gefter, "A Private View of Quantum Reality," *Quanta Magazine*, June 4, 2015, https://www.quantamagazine.org/20150604-quantum-bayesianism-qbism.

209 Maurice Walshe, trans., *The Long Discourses of the Buddha: A Translation of the Dīgha Nikāya* (Boston: Wisdom Publications, 1995), 105. *Sāmaññaphala Sutta*

in the Dīgha Nikāya 1.78.

210 Karma Chagmé, *Great Commentary to* [*Mi 'gyur rdo rje's*] *Buddhahood in the Palm of Your Hand* (*Sangs rgyas lag 'chang gi 'grel chen*) (Bylakuppe, India: Nyingmapa Monastery, date unknown), 655.

211 See Shar Khentrul Jamphel Lodrö, *Demystifying Shambhala: The Profound and Secret Nature That Is the Perfection of Peace and Harmony as Revealed by the Jonang Tradition of Kalachakra* (Belgrave, Australia: Tibetan Buddhist Rimé Institute, 2016); and Geshe Lhundup Sopa, et al., *The Wheel of Time: The Kalachakra in Context* (Ithaca, NY: Snow Lion Publications, 1991).

212 Tsongkhapa, *The Great Treatise on the Stages of the Path to Enlightenment (Lam rim chen mo)*, vol. 3, trans. The Lamrim Chenmo Translation Committee (Ithaca, NY: Snow Lion Publications, 2002), 178.

213 His Holiness the Dalai Lama, "Teachings on Lam-rim Chen-mo," http://www.lamayeshe.com/article/chapter/day-six-afternoon-session-july-15-2008.

214 James, *Principles of Psychology*, 1: 191–92.

215 "Wiles's Proof of Fermat's Last Theorem," https://en.wikipedia.org/wiki/Wiles%27s_proof_of_Fermat%27s_Last_Theorem.

216 See Simon Singh, *Fermat's Last Theorem: The Story of a Riddle That Confounded the World's Greatest Minds for 358 Years* (London: Fourth Estate, 1997). This was the first book about mathematics to become a no. 1 bestseller.

217 James, *A Pluralistic Universe*, 142.

218 *The Yogis of Tibet: A Film for Posterity*, dir. Jeffrey M. Pill (JEHM Films, 2002). This interview begins at the 35-minute mark.

219 Śāntideva, *A Guide to the Bodhisattva Way of Life: Bodhicaryāvatāra*, trans. Vesna A. Wallace and B. Alan Wallace (Ithaca, NY: Snow Lion Publications, 1997), 9.1.

220 Düdjom Lingpa, *Vajra Essence*, 171.

221 Pema Tashi, *Essence of Clear Meaning: A Short Commentary on the "Sharp Vajra of Conscious Awareness Tantra,"* in Düdjom Lingpa, *Heart of the Great Perfection*, 46.

222 Genz, *Nothingness*, 26.

223 Cole, *Hole in the Universe*, 244.

224 Ibid., 177–78.

225 Ibid., 235.

226 Steven Weinberg, *Dreams of a Final Theory: The Scientist's Search for the Ultimate Laws of Nature* (New York: Vintage Books, 1992), 196.

227 His Holiness the Dalai Lama, *The Universe in a Single Atom: The Convergence of Science and Spirituality* (New York: Morgan Road Books, 2005), 85–87.

228 See Gerardo Ceballos, Paul. R. Ehrlich, and Rodolfo Dirzo, "Biological Annihilation via the Ongoing Sixth Mass Extinction Signaled by Vertebrate Population

Losses and Declines," *Proceedings of the National Academy of Sciences* 114, no. 30 (2017): doi:10.1073/pnas.1704949114: http://www.pnas.org/content /early/2017/07/05/1704949114.full.

See also "World Wildlife Populations Halved in 40 Years," a report by Roger Harrabin, BBC environment analyst, September 30, 2014, http://www.bbc .com/news/science-environment-29418983.

229 Shabkar Tsogdruk Rangdrol, *The Life of Shabkar: The Autobiography of a Tibetan Yogi*, trans. Matthieu Ricard, Jakob Leschley, Erik Schmidt, Marilyn Silverstone, and Lodrö Palmo, ed. Constance Wilkinson, with Michal Abrams and other members of the Padmakara Translation Group (Ithaca, NY: Snow Lion Publications, 2001), 282. Translation slightly modified.

230 Tsongkhapa, *Great Treatise on the Stages of the Path to Enlightenment*, 3: 28–30.

231 Tib. *Byang chub lam gyi sgron ma*, Skt. *Bodhipathapradīpa*, v. 39.

232 Tib. *blo sbyong*, pronounced "lojong."

233 See B. Alan Wallace, *Buddhism with an Attitude: The Tibetan Seven-Point Mind-Training* (Ithaca, NY: Snow Lion Publications, 2001).

234 James, *A Pluralistic Universe*, 148.

235 William James, *The Varieties of Religious Experience: A Study in Human Nature* (New York: Penguin, 1902/1985), 456.

236 Ibid.

237 Arthur Zajonc and Anne Harrington, eds., *Investigating the Mind: The Dalai Lama at MIT* (Cambridge: Harvard University Press, 2006), 181–89.

238 Ibid., 194–98.

239 Ibid., 211–12. The reference to "MRIs in Wisconsin" pertains to studies at the University of Wisconsin, Madison.

240 Ibid., 214–15.

241 Skt. *adhisamādhiśikṣa*.

242 Skt. *adhiprajñāśikṣa*.

243 Skt. *adhiśīlaśikṣa*.

Bibliography

Source Text

Düdjom Lingpa. *The Vajra Essence: From the Matrix of Pure Appearances and Primordial Consciousness, a Tantra on the Self-Emergent Nature of Existence. Dag snang ye shes drwa ba las gnas lugs rang byung gi rgyud rdo rje'i snying po.* In vol. 17 of *Collected Works of the Emanated Great Treasures, the Secret, Profound Treasures of Düdjom Lingpa*, 48–85. Thimpu, Bhutan: Lama Kuenzang Wangdue, 2004. (Buddhist Digital Resource Center W28732.)

Citations

Abi-Rached, Joelle M., and Nikolas Rose. "The Birth of the Neuromolecular Gaze." *History of the Human Sciences* 23, no. 1 (2010): 11–36.

Amanzio, Martina, and Fabrizio Benedetti. "Neuropharmacological Dissection of Placebo Analgesia: Expectation-Activated Opioid Systems versus Conditioning-Activated Specific Subsystems." *Journal of Neuroscience* 19, no. 1 (1999): 484–94.

"Atomic Education Urged by Einstein." *New York Times*, May 25, 1946.

Bacon, Francis. "Idols Which Beset Man's Mind." http://www.sirbacon.org/baconidols.htm.

Bailey, Lee W. "A 'Little Death': The Near-Death Experience and Tibetan Delogs." *Journal of Near-Death Studies* 19, no. 3 (2001): 139–59.

Ball, Philip. "We Might Live in a Computer Program, but It May Not Matter." *BBC Earth*, September 5, 2016.

Barrow, John D., Paul C. W. Davies, and Charles L. Harper, Jr., eds. *Science and Ultimate Reality: Quantum Theory, Cosmology, and Complexity.* Cambridge: Cambridge University Press, 2004.

Bates, Marcia. "Fundamental Forms of Information." *Journal of the American Society for Information and Technology* 57, no. 8 (2006): 1033–45.

Begley, Sharon. *Train Your Mind, Change Your Brain: How a New Science Reveals Our Extraordinary Potential to Transform Ourselves.* New York: Ballantine Books, 2007.

Barsky, Robert F. *Noam Chomsky: A Life of Dissent.* Cambridge: MIT Press, 1998.

Bitbol, M., and C. Petitmengin. "On the Possibility and Reality of Introspection." *Mind and Matter* 14, no. 1 (2016): 51–75.

Bojowald, Martin. "Cosmology: Unique or Not Unique?" *Nature* 442 (August 31, 2006): 988–90.

Boorstin, Daniel J. *The Discoverers: A History of Man's Search to Know His World and Himself.* New York: Vintage Books, 1985.

Brukner, Časlav, and Anton Zeilinger. "Information and Fundamental Elements of the Structure of Quantum Theory." In *Time, Quantum and Information*, edited by Lutz Castell and Otfried Ischebeck, 323–55. Berlin: Springer-Verlag, 2003.

Caird, Edward. *Hegel.* Edinburgh: W. Blackwood, 1883.

Carroll, Sean. *The Big Picture: On the Origins of Life, Meaning, and the Universe Itself.* New York: Dutton, 2016.

Ceballos, Gerardo, Paul. R. Ehrlich, and Rodolfo Dirzo. "Biological Annihilation via the Ongoing Sixth Mass Extinction Signaled by Vertebrate Population Losses and Declines." *Proceedings of the National Academy of*

Sciences 114, no. 30 (2017): doi:10.1073/pnas.1704949114: http://www.pnas.org/content/early/2017/07/05/1704949114.full.

Chagmé, Karma. *Great Commentary to* [*Mi 'gyur rdo rje's*] *Buddhahood in the Palm of Your Hand* (*Sangs rgyas lag 'chang gi 'grel chen*). Bylakuppe, India: Nyingmapa Monastery, date unknown.

————. *Naked Awareness: Practical Instructions on the Union of Mahāmudrā and Dzogchen.* Commentary by Gyatrul Rinpoche. Translated by B. Alan Wallace. Ithaca, NY: Snow Lion Publications, 2000.

————. *A Spacious Path to Freedom.* Commentary by Gyatrul Rinpoche. Translated by B. Alan Wallace. Ithaca, NY: Snow Lion Publications, 2009.

Chökyi Gyatso, Lozang Do-ngak. "Oral Instructions of the Wise." In Wallace, *Open Mind*, 209–24.

Cole, K. C. *The Hole in the Universe: How Scientists Peered over the Edge of Emptiness and Found Everything.* New York: Harcourt, 2001.

Danziger, Kurt. "The History of Introspection Reconsidered." *Journal of the History of the Behavioral Sciences* 16 (1980): 241–62.

Davies, Paul C. W. "An Overview of the Contributions of John Archibald Wheeler." In Barrow, Davies, and Harper, *Science and Ultimate Reality*, 3–25.

————. "That Mysterious Flow." *Scientific American* 16, no. 1 (2006): 6–11.

de Lange, Catherine. "The Fragility of You and What It Says about Consciousness." In *Untold Story*, July 26, 2017, https://www.newscientist.com/article/mg23531360-600-the-fragility-of-you-and-what-it-says-about-consciousness/.

Delog Dawa Drolma. *Delog: Journey to Realms Beyond Death.* Translated by Richard Barron (Chökyi Nyima) with His Eminence Chagdud Tulku Rinpoche. Junction City, CA: Padma Publishing, 1995.

Düdjom Lingpa. *A Clear Mirror: The Visionary Autobiography of a Tibetan Master.* Translated by Chönyi Drolma. Hong Kong: Rangjung Yeshe Publications, 2011.

————. *Heart of the Great Perfection*. Vol. 1 of *Düdjom Lingpa's Visions of the Great Perfection*. 3 vols. Foreword by Sogyal Rinpoche. Translated by B. Alan Wallace. Edited by Dion Blundell. Boston: Wisdom Publications, 2015.

————. *Buddhahood without Meditation*. Vol. 2 of *Düdjom Lingpa's Visions of the Great Perfection*. 3 vols. Foreword by Sogyal Rinpoche. Translated by B. Alan Wallace. Edited by Dion Blundell. Boston: Wisdom Publications, 2015.

————. *The Vajra Essence*. Vol. 3 of *Düdjom Lingpa's Visions of the Great Perfection*. 3 vols. Foreword by Sogyal Rinpoche. Translated by B. Alan Wallace. Edited by Dion Blundell. Boston: Wisdom Publications, 2015.

Ellis, George F. R. "True Complexity and Its Associated Ontology." In Barrow, Davies, and Harper, *Science and Ultimate Reality*, 607–36.

Everett, Hugh. "Short Article." *Reviews of Modern Physics* 29 (1957): 454.

Feuerbach, Ludwig. *The Essence of Christianity*. Translated by Marian Evans. New York: Calvin Blanchard, 1855.

Feynman, Richard P. *The Character of Physical Law*. Cambridge: MIT Press, 1967.

Feynman, R. P., R. B. Leighton, and M. Sands. *The Feynman Lectures on Physics*. vol. 1. Reading, MA: Addison-Wesley, 1963.

Finkelstein, David Ritz. "Emptiness and Relativity." In Wallace, *Buddhism and Science*, 365–84.

French, Christopher C. "Near-Death Experiences in Cardiac Arrest Survivors." In *Progress in Brain Research*, vol. 150, edited by Steven Laureys, 351–67. Amsterdam: Elsevier Science, 2005.

Freud, Sigmund. "The Future of an Illusion" [1927]. In *Mass Psychology and Other Writings*, translated by J. A. Underwood, 107–64. London: Penguin Books, 2004.

Fuchs, Christopher A., N. David Mermin, and Rüdiger Schack. "An Introduction to QBism with an Application to the Locality of Quantum Mechanics." *American Journal of Physics* 82, no. 8 (2014): 749–54.

Fuente-Fernández, Raúl de la, et al. "Expectation and Dopamine Release: Mechanism of the Placebo Effect in Parkinson's Disease." *Science* 293, no. 5532 (2001): 1164–66.

Galileo Galilei. *Le opere di Galileo Galilei.* Edited by Antonio Favaro. 20 vols. Florence: Barbera, 1890–1909.

Gefter, Amanda. "A Private View of Quantum Reality." *Quanta Magazine,* June 4, 2015, https://www.quantamagazine.org/20150604-quantum--bayesianism-qbism.

Gen Lamrimpa. *Realizing Emptiness: Madhyamaka Insight Meditation.* Translated by B. Alan Wallace. Ithaca, NY: Snow Lion Publications, 2002.

Genz, Henning. *Nothingness: The Science of Empty Space.* Translated by Karin Heusch. Cambridge, MA: Perseus Books, 1999.

Geshe Lundrup Sopa, et al. *The Wheel of Time: The Kalachakra in Context.* Ithaca, NY: Snow Lion Publications, 1991.

Gould, Stephen Jay. *Ever Since Darwin: Reflections in Natural History* [1980]. New York: W. W. Norton, 1992.

———. *Rocks of Ages: Science and Religion in the Fullness of Life.* New York: Ballantine, 1999.

Graziano, Michael S. A. "Are We Really Conscious?" *New York Times,* October 10, 2014, https://www.nytimes.com/2014/10/12/opinion/sunday/are-we-really-conscious.html.

Greyson, Bruce. "The Near-Death Experience Scale: Construction, Reliability, and Validity." *Journal of Nervous and Mental Disease* 171, no. 6 (1983): 369–75.

Harrington, Anne, ed. *The Placebo Effect: An Interdisciplinary Exploration.* Cambridge: Harvard University Press, 1997.

Harvey, Peter. *The Selfless Mind: Personality, Time, Consciousness and Nirvana in Early Buddhism.* Surrey, England: Curzon Press, 1995.

Hawking, Stephen. "Interview with Ken Campbell." *Reality on the Rocks: Beyond Our Ken,* aired February 26, 1995.

———. "10 Questions for Stephen Hawking." *Time*, November 15, 2010, http://content.time.com/time/magazine/article/0,9171,2029483,00.html.

Hawking, S. W., and Thomas Hertog. "Populating the Landscape: A Top Down Approach." *Physical Review D* 73, no. 12 (2006): 123527-1–9.

Heisenberg, Werner. *Physics and Philosophy: The Revolution in Modern Science*. New York: Harper & Row, 1962.

Henry, Richard Conn. "The Mental Universe." *Nature* 436 (July 7, 2005): 29.

His Holiness the Dalai Lama. *The Universe in a Single Atom: The Convergence of Science and Spirituality*. New York: Morgan Road Books, 2005.

Hoffman, Donald. "Do We See Reality as It Is?" June 11, 2015. https://www.ted.com/talks/donald_hoffman_do_we_see_reality_as_it_is/transcript?language=en.

Houshmand, Zara, Robert B. Livingston, and B. Alan Wallace, eds. *Consciousness at the Crossroads: Conversations with the Dalai Lama on Brain Science and Buddhism*. Translations by Geshe Thubten Jinpa and B. Alan Wallace. Ithaca, NY: Snow Lion Publications, 1999.

Huxley, Thomas H. *The Elements of Physiology and Hygiene: A Text-Book for Educational Institutions*. New York: D. Appleton & Co., 1868.

———. "Materialism and Idealism." In *Collected Essays*, vol. 1, *Methods and Results*. New York: Cambridge University Press, 2011. http://www.bartleby.com/library/prose/2766.html.

———. "On the Physical Basis of Life." *Fortnightly Review* 5 (1868).

———. "Science and 'Church Policy.'" *The Reader*, December 1864.

———. "Science and Religion." *The Builder* 17 (January 1859).

James, William. "A Plea for Psychology as a 'Natural Science.'" *The Philosophical Review* 1, no. 2 (1892): 146–53.

———. *A Pluralistic Universe* [1909]. Cambridge: Harvard University Press, 1977.

———. *The Principles of Psychology*. 2 vols. New York: Dover Publications, 1950.

———. *The Varieties of Religious Experience: A Study in Human Nature* [1902]. New York: Penguin, 1985.

Kaku, Michio. "Consciousness Can Be Quantified." April 13, 2015. https://www.youtube.com/watch?v=oGS2rxROcP0&feature=youtu.be.

Kandel, Eric R. "The New Science of Mind." *New York Times*, September 6, 2013, http://www.nytimes.com/2013/09/08/opinion/sunday/the-new-science-of-mind.html.

———. "The Origins of Modern Neuroscience." *Annual Review of Neuroscience* 5 (1982): 299–303.

Kelly, Edward F., Emily Williams Kelly, Adam Crabtree, Alan Gauld, Michael Grosso, and Bruce Greyson. *Irreducible Mind: Toward a Psychology for the 21st Century*. Lanham, MD: Rowman & Littlefield, 2007.

Kirsch, Irving. "Conditioning, Expectancy, and the Placebo Effect: Comment on Stewart-Williams and Podd (2004)." *Psychological Bulletin* 130, no. 2 (2004): 341–43.

Koch, Cristof. *The Quest for Consciousness: A Neurobiological Approach*. Englewood, CO: Roberts and Company Publishers, 2004.

LaBerge, Stephen, and Howard Rheingold. *Exploring the World of Lucid Dreaming*. New York: Ballantine Books, 1990.

Lerab Lingpa. "The Vital Essence of Primordial Consciousness." In Wallace, *Open Mind*, 3–120.

Lewin, Roger. "Is Your Brain Really Necessary?" *Science* 210 (December 12, 1980): 1232–34.

Linde, Andrei. "Inflation, Quantum Cosmology and the Anthropic Principle." In Barrow, Davies, and Harper, *Science and Ultimate Reality*, 426–58.

LiveScience Staff. "Girl Sees Fine with Half a Brain." LiveScience.com, July 27, 2009, http://www.livescience.com/health/090727-one-eye-vision.html.

Lozang Chökyi Gyaltsen. *Collected Works (Gsung 'bum) of Blo bzang chos kyi rgyal mtshan, the 1st Panchen Lama, Reproduced from Tracings from Prints of the Bkar shis lhun po Blocks*. New Delhi: Mongolian

Lama Gurudeva, 1973. Also published as *The Autobiography of the First Paṇchen Lama Blo bzang chos kyi rgyal mtshan*. New Delhi: Ngawang Gelek Demo, 1969.

Ma, Xiao-song, et al. "Experimental Delayed-Choice Entanglement Swapping." *Nature Physics* 8, no. 6 (2012): 479–84.

Mermin, David N. "Physics: QBism Puts the Scientist Back into Science." *Nature* 507, no. 7493 (2014): 421–23.

Muckli, Lars, et al. "Bilateral Visual Field Maps in a Patient with Only One Hemisphere." *PNAS* 106, no. 31 (2009): 13034–39, doi:10.1073 /pnas.0809688106.

Nagel, Thomas. *The View from Nowhere*. New York: Oxford University Press, 1986.

Ñāṇamoli, Bhikkhu, and Bhikkhu Bodhi, trans. *The Middle Length Discourses of the Buddha: A Translation of the Majjhima Nikāya*. Boston: Wisdom Publications, 1995.

Nyanaponika Thera. *The Heart of Buddhist Meditation: Satipaṭṭhāna*. San Francisco: Red Wheel/Weiser, 1996.

Padma Sambhava and Karma Lingpa. *The Tibetan Book of the Dead: Liberation through Understanding in the Between*. Translated by Robert A. F. Thurman. New York: Bantam Books, 1994.

Padmasambhava. *Natural Liberation: Padmasambhava's Teachings on the Six Bardos*. Commentary by Gyatrul Rinpoche. Translated by B. Alan Wallace. Boston: Wisdom Publications, 2015.

Pema Tashi. *Essence of Clear Meaning: A Short Commentary on the "Sharp Vajra of Conscious Awareness Tantra."* In Düdjom Lingpa, *Heart of the Great Perfection*, 39–138.

Petersen, Aage. "The Philosophy of Niels Bohr." *Bulletin of the Atomic Scientists* 19, no. 7 (1963): 8–14.

Petitmengin, Claire. "Describing One's Subjective Experience in the Second Person: An Interview Method for the Science of Consciousness." *Phenom. Cogn. Sci.* 5 (2006): 229–69.

Petitmengin, C., A. Remillieux, B. Cahour, and S. Carter-Thomas. "A Gap in Nisbett and Wilson's Findings? A First-Person Access to Our Cognitive Processes." *Consciousness and Cognition* 22, no. 2 (2013): 654–69.

Probability and Uncertainty: The Quantum Mechanical View of Nature. Directed by Richard P. Feynman. Produced by the British Broadcasting Corp. Television, London, November 18, 1964, http://www.richard-feynman.net/videos.htm.

Putnam, Hilary. *Realism with a Human Face.* Edited by James Conant. Cambridge: Harvard University Press, 1990.

Rosenberg, Alex. *The Atheist's Guide to Reality: Enjoying Life without Illusions.* New York: W. W. Norton, 2011.

———. "Why You Don't Know Your Own Mind." *New York Times*, July 18, 2016, http://www.nytimes.com/2016/07/18/opinion/why-you-dont-know-your-own-mind.html.

Śāntarakṣita. *Tattvasaṃgraha.* Edited by D. Shastri. Varanasi, India: Bauddhabharati, 1968.

Śāntideva. *A Guide to the Bodhisattva Way of Life: Bodhicaryāvatāra.* Translated by Vesna A. Wallace and B. Alan Wallace. Ithaca, NY: Snow Lion Publications, 1997.

Searle, John R. *Consciousness and Language.* Cambridge: Cambridge University Press, 2002.

———. *Mind: A Brief Introduction.* New York: Oxford University Press, 2004.

———. *The Rediscovery of the Mind.* Cambridge: MIT Press, 1994.

Shabkar Tsogdruk Rangdrol. *The Life of Shabkar: The Autobiography of a Tibetan Yogi.* Foreword by His Holiness the Dalai Lama. Translated from the Tibetan by Matthieu Ricard, Jakob Leschley, Erik Schmidt, Marilyn Silverstone, and Lodrö Palmo. Edited by Constance Wilkinson, with Michal Abrams and other members of the Padmakara Translation Group. Ithaca, NY: Snow Lion Publications, 2001.

Shar Khentrul Jamphel Lodrö. *Demystifying Shambhala: The Profound and*

Secret Nature That Is the Perfection of Peace and Harmony as Revealed by the Jonang Tradition of Kalachakra. Belgrave, Australia: Tibetan Buddhist Rimé Institute, 2016.

Singh, Simon. *Fermat's Last Theorem: The Story of a Riddle That Confounded the World's Greatest Minds for 358 Years.* London: Fourth Estate, 1997.

Skinner, B. F. *About Behaviorism.* New York: Alfred A. Knopf, 1974.

———. *Science and Human Behavior.* New York: Macmillan, 1953.

Steering Committee on Science and Creationism. "Science and Creationism: A View from the National Academy of Sciences." Washington, DC: NAS Press, 1999.

Stewart, Ian. *Concepts of Modern Mathematics.* New York: Dover Publications, 1995.

Susskind, Leonard. "The World as a Hologram." SU-ITP-94-33, September 1994, arXiv:hep-th/9409089.

Titchener, Edward B. *Experimental Psychology: A Manual of Laboratory Practice.* New York: Macmillan, 1901–5.

———. *A Primer of Psychology.* Revised edition. New York: Macmillan, 1899.

Tsongkhapa. *The Great Treatise on the Stages of the Path to Enlightenment (Lam rim chen mo).* vol. 3. Translated by The Lamrim Chenmo Translation Committee. Ithaca, NY: Snow Lion Publications, 2002.

———. *Illumination of the True Thought. An Extensive Explanation of "Entering the Middle Way"* (Tib. *Dbu ma la 'jug pa'i rgya cher bshad pa dgongs pa rab gsal*). In vol. *ma* of the Tashi Lhunpo block-print edition of the *Collected Works of the Lord* (*Rje'i gsung 'bum*). Dharamsala, India: Sherig Parkhang, 1997.

Tsultrim Zangpo. "An Ornament of the Enlightened View of Samantabhadra." In Wallace, *Open Mind,* 159–208.

Van Lommel, Pim. *Consciousness Beyond Life: The Science of Near-Death Experience.* New York: HarperOne, 2010.

Von Baeyer, Hans Christian. *QBism: The Future of Quantum Physics*. Cambridge: Harvard University Press, 2016.

Wall, Patrick David. "Pain and the Placebo Response." In *Experimental and Theoretical Studies of Consciousness*, edited by G. R. Bock and J. Marsh, 187–211. Chichester, UK: John Wiley & Sons, 1993.

Wallace, B. Alan. *The Attention Revolution: Unlocking the Power of the Focused Mind*. Boston: Wisdom Publications, 2006.

———. *Balancing the Mind: A Tibetan Buddhist Approach to Refining Attention*. Ithaca, NY: Snow Lion Publications, 2005.

———, ed. *Buddhism and Science: Breaking New Ground*. New York: Columbia University Press, 2003.

———. *Buddhism with an Attitude: The Tibetan Seven-Point Mind-Training*. Ithaca, NY: Snow Lion Publications, 2001.

———. *Choosing Reality: A Buddhist View of Physics and the Mind*. Ithaca, NY: Snow Lion Publications, 1996.

———. *Dreaming Yourself Awake: Lucid Dreaming and Tibetan Dream Yoga for Insight and Transformation*. Boston: Shambhala Publications, 2012.

———. "A General Theory of Ontological Relativity." In Wallace, *Hidden Dimensions: The Unification of Physics and Consciousness*, 70–84. New York: Columbia University Press, 2007.

———. *Minding Closely: The Four Applications of Mindfulness*. Ithaca, NY: Snow Lion Publications, 2011.

———, trans. *Open Mind: View and Meditation in the Lineage of Lerab Lingpa*. Boston: Wisdom Publications, 2017.

———. *Stilling the Mind: Shamatha Teachings from Düdjom Lingpa's Vajra Essence*. Boston: Wisdom Publications, 2011.

———. *The Taboo of Subjectivity: Toward a New Science of Consciousness*. Oxford: Oxford University Press, 2000.

———. "Vacuum States of Consciousness: A Tibetan Buddhist View." In

Buddhist Thought and Applied Psychological Research: Transcending the Boundaries, edited by D. K. Nauriyal, 112–21. London: Routledge, 2006.

Walshe, Maurice, trans. *The Long Discourses of the Buddha: A Translation of the Dīgha Nikāya*. Boston: Wisdom Publications, 1995.

Watson, John B. "Psychology as the Behaviorist Views It." *Psych. Rev.* 20 (1913): 158–77.

———. *Psychology from the Standpoint of a Behaviorist*. London: Frances Pinter, 1983.

Wegner, Daniel M. *The Illusion of Conscious Will*. Cambridge: MIT Press, 2003.

Weinberg, Steven. *Dreams of a Final Theory: The Scientist's Search for the Ultimate Laws of Nature*. New York: Vintage Books, 1992.

———. *The First Three Minutes: A Modern View of the Origin of the Universe*. New York: Basic Books, 1993.

Weragoda Sarada Maha Thero. *Treasury of Truth: Illustrated Dhammapada*. Taipei, Taiwan: The Corporate Body of the Buddha Education Foundation, 1993.

Wheeler, John Archibald. "Law without Law." In *Quantum Theory and Measurement*, edited by John Archibald Wheeler and Wojciech Hubert Zurek, 182–213. Princeton, NJ: Princeton University Press, 1983.

Wiener, Norbert. *Cybernetics: Or Control and Communication in the Animal and the Machine* [1948]. Cambridge: MIT Press, 1961.

Yin, Juan, et al. "Bounding the Speed of 'Spooky Action at a Distance.'" *Phys. Rev. Lett.* 110, no. 26 (2013): http://arxiv.org/abs/1303.0614.

The Yogis of Tibet: A Film for Posterity. Directed by Jeffrey M. Pill. JEHM Films, 2002.

Zajonc, Arthur, ed. *The New Physics and Cosmology: Dialogues with the Dalai Lama*. New York: Oxford University Press, 2004.

Zajonc, Arthur, and Anne Harrington, eds. *Investigating the Mind: The Dalai Lama at MIT*. Cambridge: Harvard University Press, 2006.

Index

A

absence of mindfulness, 7

afflictive mentation, 74, 83, 125

ahaṃkāra, 74, 125

anthropic principle, 153

appearances, 124–80

  of city of gandharvas, 113, 130

  delusion of, 163, 166–67, 170–71

  emptiness of, 91, 97, 134

  grasping at, 129

  identity and arising of, 124–26

  karmas and, 134–35

  Pāli concept of, 38

  taking as the path with awareness, 117–18

  validity of, 174–80

arhat, 52

Association for Research in Contemplative Science (ARCS), 207

Atīśa, 92, 194

atomism, 106

awareness

  appearances perceived by, 85

  awareness of, 4, 5, 30–31, 63, 66

  nonconceptual, 10, 57, 117

  objects arising in, 74, 126

  space of, 40, 60, 74, 82, 85, 131–34, 145, 175–77

  stillness and movements of mind in, 6

  See also pristine awareness

B

Bacon, Francis, 19–20

Baeyer, Hans Christian von, 160

balance

  emotional, 185, 206–7

  mental, 30, 193, 206

  mindfulness of breathing and, 9–10

  śamatha as cultivating, 5, 9

Begley, Sharon, 18

behaviorism, 21–22

Big Bang, 34–35, 124

Big Picture, The (Carroll), 16

birth. *See* rebirth

bodhisattva paths of Mahāyāna Buddhism, 181–82

Bodhisattva Faculties. *See specific faculty*

body

  analogy of rider and horse, 42–43

  behaviorists' view of, 15, 21–23

  examining components of, 87–91, 93–97

finding source of "I" in, 75–79
location of dreams within, 141–42
materialistic beliefs about, 12–15, 24
Pāli concept of mind and, 38
perceiving emptiness of, 85–87
questioning arising of, 145–46
scientific dichotomy of mind and,
    31–32
serviceable pliancy of, 8
tukdam at death of, 144
Bohr, Niels, 115–16, 159, 201
Bostrom, Nick, 111
brain
    abnormalities and functioning of,
        77–78
    consciousness in neurons of, 32–33
    nihilism and views of, 25–26
    regarded as equivalent with identity, 76
    reports of out-of-body phenomenon,
        91–92, 102
    studying placebo effects on, 17–18
    substituting for mind, 23–24
    understanding meditation with
        research on, 57–58
breathing. *See* mindfulness of breathing
Brukner, Časlav, 33, 36, 137
Buddha
    on essential nature of mind, 44
    on mindfulness of breathing, 8–9
    testing teachings of, 51, 52
Buddhahood Without Meditation
    (Düdjom Lingpa), 49, 50, 206
Buddhism
    benefiting future disciples, 183–84
    collaborating with science, 197–207
    countering materialistic views, 24,
        27–28
    explaining perceptions of reality,
        110–11
    finding ultimate nature of mind,
        44–48
    incompatible with scientific material-
        ism, 199–200
    samādhi as technology of, 149
    scientific depictions added to views
        of, 179
    theories of cosmogony, 148–49
    transcendent nature of consciousness,
        48–54
    understanding essential nature of
        mind, 38–44
    views of Vaibhaṣika, 106–7
    *See also specific Buddhist practices and
        schools*

C

Caird, Edward, 36–37
Carroll, Sean, 16, 17, 20
causality, consciousness and, 41–42
cause
    contributing conditions and, 125,
        128–31
    cooperative condition and, 41–43
    primary, 125, 129
    substantial, 41–43, 101
Center for Contemplative Research
    (CCR), 204, 205–6
Chomsky, Noam, 140
cittatā, 65
city of gandharvas, 113, 130
clear light of death, 100–101, 144
Clear Mirror, A (Düdjom Lingpa), 1
cognizance, 30, 31, 45, 106
Cole, K. C., 187
collaboration of Buddhism and science,
    197–207
    examples of, 204–7
    incompatibilities in, 199–200
    using Buddhism in scientific meth-
        ods, 200–202
Commentary on Bodhicitta (Nāgār-
    juna), 43

Concepts of Modern Mathematics (Stewart), 90
conscious awareness, 57–60.
consciousness
   after death of arhat, 52
   analogy of rider and horse, 42–43
   awareness as, 32–33
   causality and, 41–42
   conservation of energy and, 41
   identifying unstructured awareness
      of, 65–66
   karma accumulated by practice,
      61–62
   materialists' view of, 25–26, 140–41
   phenomenological nature of, 30–38
   primordial vs. substrate, 58–59
   qualities of self-illuminating mindfulness as, 7–8
   scientific reductionism of, 128
   Searle's scientific explanations of,
      12–13, 26, 126
   subjective nature of, 76–77
   transcendent nature of, 48–54
   traveling to location in dreams, 145
   See also primordial consciousness;
      substrate consciousness
conservation of energy, 41
Copenhagen Theory, 42
corpse pose, 10
cosmology
   Buddhist theories of, 148–49
   theories of quantum, 33–34, 37,
      139–40
Cremonini, Cesare, 127
cutting through, 2, 50, 53, 60–62, 68, 100

D

Dalai Lama, 114
   combining spiritual traditions in
      research, 202–3
   on configuration of matter and
      energy, 188
   encouraging collaboration with science, 197–207
   on essence of Madhyamaka philosophy, 107
   on mental training, 18–19
   three criteria for existence, 172–73
Damasio, Antonio, 76, 78
Danzan Ravjaa, 163
Darwin, Charles, 151, 152
Davies, Paul C. W., 152
Dawa Drolma, 102
death
   clear light of, 100–101, 144
   consciousness of arhat after, 52
   expansion of perceptions after, 92
   nature of consciousness at, 126
   NDEs and OBE, 101–3
   returning to substrate at, 99–100
   transference of consciousness at, 144
delayed-choice entanglement swapping,
   137
Della Porta, Giovanni Baptista, 127
delog, 102
delusion
   appearances and, 163, 166–67, 170–71
   examining, 71–73
   recognizing in waking state, 72–73, 75
   reification and, 135
dependent origination of objects,
   131–33
Descartes, René, 31
DeWitt, Bryce, 34
Dhammapada, 12
dharmadhātu, 65, 122, 131–32, 134, 170,
   188–89
dharmakāya, 51, 52, 57–59, 66
Dharmasāra, 47
dharmatā
   defined, 64, 65
   emptiness of phenomena and, 134
direct crossing over, 2, 53
Doṇa Sutta, 119

dreaming
  as analogy of illusion, 112–13
  comparing phenomena in waking
    and, 143–44
  determining validity of waking or,
    174–76
  emptiness of appearances in, 91, 97,
    134, 165–66
  experience in waking and, 118, 168–69
  identity in, 80, 82, 147
  location and existence of, 84
  perceiving emptiness of body via,
    85–86
  questioning location of phenomena
    in, 141–45
  recognizing delusion of, 72–73, 75
  traveling of consciousness to location
    in, 145
  See also lucid dreaming
Drubwang Konchok Norbu Rinpoché,
    179–80
Düdjom Lingpa, 3, 53, 105
  commentary on sharp vajra, 44
  on existence of particles, 106
  on Great Perfection, 52, 53–54, 183
  retreats transmitting works of, 206
  revelation of, 1–2
  taking appearances and awareness as
    path, 117–18
  on truth of emptiness and phenom-
    ena, 188–89
  vision of Samantabhadra and circle of
    bodhisattvas, 55–56
Düdjom Lingpa's Visions of the Great
    Perfection (Sogyal Rinpoché), 53

E
echo, 113, 130
Einstein, Albert, 42, 124, 137
"Elliptic Curves and Galois Representa-
    tions" (Wiles), 173
Ellis, George F. R., 32

empiricism
  explaining perceptions of reality via,
    109
  James on, 14–15, 174
  need for, 175, 186, 205
  negating introspection and conscious-
    ness with, 22
emptiness
  all phenomena as, 156–57, 165, 180–89
  āryabodhisattva's realization of, 168
  coarse and subtle considerations for,
    116–24
  defined, 64–65, 115
  dharmadhātu and, 65, 187
  dream appearances and, 91, 97, 134,
    165–66
  Düdjom Lingpa on truth of, 188–89
  grasping at identity and, 80, 82
  impermanence of tree trunk and, 119,
    120–21, 123
  meditating on, 125–26
  as path to Great Perfection, 72
  personal identitylessness and, 156–57
  phenomena and, 134
  point of realizing, 180–89
  śamatha and meditation on, 69
  as source of objects, 74
  treating objects as abstraction, 180–82
Englishman Who Went Up a Hill but
    Came Down a Mountain, The, 105
Enlightened View of Samantabhadra
    (Düdjom Lingpa), 2, 206
Essence of Christianity, The (Feuer-
    bach), 151
Essence of Clear Meaning (Düdjom
    Lingpa), 206
essential nature of mind, 44
Everett, Hugh, 109

F
Faculty Displaying All Appearances. See
    Faculty of Appearances

Faculty of Appearances, 4, 135–36, 141–
  46, 155, 157, 158, 164, 168, 169, 175,
  176–77, 181, 183, 185, 186
Faculty of Luminosity, 55–57, 71, 81, 82,
  87–88, 118, 124–25
Fermat, Pierre de, 173
Fermat's Last Theorem, 173
Feuerbach, Ludwig, 151, 152, 153–54
Feynman, Richard, 16, 91–92, 116
Finkelstein, David, 20
first dhyāna
  realizing, 7–8
  respiration and, 11
  substrate consciousness and threshold
    of, 43–44
*Foolish Dharma of an Idiot Clothed
  in Mud and Feathers* (Düdjom
  Lingpa), 3, 206
Freud, Sigmund, 27, 128
Fuchs, Christopher, 160
Future of an Illusion, The (Freud), 27

G

Galileo, 127, 152
Gangteng Tulku Rinpoché, 128
Gates, James, 111
Gefter, Amanda, 160
Gen Lamrimpa, 125
Genz, Henning, 187
Gould, Stephen J., 16, 25
grasping at identity of person, 82
Graziano, Michael, 25
Great Perfection
  Düdjom Lingpa's teaching on, 52,
    53–54, 183
  effortless path of, 72
  examining delusion of self, 71–73
  practicing, 63–64, 66, 67–68
  rigpa in reference to, 57
*Guide to the Bodhisattva Way of Life,
  The* (Śāntideva), 181
Guth, Alan, 111

Gyatrul Rinpoché, 2, 168

H

hallucination, 114, 131
Harrington, Anne, 18
Hawking, Stephen, 25, 116, 126, 139–
  40, 148
Heart Sūtra, 126, 156–57, 165
Heisenberg uncertainty principle, 137
Heisenberg, Werner, 108, 110, 115, 148
Helmholtz, Hermann von, 41
Hertog, Thomas, 139–40
Higgs boson, 64–65, 180
Hoffman, Donald, 22
Huxley, Thomas H., 13, 22, 31, 52, 53, 152

I

"I." *See* identity
"I-maker," 125
identity
  arising of appearances and, 124–26
  continuity in lives and, 81–82
  creating division in consciousness
    with, 132
  emptiness and grasping at, 80, 82, 129
  equivalence with brain, 76
  examining body's components to
    find, 87–91, 93–95, 96–97
  existence of phenomena and, 47–48
  finding source of "I," 72, 74–80
  forgetting one's, 146–47
  locating referent for "I," 158
  object's components examined to
    find, 103–6
identitylessness
  determining as objects, 85–116
  determining as subjects, 71–85
  emptiness and personal, 156–57
  Theravāda and Mahāyāna views on, 48
idol, 20
Idols of the Cave, 19–20
Idols of the Marketplace, 20

Idols of the Theater, 20
Idols of the Tribe, 19, 20
illusion
  analogies for, 111–15
  analogies illustrating emptiness of
    phenomena, 128–35
  grasping at identity and appearance
    of, 129
impermanence of tree trunk, 119,
  120–21, 123
intellect, transcending, 49, 50
introspection
  empiricism's negation of, 22
  scientific attempts at, 29–30
  skepticism of, 126–28

J
James, William, 14–15, 20–21, 22,
  26–27, 29, 36, 116, 173, 174, 194, 195
Jé Khenpo Rinpoché, 128
Jé Tsongkhapa, 43, 106, 172, 173
Jé Tsultrim Zangpo, 46
Jung, Carl, 128

K
Kagan, Jerome, 200, 201, 203
Kaku, Michio, 25–26
Kālacakra Tantra, 148–49, 162, 163, 188
Kandel, Eric R., 23
Karma Chagmé, 45, 161
karmas
  accumulated in substrate conscious-
    ness, 61
  appearance and arising of phenom-
    ena, 134–35
  as seeds of worlds, 111
  shared, 134
Katz, Nick, 173–74
Kirsch, Irving, 18
Kurzweil, Ray, 111

L
LaBerge, Steven, 138, 178
Lama Tsong Khapa Institute, 204, 207
Lamp for the Path of Enlightenment
  (Atīśa), 92, 194
Lander, Eric, 200–201, 202, 203
Leibniz, Gottfried, 152
Lerab Lingpa, 46, 117
Letter to a King (Nāgārjuna), 105–6
Libri, Giulio, 117
Lozang Chökyi Gyaltsen, 73
Lozang Do-ngak Chökyi Gyatso Chok
  (a.k.a. Dharmasāra), 47
lucid dreaming
  keys to, 16–19
  parallelism with quantum system, 138
  practice of Great Perfection like, 67–68
  prospective memory in, 169
  respiration during, 11
  usefulness in vipaśyanā, 166–67
  viewing world as in, 119–20
luminosity, 30–31, 44–45

M
Madhyamaka (Middle Way) philosophy, 3, 107
  determining validity of existence,
    172–74
  impermanence of tree trunk, 121–22
  perception in, 154
  view of phenomena in, 150–51
Mahāparinirvāṇasūtra, 52
manas, 74, 84
manifest mindfulness, 7
manifestation
  nature of, 63–64
  of primordial consciousness, 61–63,
    65–66
March-Russell, John, 187–88
materialism, 11–28
  beliefs of body, 12, 24

consciousness as physical phenomenon, 41
countering views of, 24, 27–28
delegitimization of subjective perception, 164
effect on civilization's values, 191–92
Huxley's views on, 13–14
incompatibility with Buddhism,
199–200
James as pioneer in, 14–15
perceptions of consciousness in,
25–26, 140–41
role of brain in theories of, 24
science and, 12–14, 16
skepticism of introspective observations, 126–28
views challenged by substrate consciousness, 82–83
Maudgalyāyana, 162
meditation
CCR's proposed research in, 206–7
on emptiness, 69
finding primordial consciousness via,
59–62, 66
human need for freedom and, 192–93
nonmeditation of Great Perfection,
66–68
Padmasambhava on, 77
purpose of Zen kōan, 65, 68
theory of view and practice of, 73
meditative equipose, 48–49
memory in waking and dreaming,
169–70
mental afflictions, 97–98, 180, 192
mentation, 74, 84
metaphysical realism, 96–97, 135–37, 156
mind
Buddhism on essential nature of, 38–44
effect on body, 18–19
finding ultimate nature of, 44–48
James on exploration of, 29

Mahāmudrā and Dzokchen traditions
on, 45–47
manifest vs. essential nature of, 38–39
meditative equipose, 49–50
Pāli concept of body and, 38
as primary agent, 11–12
Sanskrit terms related to nature of, 65
scientific dichotomies of body and,
31–32
scientific explanations of, 12–21
serviceable pliancy of, 8
settling in natural state, 39
space of, 4–7, 45, 83–85, 117–18,
145–46, 149–50
substituting brain for, 23–24
supernormal powers of, 160–62
taking the impure mind as the path,
3–4, 5, 6
ultimate nature of, 44–48, 65
witnessing arising in, 9
mind-body problem. *See* body; mind;
science
mindfulness
absence of, 7
manifest, 7
self-illuminating, 7–8
single-pointed, 6
mindfulness of breathing
balance reached with, 9–10
Buddha's teaching of, 8–9
frequency of respiration, 10–11
relaxation and, 5–6
teaching, 3
Minsky, Marvin, 111
mirage, 82, 112
mountain, 104–5
Mt. Meru, 161, 162
Muckli, Lars, 77–78
Musk, Elon, 111

N
Nāgārjuna, 43, 115, 121

Nāgasena, 48
Nagel, Thomas, 110
naïve realism, 145
names, 114–15
Nasruddin, Mullah, 140
Natural Liberation (Padmasambhava), 4
Natural Magic (Della Porta), 127
near-death experiences (NDEs), 101–3
neuroscience, 22–23
nihilism, 118, 120, 156
nirmānakāyas, 51, 67
nonmeditation of Great Perfection,
    66–68
nonoverlapping magisteria, 16, 17

O
object permanence, 177
objects
    act of designating, 95–96
    appearance of city of gandharvas, 113,
        130
    arising in awareness, 74, 126
    dependent origination of, 131, 133
    designated as other, 98–99
    examining components of, 103–6
    light and entanglement of quantum,
        136–38
    Pāli concept of appearing forms, 38
    reality of dream objects, 159
    regarded as permanent, 177
    relation to subjects, 159–60
    science and relation to part or whole,
        36–37
    See also identitylessness
ontological relativity, 109
organicism, 152
Origin of Species (Darwin), 151
other
    designating objects as, 98–99
    pairing with subject, 79
out-of-body experiences (OBEs),
    91–92, 102

P
Padmasambhava
    examples of bodies arising without
        parents, 146
    explanation of death process, 100–101
    finding source of "I," 74, 77
    on practice of awareness of awareness,
        66
    on śamatha, 4, 73
    taking the mind as the path, 117
parents, bodies without, 146, 155
Pema Tashi, 55
permanence
    considering tree trunk and, 119,
        120–21, 123
    object, 177
    vajra qualities of, 122–24
personal identity. *See* identity; identi-
    tylessness
phenomena, 124–80
    absolute space of, 65, 120, 122
    believing reality of, 136
    delusion of appearances, 163, 166–67
    determining validity of existence,
        172–74
    Düdjom Lingpa on emptiness and,
        188–89
    emergence from substrate, 81
    emptiness and, 134
    establishing existence of deceptive, 172
    existence of identity and, 47–48, 131,
        133
    fathoming appearances in, 174–80
    karmas and arising of, 134–35
    Madhyamaka view of, 150–51
    questioning location of in dreams,
        141–45
    realizing emptiness of, 180–89
    scientific approach to, 116–17, 126–27
    seen from pristine awareness, 155–74
    viewing from realist viewpoint, 135–55

phenomenological nature of consciousness, 30–38
phowa, 144
physics
  existence of particles, 106
  measuring attributes of electrons, 108
  perceptions of reality explained, 109–11
Piaget, Jean, 177
placebo effects, 17–18
Plato, 152
possibility, 108
power
  of emanation, 114–15
  supernormal, 160–62
practicing
  Great Perfection, 63–64, 66, 67–68
  karma accumulated in consciousness by, 61–62
  primordial consciousness, 61–62
  śamatha, 3–4, 66, 194–95
pratītyasamutpāda, 31
preliminary practices for Great Perfection, 68
primordial, 56
primordial consciousness
  alternate terms for, 60–61
  emptiness and, 131–32
  practice vs. manifesting, 61–62, 64
  questions on achieving, 56–57
  remaining in heart at death, 144
  substrate vs., 58–59
pristine awareness, 155–74
  fantasy of subjective perception viewed from, 164–65
  "I" referring to, 158
  view of phenomena from, 158–59
Probability and Uncertainty, 116
prospective memory, 169
Protagoras, 154
pure visions, 1
Putnam, Hilary, 116, 184
Pythagoras, 150

Q
QBism, 160
quantum physics
  Bohr on worlds of, 115–16
  Copenhagen Theory and, 42
  cosmology and, 33–34, 37, 139–40
  decoherence of systems, 139
  light and entanglement of quantum objects, 136–38
  "many-worlds" interpretation of, 109
  zero-point energy, 124

R
rainbow, 132–33
rainbow body, 2, 53
Ramachandra, V.S., 76
Ratnamegha Sūtra, 12
reality
  believing phenomena to be, 136
  Buddhism's explanations of, 110–11
  delusive appearances and, 170–71
  of dream objects, 159
  empiricism's explanations of, 109
  explained by physics, 109–11
  ultimate reality, 64, 65
reality check, 169
rebirth
  karma and, 111
  once achieving śamatha, 58, 84
  process of becoming human, 101
  See also substrate consciousness
reductionism. *See* materialism
reflection, 113–14, 130
reification
  of another person, 98–99
  effects of, 95–96, 97–98, 120
  grasping appearances, 159
  impact on daily life, 180–81
  permanence of phenomena and, 17
  root of all delusion, 135
relaxation, 5
religion, separation of science and, 16–17

rigpa, 57
Rosenberg, Alex, 22, 126
rūpa, 38

S
samādhi
    siddhis of, 160–61
    as technology of Buddhism, 149
    using powers of, 168
Saṃadhinirmocanasūtra, 8
Samantabhadra, 11, 39–40, 53–54
    Düdjom Lingpa's vision of bodhisat-
        tvas, 1–2, 55–56
śamatha
    achieving, 194
    cultivating, 5, 193–94
    focused on the mind, 47
    importance of, 192–93
    introspection available via, 30
    in Mahāmudrā and Dzokchen tradi-
        tions, 45–47
    necessary foundation in practice of, 83
    Padmasambhava on, 73
    practices of, 3–4, 66
    rebirths once achieving, 58, 84
    substrate consciousness and, 57–58, 99
    Vajra Essence on, 2
    See also awareness; meditation; mind-
        fulness of breathing
sambhogakāya, 51, 67
Santa Barbara Institute for Conscious-
    ness Studies, 204, 207
Śāntideva, 181
Schrödinger, Erwin, 108, 159–60
science, 12–21
    approach to phenomena via, 116–17,
        126–27
    Bacon's four idols, 19–20
    behaviorists view of body, 21–23
    biasing results by methods of, 148
    brain research to understand medita-
        tion, 57–58

defining consciousness, 30–38
delegitimization of subjective percep-
    tion by, 164
discovery of "god particle," 64–65
effect of values on civilization, 191–92
on emergence of physical phenomena
    from space, 187–88
equating mental with neural pro-
    cesses, 76–77
explaining death and NDEs, 101–2
ideals of inquiry in, 91–92
impact of studies in, 197–98
implications of quantum physics,
    33–34, 37
incorporating Buddhism into meth-
    ods, 200–202
nihilism and materialistic views of
    brain, 25–26
path of empiricism, 14
scientific materialism, 12–14, 16
separation of religion and, 16–17
skepticism of introspection, 126–28
story of world and development of,
    151–55
twentieth-century questions about
    existence, 107, 136
views in metaphysical realism, 96–97
See also empiricism; materialism;
    quantum physics
Searle, John R., 12–13, 26, 32, 126
self-emergent, 56
self-identity. See identity
self-illuminating mindfulness, 7–8
Sera Khandro Dewé Dorjé, 50
settling mind in natural state, 39–40
Seven-Point Mind Training (Atīśa), 194
Shabkar Tsokdruk Rangdröl, 192–93
Shambhala, 162–63
*Sharp Vajra of Consciousness Awareness
    Tantra* (Düdjom Lingpa), 2, 6, 55,
    183, 206
siddhis, 160–61

single-pointed mindfulness, 6
sipa, 108
Skinner, B. F., 21–22, 23
sleeping
  lucidity during, 11
  nonconceptual awareness in, 10
  substrate consciousness and, 73–74
Smoot, George, 111
solipsism, 118, 157
space, 186–89
śrāvaka view, 156
stability, 5
Stewart, Ian, 90
Stilling the Mind (Wallace), 55
subjects
  determining identitylessness of, 71–85
  pairing other with, 79
  See also identitylessness
substantialism, 120, 156
substrate, 74–75
  defined, 7
  emergence of phenomena from, 81
  exploring via śamatha, 99
  giving rise to substrate consciousness, 81
  returning to at death, 99–100
substrate consciousness
  awareness of respiration in, 11
  as cause for consciousness, 43
  characteristics of, 7, 40, 57–58
  death and experience of, 99–100
  examining mind from, 50–51
  finding essential nature of mind, 39, 40
  finding source of "I" in, 81
  as foundation for vipaśyanā, 83–84
  karmas accumulated in, 61
  limitations of, 59–61, 66
  materialist views challenged by, 82–83
  primordial vs., 58–59
  sleep and, 73–74
  various names of, 43–44
suchness, 64, 65
śūnyatā, 65, 115, 122

supernormal powers, 160–62
Susskind, Leonard, 111
svabhāvikakāya, 51

T
taking appearances and awareness as
  path, 117–18
taking mind as the path, 3–4, 5, 6, 38, 117
tathāgatagarbha, 52
tathatā, 64, 65
Tegmark, Max, 111
tertön, 1
Tertön Sogyal, 46
testing Buddha's teachings, 51, 52
thoughts, observing, 3–4
Thurman, Robert, 102
Tibetan Book of the Dead, The (trans.
  Thurman), 102
Titchener, Edward B., 29–30
Train Your Mind, Change Your Brain
  (Begley), 18
transcendent nature of consciousness,
  48–54
Treisman, Anne, 114
Tsongkhapa. *See* Jé Tsongkhapa
tukdam, 144

U
ultimate nature of mind, 44–48, 65
ultimate reality, 64, 65
universe
  Buddhist views of, 148–49, 162–63
  phenomenological nature of con-
    sciousness and, 31–32
  quantum cosmology, 33–34, 37, 139–40
Universe in a Single Atom, The (Dalai
  Lama), 188
US Geological Survey, 105
Uttara Kuru, 162

V
Vaibhāṣika Buddhism, 106–7

Vajirā, 48

Vajra Essence

analyzing mind in, 45

considering qualities of vajras, 122–24

on meditative equipose, 48–49

practice for fluctuating thoughts,
39–40

on rebirths once achieving śamatha,
58, 84

retreats on, 206

revelation of, 1–2

vipaśyanā

experience in lucid dreaming for,
166–67

metaphor and benefits of, 2–3

practicing, 66

śamatha foundation for, 83–84

vitalism, 152

W

waking state

comparing phenomena of dream state
and, 143–44

determining validity of dream or,
174–76

dissimilarity of people in dream and,
178

experience in dreams and, 118, 168–69

recognizing delusions of dreams in,
72–73, 75

Wall, Patrick David, 18, 78

Wallace, B. Alan, 55

Wallace, Vesna, 163

water, analogy of, 113–14

water bubble, 114, 130, 132

Watson, John B., 15

Wegner, Daniel M., 24

Weinberg, Steven, 25, 188

Weragoda Sarada Maha Thero, 38

Wheeler, John Archibald, 34, 35–36,
109, 139, 140, 160

Wiener, Norbert, 33

Wiles, Andrew, 173–74

world

Bohr on quantum mechanics, 115–16

as each one's own maṇḍala, 133

Freud's view of mind and, 27

karmas as seeds of, 111

"many-worlds" of quantum mechanics, 109

viewing as in lucid dreaming, 119–20

Y

Yangthang Rinpoché, 168

Yogis of Tibet, The, 179

Z

Zeilinger, Anton, 33, 36, 107, 137, 140

zero-point energy, 124

About the Translator

B. ALAN WALLACE is president of the Santa Barbara Institute for Consciousness Studies. He trained for many years as a monk in Buddhist monasteries in India and Switzerland. He has taught Buddhist theory and practice in Europe and America since 1976 and has served as interpreter for numerous Tibetan scholars and contemplatives, including His Holiness the Dalai Lama. After graduating summa cum laude from Amherst College, where he studied physics and the philosophy of science, he earned his MA and PhD in religious studies at Stanford University. He has edited, translated, authored, and contributed to more than forty books on Tibetan Buddhism, medicine, language, and culture, and on the interface between science and religion.

What to Read Next
from Wisdom Publications

Stilling the Mind
Shamatha Teachings from Dudjom Lingpa's Vajra Essence
B. Alan Wallace and Brian Hodel

"A much needed, very welcome book."—Jetsün Khandro Rinpoche

Open Mind
View and Meditation in the Lineage of Lerab Linga
B. Alan Wallace
Foreword by His Holiness the Dalai Lama

"*Open Mind* is a gift to those who have affinity with the way of Dzogchen."
—Anam Thubten, author of *The Magic of Awareness*

Buddhahood Without Meditation
B. Alan Wallace and Sera Khandro

The revelations of Düdjom Lingpa, a highly influential mystic of
nineteenth-century Tibet, translated by B. Alan Wallace.

Heart of the Great Perfection
Dudjom Lingpa's Visions of the Great Perfection
B. Alan Wallace

"Superb . . . we are indebted to Wallace, and to those who inspired and assisted him, for providing us with such a rich and vital resource for coming to terms with the profundities and puzzles of the Great Perfection."
—*Buddhadharma*

About Wisdom Publications

Wisdom Publications is the leading publisher of classic and contemporary Buddhist books and practical works on mindfulness. To learn more about us or to explore our other books, please visit our website at wisdompubs.org or contact us at the address below.

Wisdom Publications
199 Elm Street
Somerville, MA 02144 USA

We are a 501(c)(3) organization, and donations in support of our mission are tax deductible.

Wisdom Publications is affiliated with the Foundation for the Preservation of the Mahayana Tradition (FPMT).